Marketing Strategy in International Business

Marketing Strategy in International Business

E. P. Hibbert MA, PhD, F Inst M, MIEx
Durham University Business School

McGRAW-HILL BOOK COMPANY

London · New York · St Louis · San Francisco · Auckland · Bogotá
Guatemala · Hamburg · Lisbon · Madrid · Mexico · Montreal
New Delhi · Panama · Paris · San Juan · São Paulo · Singapore
Sydney · Tokyo · Toronto

Published by
McGRAW-HILL Book Company (UK) Limited
MAIDENHEAD · BERKSHIRE · ENGLAND

British Library Cataloguing in Publication Data
Hibbert, E. P. (Edgar P.)
  Marketing strategy in international business.
  1. International marketing
  I. Title
  658.8'48
  ISBN 0-07-084189-6

Library of Congress Cataloging-in-Publication Data
Hibbert, E. P. (Edgar P.)
  Marketing strategy in international business / E. P. Hibbert.
     p.   cm.
  Bibliography: p.
  Includes index.
  ISBN 0-07-084189-6
  1. International business enterprises—Management. 2. Export
marketing.   I. Title.
HD62.4.H53 1989
658.8'48—dc19   88-21577

1234 WL9089

Typeset by Eta Services (Typesetters) Ltd, Beccles, Suffolk and printed and bound in Great
Britain by Whitstable Litho Printers Ltd, Whitstable, Kent

To my parents

Contents

Foreword

Cohesion and relevance to corporate objectives is best achieved by explicit marketing strategies, through which top management directs the business and its resources, while encouraging individual initiative close to the customer, and in the specific market environment. Dr Hibbert beautifully illustrates the dangers of transporting a marketing strategy successful in one country, intact to another—whether the product be engagement rings or credit cards.

Dr Hibbert's valuable book gives sound advice illustrated by well chosen and pithy case examples. Whether calling on Cinzano, American Express or Unilever to demonstrate his points, he affirms the crucial need to keep local marketing relevant to local perceptions and customer values.

The central theme of this book—devolved decision making within a sound strategic framework inspired by the chief executive—is relevant and valuable in other aspects of modern management too. In today's turbulent markets, harnessing the sensitivity and creative power of the individual to the objectives of the enterprise is the formula for corporate success.

Peter Benton
Director General
British Institute of Management

Acknowledgements

The author has made use of a large amount of primary and secondary data as source materials. He wishes to acknowledge fully the following published material which he has quoted in full or in part. Permission to use this material has been obtained as follows:

- Saatchi and Saatchi, Garland-Compton, 15 Lower Regent Street, London W1. *Review of Operations—Worldwide* (*International Branding and Advertising*).

- *Handbook of International Trade*, Vol. I. Selected passages as follows: pp. 1.2-01– 1.2-12, 'The Options Available'; 3.7-01–3.7-09, 'Management Contracts'; pp. 4.1- 15, 4.1-16, 4.2-02 and 4.2-03, 4.2-06 and 4.2-12, 'Investment and Acquisitions Policies', by M. Brooke and P. T. Buckley, by permission of Macmillan, London and Basingstoke.

- International Trade Centre UNCTAD/GATT, Geneva, Switzerland. *Comparability: Sacred Principle*. Originally published as a paper for European Society for Opinion and Market Research (ESOMAR) and reprinted from International Trade Forum, issued by ITC.

- Institute of Export, Export House, 64 Clifton Street, London EC2. 'Agents and Distributors' by Professor C. M. Schmitthoff, in journal *Export*, July/August 1979.

- C. G. Alexandrides and G. P. Moschis, *Export Marketing Management*, pp. 24 and 25, and Table 1. Copyright © 1977 by Praeger Publishers, a division of Greenwood Press Inc. New York City.

A note about the 'case examples' (of which there are 73). These have been collected by the author from a wide spectrum of the trade, business and management press over a lengthy period. Every effort has been made to cite the sources in each case, and the author has tried to contact each of the companies and publications concerned. The case examples are not intended to show correct or incorrect handling of situations, but to illustrate contrasting management and trade policies.

Particular acknowledgement is due to Heinemann Professional Publishing, 22 Bedford Square, London W1, for permission to quote from author's copyright material *Principles and Practice of Export Marketing*, pp. 116–18, 114, 154, 161–7 and 225–31.

The author is also indebted to both students and managers who, over many years, have indirectly contributed to this book.

Introduction

This textbook covers all main aspects of developing international business, concisely and in an integrated way not generally available in existing literature. The main theme of the text is that, in order to develop profitable business internationally, in increasingly competitive conditions, it is essential to adopt an integrated management approach, one that brings together under the chief executive such major management disciplines as marketing, design, business policy and operations management. The applications of this approach range from the promotion of finished goods to licensing technology, investment in overseas operations and multi-sourcing. The text also contains many practical applications of sound international business management, particularly in implementing competitive marketing strategies.

The intended readership is degree-level students of business/management, particularly those taking options or electives in international aspects, especially at Masters level, and managers in industry who are responsible for, or are in a position to influence, the development of their companies' international operations or policies.

1
Researching international markets

1.1 Some strategic factors in world trade

Introduction

Many factors affect the relationships world-wide between marketing, as a process by which goods and services originate from producer to reach the foreign customer, and economic development. Certainly, trade promotion is an integral but critical component of the whole marketing process, and as such has a vital contribution to make both to economic development and to world trade expansion. This Section explores therefore, the role of trade promotion and particularly industrial manufactures and materials, and other strategic aspects and their impact on marketing practice.

Marketing and trade promotion

Both government and industry need to work effectively to improve all aspects of trade promotion in order to open up and maintain international market access. And another factor influencing the relationship between marketing and economic development has been the increasing role of statutory marketing organizations in many countries, particularly those handling commodities, minerals and other products providing the bulk of national export earnings. Both co-operatives and marketing boards can contribute to an expansion of the marketing system in developing countries, with, most importantly, the organization and development of efficient internal distribution systems that can serve the export trade as an integral part of trade promotion strategy. In the EEC, there is a move towards a single European market in 1992 to be reconciled with the continued market distortions of the Common Agricultural Policy (CAP).

In national trade promotion policy, dilemmas face many governments attempting to improve their trade balance in terms of import substitution or export promotion. The topical importance of such dilemmas to all organizations involved in overseas trade is illustrated by the stresses currently afflicting the world system. Domestic unemployment and inflation have caused some countries to become protectionist in their overseas trade policies. Other governments, many with substantial payments surpluses, have been reluctant to reflate, or pursue economic growth, for fear of accelerating their own inflation rate. Yet only if there is growth in world trade will prosperous industrialized nations be in a position to absorb more imports from countries with balance of payments problems. Also, there needs to be continuing co-

Table 1.1 Foreign trade by value as a percentage of GNP

	%	
USSR	2.6	Low
USA	2.9	
Japan	7.7	
France	11.0	↓
West Germany	13.8	
Canada	15.2	
UK	17.0	High

operation between government and business in undertaking research into new product uses in new markets for traditional exports and in diversifying industrial goods for export. Particularly vital is the provision of venture capital for investment in new industrial plant and processes. (Even the UK compares unfavourably with some other countries, particularly the USA.) The limited availability of and high interest rates for loan capital and technical services of both the National Research and Development Corporation (NRDC) and the Industrial and Commercial Finance Corporation (ICFC) require review by government.

The role of national trade promotion organizations, both in function and in organization, is to promote their countries' exports cost-effectively. Particular reference is made here to the UK, since that country is singularly dependent for economic solvency on foreign trade (see Table 1.1).[1]

Industrialists must not, however, rely on governments to do their exporting for them; much can be achieved, both at home and abroad, by the activities of national trade or industry exporters' associations. Indeed, the discipline of a pricing policy for all government export services in many countries is now widely recognized: it ensures more cost-effective use of these services, particularly those involving commercial risks.

Expansion in world trade

Multilateral trade and regional trading blocs are the focus for collective action by developing countries producing and exporting essential raw materials and commodities to industrialized countries. An important aspect of this is what is termed the 'North–South dialogue', and its significance lies in the balance of power in world trade between the producer countries of the Third World and the industrialized consuming countries in terms of preferential tariffs, debt relief and investment. The need of Third World countries to derive higher levels of export earnings from new industrial development projects is urgent, because only in this way can they increase earnings of hard currencies with which to purchase industrial goods and services and technology from the industrialized countries. The capacity of Third World countries to continue to

Table 1.2 Growth in world trade 1962–1987[2]

Year	Volume (%)	Value (%)
1962–71	9	2.5
1973	13	22.5
1974	5	41.0
1975	− 4.5	8.0
1976	11.5	2.0
1977	7	N/A
1977–82	4.5–5	2.5
1983–87	4	3.0

finance imports of technology from the Western industrialized world will also rest on their improved promotion of the whole range of commodities and produce, and on the increased purchasing capacity of the industrialized countries themselves.

Both Tokyo Round and Bonn Summit conferences sought to ensure some continuing and measurable growth in world trade, and above all increased domestic industrial output levels which will have some impact on reducing both inflation and unemployment. The significance of movements in world trade in this context is illustrated in Table 1.2.

The strategic importance of expanding trade has been spelt out as a result of these conferences in terms of (1) monetary stability and (2) economic growth. West Germany pledged to stimulate demand by the equivalent of 1 per cent of its GNP, and Japan undertook to stabilize the volume of its exports while achieving a real growth rate of 7 per cent. The OECD reckons that, unless these two pledges are fulfilled, the growth rate of OECD member countries will have been only 2 per cent in 1987. The Tokyo Round, which originated as the seventh round of GATT negotiations, is concerned not only with the further liberalization of international trade within the framework of the General Agreement on Tariffs and Trade (GATT), but also with the rules of GATT itself, some of which have been increasingly breached or abused, such as Article 24, which sets out the principle of 'non-discrimination', and Article 19, dealing with emergency protection against 'market disruption', which has become too complex to be administered under a single Article. Nevertheless, the Tokyo Declaration recognized the need for

special measures to be taken in the negotiations to assist the developing countries in their efforts to increase their export earnings through mechanisms such as the General System of Preferences (GSP), reduction of Most Favoured Nation (MFN) tariffs and specific measures such as STABEX.

World-wide supply situation

Other strategic factors in world trade concern the critical importance of the supply situation of commodities, minerals and other raw materials essential to the continued

Table 1.3 Reserves of strategic minerals

Resource	Estimated African % of world production	Years remaining with 5 times present known reserves
Cobalt	80	148
Chrome	50	154
Platinum	80	85
Asbestos	60	N/A
Gold	82	29
Manganese	50	94
Vanadium	40	N/A
Copper	25	48
Tungsten	N/A	72
Zinc	N/A	50
Tin	N/A	61
Titanium	20	N/A
Nickel	20	96
Aluminium	15	55
Uranium	25	N/A

functioning of the manufacturing industries and technologies of the Western industrialized world. The commercial and, indeed, strategic implications of this supply situation world-wide are illustrated in Table 1.3.[3]

Thus, it is essential that the marketing system should be used to contribute to economic development by encompassing an orderly approach to world trade in raw materials, commodities and semi-manufactures, and should not be used so often as in the past to gain advantages of price manipulation. There must be recognition that developing countries need to industrialize on the basis of their comparative advantage, if only to accommodate productively the large increases in their population. GATT has therefore proposed that an important component of multilateral trade rounds must be a negotiated 'trade-off' in terms of assurance of unimpeded access to markets by a quid pro quo for assurances of unimpeded access to supplies.

Indeed, this proposal has focused on the impact of changing technology on world trade, and on the need for a new approach to the 'inputs' and 'outputs' of marketing, both in terms of internal consumption and distribution, and in terms of resources being more widely shared and controlled world-wide. Socioeconomic needs, for instance, have themselves generated much new technology in the last 30 years: agricultural techniques which improve per-acre productivity, new processes for recycling waste, improvements in energy technology leading to more cost-effective energy consumption.

One analysis has drawn attention to the implications for marketing management of finite resources:[4]

The historical task of marketing has been to identify saleable products and services and to find buyers for them. A new task may be added based on the increasing difficulty of obtaining raw materials and other input supplies. The question may become not 'What can we make and sell?' but, 'Given what can we buy, what are the highest order uses we can make of our supplies?'

Conclusion

The marketing process clearly encompasses the spectrum from point of supply or production in the country of origin through the internal distribution network to export ports and through to the final customer overseas. The foregoing analysis has highlighted the importance of trade promotion within the marketing process.

It follows, therefore, that the marketing process itself can contribute directly to economic development. Above all, there must be a clearer recognition by government and by business that the marketing concept must be paramount in the development of overseas trade—investigating new product applications in overseas markets and researching new and changing overseas customer requirements; diversifying industries to broaden the exporting base; applying sound promotional pricing and distribution policies in overseas markets; above all, implementing a joint approach to trade promotion overseas by government and by the business community as a means to an end, that end being steady economic growth by the orderly expansion of world trade so as to bring about sustained prosperity for all trading nations.

All this requires a comprehensive and up-to-date data base, and this research aspect is accordingly discussed in the next section.

1.2   Analysing trade data

Trade classifications

To undertake any analysis of international trade data, some understanding of what trade classifications are and how they work is essential. These classifications refer particularly to product codes. Until a few years ago, specific duties on imported products were imposed widely, and the tariffs of many countries, particularly those in the Middle East and Latin America, were very complex. In addition, there has been a more recent trend towards the 'ad valorem' system. However, tariff administration has now been standardized by the adoption of two main trade classifications.

1. *Standard International Trade Classification (SITC) Revised.* This has ten divisions split up into 625 sub-groups, and these include all commodities of international trade, numbering more than 40 000 separate products. These are further subdivided into over 2000 items, designated by five-digit code numbers, thus enabling the exporting company to pinpoint data on a specific product.

   Currently, some 120 countries, accounting for nearly 90 per cent of world trade, report their trade statistics to the United Nations using the SITC code; these statistics are published regularly and represent the most complete set of international trade statistics in existence. The statistical values of goods for all countries are reported in US dollars, giving even greater comparability. SITC is fully compatible with major commodity nomenclature systems used in international trade.

2. *Customs Co-operation Council Nomenclature (CCCN).* This came into force, with the setting up of the EEC, as a four-digit customs tariff nomenclature in which all products entering international trade are grouped according to the nature of the material from which they are made, and are easily identifiable. This facilitates a comparison between the duties applied by different countries, and simplifies international tariff negotiations. Over two-thirds of world trade is now conducted under tariffs that are based on CCCN, and this includes almost all signatories to the General Agreement on Tariffs and Trade (GATT). Over 90 countries use CCCN for customs tariff purposes, but they submit trade statistics to the UN using the SITC code above. And in the SITC Manual the CCCN code number appears opposite each SITC number. Thus, by using this key, it is a simple matter to obtain the customs import duty for any product in any country.

A development of CCCN is used to classify external and internal trade of all member countries of the EEC under a system called NIMEXE.

Here are two examples of SITC and CCCN:

Product	SITC	CCCN
Commercial vehicles	783.10	87.02
Electrical machinery	716.21	85.01

It is essential for international companies to understand these classifications, particularly CCCN, and the practical advantages they offer. For example, they guarantee, to both government and business, maximum uniformity in the classification of goods in the national customs tariffs of target markets overseas. Management, therefore, can know in advance how their goods will be classified for customs purposes, and what tariffs their goods will be subject to. This is essential for the purpose of marketing planning, and in particular pricing policy. Further accurate measurement by volume and value is ensured not only for exports, but also for imports and re-exports. The language problem is practically eliminated, and the company can identify the movements of a highly specific sub-group of products in overseas markets. Also provided is a standard measure for comparing export and import statistics of different countries and trading blocs.

Two further, but less important, classifications are worthy of mention.

3. *International Standard Industrial Classification (ISIC).* ISIC is often confused with SITC, but the two coding systems were designed for different purposes. The ISIC is a system for classifying commodities by the industries that produce them and is widely used in reporting employment statistics, labour rates and other economic data related to industry classifications. The UN has published a key showing the relationship of ISIC code numbers to the corresponding SITC numbers.

Since many trade directories are published according to ISIC codes, this conversion key is particularly helpful for finding the names of importers or buyers for a particular commodity.

4. *ETNVT (Edinaia Tovarnaia Nomenklatura Vneshney Torgovli).* This classification is used by the USSR and countries of Eastern Europe (COMECON) in reporting international trade statistics. This group is the only major trading bloc that does not report trade statistics according to SITC. This failure does not represent any major problem, however, since the UN converts the data into SITC code in its published statistics. The UN also has developed a conversion key from the ETNVT to the SITC.

Market selection criteria

In applying these international codes, and in the use of statistical methods, some significant techniques have been developed by International Trade Centre UNCTAD/GATT, Geneva. ITC has published a manual on the procedures for selecting potential export markets. A summary of market selection criteria in this manual is shown in Table 1.4. Later in this section, another analytical approach (sectoral analysis), using codes, will be explained.

The data in Table 1.4 have been analysed in a study by Alexandrides and Moschis[5] aimed at identifying attractive and unattractive markets for product A. In this interesting analysis, the figures in the table have been used to make a decision on each market by determining an elimination threshold in respect to each criterion shown. The criteria have been organized in relation to the following three major areas:

1. *dimension*, having two criteria: the value in dollars of product A by each country in the region considered, for the most recent year analysed; and the percentage share of the target country in each of these markets;
2. *evolution*, having three criteria: value indices during the period considered for exports of product A by the target country to each of the markets considered; value indices over the period considered for total imports of product A by each of the markets examined; and the quotient of these two indices;
3. *competition*, having two criteria: the proportion of imports to domestic production in the markets studied; and the position of the competing countries in relation to the target country in the markets studied.

This analysis has extracted the figures shown in columns (2), (3), (5), (6), (7), (9) and (12) from four preceding tables; the figures for columns (4), (8) and (11) have been compiled from the data shown in the other columns in Table 1.4, and the figures for column (10) have been taken from production statistics.

Under the 'Dimension' section of this sample table, in column (3) those importing countries that account for more than 5 per cent of the total imports of product A into the region are encircled. Also encircled are the non-importing countries, which, as they cannot be dealt with by statistical methods, will be subject to special treatment. In column (4) the analysis refers to the average share obtained by the country in the

Table 1.4 Summary of market selection criteria (*Source*: 'The Compilation of Basic Information on Export Markets', International Trade Centre UNCTAD/GATT, Geneva, 1968. Adapted by C. G. Alexandrides and G. P. Moschis, *Export Marketing Management*, Praeger, New York, 1977)

(1)	(2) Criterion 1 — Imports by countries of the area: Value 1967	(3) Criterion 1: Percentage share	(4) Criterion 2 — Exporting country's share of imports into countries of the area in 1967: Above the average	(5) Criterion 2 — Exports: value in 1967 of the exporting country	(6) Criteria 3,4 — Value indices, 1967/1963: Of exporting of exporting country	(7) Criteria 3,4: Of imports into countries of the area	(8) Criterion 5 — Index quotient: (6)÷(7)	(9) Imports 1967 quantity	(10) Criterion 6 — Proportion imports/production: Domestic production 1967	(11) Criterion 6 — Relation between imports and production: % of production	(12) Criterion 7 — Main competing countries and their share in total imports of each country of the area	(13) Decision under criterion (7)	(14) No. of circles marked in preceding columns	(15) Conclusion — Final decision
Unit	Hundreds of dollars	%	—	Hundreds of dollars	1963 = 100	—	1.0 greater than 1	Tons	Tons	% of production			(Maximum: 7 Minimum: 0)	
Elimination threshold		Less than 5.0%	Above the average		Value greater than that in column (7)	Indices below 110				Less than 10%	Based on qualitative considerations			
Total for region	522 000	100.0	2.80	14 000	118	140	0.84	133 400	1 422 500	9.3%				
Importing countries Country I	25 320	4.85	8.29	2 100	(108)	(125)	(0.86)	2 000	100 000	2.0%	Country X 50%, country Z 20%, country Y 20%, others 10%	−	3	Eliminated
II	6 190	1.18	44.10	2 730	115	105	1.09	600	20 000	3.0%	Country X 40%, country Z 10%, 3 others 50%	−	0	Eliminated
III	11 420	2.19	(—)	(—)	(—)	(133)	(—)	1 100	10 000	(11.0%)	Country X 30%, 10 other countries 70%	+	6	Priority
IV	82 330	4.21	3.98	2 680	(113)	(149)	(0.76)	2 000	30 000	6.6%	Country X 85%, country Z 10%, 3 others 5%	−	3	Eliminated
V	113 940	(21.87)	(0.90)	1 030	(142)	(128)	1.11	95 000	190 000	(50.0%)	Country X 30%, 15 other countries 70%	+	5	Pending
VI	15 270	2.92	3.79	580	83	80	1.04	1 200	20 000	6.0%	Country Z 50%, country Y 40%, 2 others 10%	−	0	Eliminated
VII	26 900	(5.15)	(—)	(—)	(—)	(329)	(—)	1 500	2 000	(75.0%)	Country X 10%, 15 other countries 90%	+	7	Priority
VIII	9 300	1.78	5.37	500	150	(128)	1.17	1 000	100 000	1.0%	Country Y 50%, 5 other countries 50%	+	2	Eliminated
IX	77 400	(14.82)	(0.51)	400	120	(117)	1.03	8 000	160 000	2.0%	Country X 30%, 10 other countries 70%	+	4	Pending
X	48 000	(9.19)	2.87	1 380	175	(128)	1.37	5 000	200 000	2.5%	Country X 20%, country Y 15%, country Z 5%, 10 others 60%	+	3	Eliminated
XI	7 900	1.51	(—)	—	(—)	108	—	500	100 000	0.5%	Country Z 50%, country Y 30%, 5 others 20%	−	2	Eliminated
XII	37 100	(7.11)	2.96	1 100	106	104	1.02	3 000	9 000	(33.3%)	Country Y 80%, country Z 15%, others 5%	−	2	Eliminated
XIII	92 900	(17.80)	(0.32)	300	(130)	(217)	(0.60)	10 000	50 000	(20.0%)	Country Z 25%, country Z 0%, country Y 15%, others 40%	+	7	Priority
XIV	16 300	3.12	3.68	600	85	105	(0.81)	1 500	300 000	0.5%	Country X 100%	−	1	Eliminated
XV	11 730	2.24	10.23	1 200	(140)	(180)	(0.77)	1 000	1 000	(66.6%)	Country X 20%, country Y 15%, country Z 5%, 10 others 60%	+	5	Pending
XVI	—	(○)	(○)	—	—	—	(○○)	—	30 000	90.0		+	+	Special investigations
XVII etc.	—	(○)	(○)	—	—	—	(○○)	—	100 000	0.0		+	+	

region's imports as a whole (an average of 2.8 per cent in the table), and figures pertaining to those countries where that share is below the average are encircled. Similarly indicated are the countries that have not yet imported product A from the analyst's country.

Column (6), in the 'Evolution' section, lists figures showing the average price (based on 100) of exports of product A into each country by the exporting/supplying country that is the subject of this analysis. Column (7) shows the average price of exports of product A to the same markets from all countries; in this column figures are circled where the indices exceed 110 thus indicating high growth. The analysis, by dividing each column (6) figure by its corresponding column (7) figure, can then determine the rate of the country's price for product A in relation to its average price from the other countries; these quotients are entered in column (8), and each figure lower than 1.00 is encircled as this indicates that the country's price is very competitive in that market. A price of zero (−) is entered in column (6), and thus also in column (8), for markets to which the country has not exported product A at all; these are encircled in column (8) to denote a need for further investigation.

Under the 'Competition' section, column (9) lists the amount of imports (in tons) of product A into each country over the period under consideration. Corresponding figures in column (10) show the amount of domestic production of product A. The analysis calculates the ratio between imports and production for each country and enters the figures in column (11). Any country showing a good volume of imports in relation to domestic production has been marked by encircling the relevant figures as an attractive market.

Data shown in column (12) are based on qualitative aspects of the position of the competing exporters in each market. In calculating these figures, non-statistical elements including the following are taken into consideration: political ties between importing countries and competing exporting countries, trade agreements, preferential arrangements, geographical distances between customers and suppliers, commercial traditions, and the number of suppliers to each market. (It is more difficult to penetrate a market dominated by one or two exporting countries than one that has many suppliers.) This analysis requires a judgement on each market, with an entry of a positive or negative notation in column (13).

In column (14), the analysis totals all figures encircled in the table, country by country. A 'priority' rating is listed for each market showing six or seven notations; these are targets for future trade promotion. Countries having four or five circles are marked 'pending' for subsidiary action. The remaining countries have been 'eliminated' as unattractive markets. The analysis notes at the bottom of column (15) those countries where there are no imports at all of product A, so that a 'special investigation' may be conducted to determine why this is so.

Sectoral analysis

This approach to data analysis shows how management can identify and quantify actual and potential country markets. Another, more recent, approach has been developed by International Trade Centre UNCTAD/GATT: this is sectoral analysis for international market planning.[6] The principal aim of this approach is to indicate to management how to plan where best to allocate resources for product development, supply, promotion and market follow-up in those countries that offer the best growth prospects. Sectoral analysis determines growth rates, and therefore sales potential overseas, over a trading period in which the exports of one country, or one industry sector, can be compared with the growth of total imports into target countries overseas (by product code); this analysis cannot be done accurately without the use of product and country codes already explained.

Case example 1.1

A company in the British Midlands was manufacturing the complete range of electrical heaters (blow heaters, convectors, etc.); a company in Yorkshire was manufacturing refractory bricks, sold primarily to the steel industry to line furnaces. Using the SITC and CCCN codes, the marketing managers of these companies, quite independently, investigated the movements of their product codes into foreign markets where their companies had never previously operated, largely for historical reasons.

In the case of the heater manufacturer, it was found that Venezuela, Brazil and Jordan imported large quantities of heaters; on the face of it, this was surprising. By subsequent research, and a personal visit overseas, it was ascertained that Venezuelan and Brazilian coffee growers found a certain type of heater, similar to that already manufactured by the company, highly suitable for drying coffee beans quickly, thus avoiding the onset of rot or disease in storage; in the case of Jordan, another type of heater was already selling well for use at night, when there is a sharp drop in temperature.

The refractory brick company found that there were substantial imports of refractory bricks throughout the Caribbean territories, a region never previously sold to by the company. Again, further investigation by the marketing manager revealed that refractory bricks manufactured to European specifications were widely used to line the furnaces in sugarcane processing plants.

As a result of identifying new markets by use of product codes, both these companies have in the last three years developed substantial and profitable business, not only in completely new markets; but for new product applications.

The exercise that follows shows the results of applying sectoral analysis to the performance of four sectors of UK industry. Data from both the UK Customs Statistical Office and the BOTB Export Intelligence Service have been retrieved, using the SITC and CCCN product codes and the UN country code. The following products have been taken from the Overseas Trade Statistics (OTS) at BOTB, comprising the 30 major export product categories:

– Packaging Machinery
– Electrical Machinery
– Commercial Vehicles
– Building Materials and Fabricated Components

Furthermore, 10 of the top 50 UK overseas markets have been selected.

The first step is to make a statistical analysis, using the codes referred to, which shows (1) total imports by value (c.i.f.) of these products into other countries, (2) exports by value (f.o.b.) from the UK of these products to each country, and (3) the index over five years showing rates of growth or decline in (1) and (2). This statistical analysis is shown in Tables 1.5 and 1.6 as follows:

Table 1.5: Sector 1—High demand/High supply
             Sector 2—Low demand/High supply
Table 1.6: Sector 3—Low demand/Low supply
             Sector 4—High demand/Low supply

The second step is to construct a 'grid' which will give, at a glance, some important indications of the prospects of this country's exports in target markets overseas. The location of the product on this grid is the key to a rapid reading of how it is positioned overseas and what the implications are for promotion, competition, product development and market follow-up.

The grids for the four products selected are shown as follows:

– Packaging Machinery   Fig. 1.1
– Electrical Machinery   Fig. 1.2
– Commercial Vehicles   Fig. 1.3
– Building Materials and Fabricated Components   Fig. 1.4

The positions of these products on the grid are plotted by reading off the supply and demand index values shown in Tables 1.5 and 1.6. Clearly, it follows from the positions plotted on the grid that the growth or decline in the exporting country's market share for each product is determined on the grid by its distance from the diagonal axis. This axis represents a constant market share situation. Points to the right of the diagonal line represent an increasing market share, while those on the left indicate a decreasing market share.

The following indicators can now be highlighted on the four products and ten overseas markets in Figs 1.1–1.4.

In those countries with rapidly rising demand (sector 1), UK market shares have remained fairly stable in Greece and South Africa for building materials and fabricated components and in Sweden and West Germany for packaging machinery; exports of commercial vehicles to Greece and West Germany have also maintained market share. Demand is lower in sector 3 for electrical machinery in South Africa and the USA, and for commercial vehicles in Switzerland. With effective promotional activ-

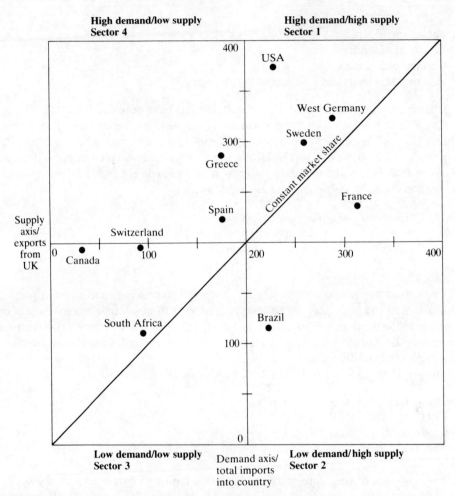

Fig. 1.1 Sectoral analysis of export markets for packaging machinery.

ities, it should be possible to increase market shares in sector 1, where demand is clearly rising faster than in sector 3, where it is particularly low, for packaging machinery in South Africa and for commercial vehicles in Brazil.

UK market shares have increased markedly for packaging machinery to France, for electrical machinery to West Germany, France and Brazil, and for commercial vehicles to the USA. (That is, these markets are plotted farthest to the right of the diagonal axis.) High performance in these markets suggests strong competitive advantage, which should be analysed and strengthened by management. This means planning a high level of promotional activity in markets where demand is already high and justifies further investment. In the case of sector 3, a very low level of demand for

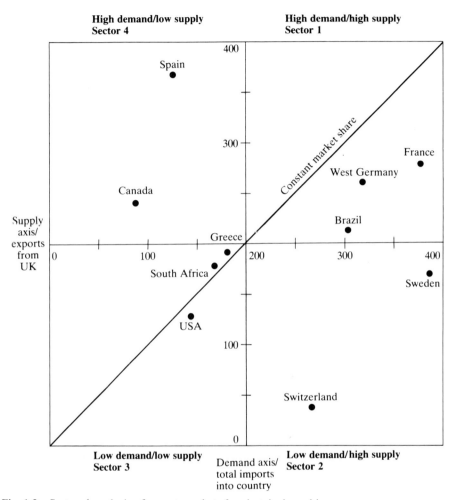

Fig. 1.2 Sectoral analysis of export markets for electrical machinery.

packaging machinery in Canada and Switzerland, and for commercial vehicles in Spain, does not offer good prospects for a fast recovery, and these are not products which, at present, would appear to warrant strong marketing campaigns.

Most significant for UK export promotion strategy is the group of overseas markets in sector 4 for which demand is clearly high and UK's supply is currently low. For example, there is low export performance by UK industry in the supply of packaging machinery to Greece and Spain, of commercial vehicles to Canada and Sweden, electrical machinery to Canada and Spain, and building materials and fabricated components to the USA, Canada and France. These indicators suggest that there are some marketing weaknesses in UK exporting to countries where demand is high,

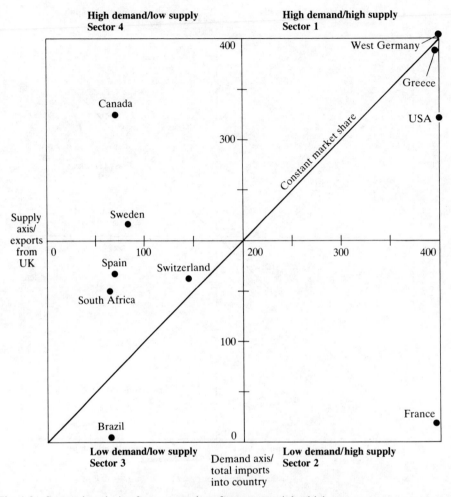

High demand/low supply
Sector 4

High demand/high supply
Sector 1

Low demand/low supply
Sector 3

Demand axis/
total imports
into country

Low demand/high supply
Sector 2

Fig. 1.3 Sectoral analysis of export markets for commercial vehicles.

whether in product design and adaptation, in supply and delivery, in pricing or in effective promotion, compared with other countries supplying these products. Sector 4 demands, and indeed should repay, detailed investigation by management of why their particular industry has actually fallen behind in high growth markets.

In general terms, therefore, sectoral analysis can be applied precisely to countries and products. In fact, it offers two dimensions for analysis and planning:

1a. the growth or decline in value of UK exports of one product to selected overseas markets (horizontal supply axis);
1b. the growth or decline in value of imports of a selected product into a group of overseas markets (vertical demand axis);

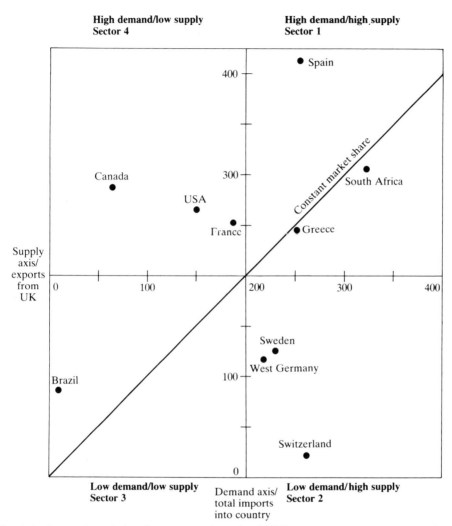

Fig. 1.4 Sectoral analysis of export markets for building materials and fabricated components.

2a. the growth or decline in value of UK exports to one selected overseas market of a number of products (horizontal supply axis);

2b. the growth or decline in value of imports into one selected market of a group of export products (vertical demand axis).

For example, while some well established overseas markets can be clearly positioned in sector 1 for a particular product, other overseas markets may be located in sector 2 of the grid, perhaps because of foreign exchange problems or new local indus-

Table 1.5 Sectoral analysis of export markets

SITC	CCCN	Product	UN CC	Country	Demand — Total imports of product into country Value (£m) 1979	Demand — Index* 1974–9	Supply — Product exports to country from UK Value (£m) 1979	Supply — Index* 1974–9
Sector 1: High demand/high supply								
745.20	84.19	Packaging machinery	21 840	USA	37.1	371	3.08	218
			55 752	Sweden	3.61	292	0.177	256
			53 280	West Germany	23.34	318	1.24	284
			53 250	France	12.64	234	0.395	312
716.21	85.01	Electrical machinery	53 250	France	19.7	277	1.26	374
			53 280	West Germany	80.79	257	4.44	314
			33 076	Brazil	2.77	211	0.052	301
783.10	87.02	Commercial vehicles	53 280	West Germany	674	409	12.0	402
			53 300	Greece	4.6	406	0.26	398
			21 840	USA	909.5	311	2.81	406
278.12	25.02– 25.10	Building materials and fabricated components	57 724	Spain	0.556	410	0.042	252
			11 710	South Africa	9.03	300	0.484	320
			53 300	Greece	0.192	246	0.025	245
Sector 2: Low demand/high supply								
745.20	84.19	Packaging machinery	33 076	Brazil	0.389	114	0.044	219
716.21	85.01	Electrical machinery	55 752	Sweden	10.89	158	3.17	398
			55 756	Switzerland	1.86	37	0.50	264
783.10	87.02	Commercial Vehicles	53 250	France	168.8	14	6.17	400
278.12	25.02– 25.10	Building materials and fabricated components	55 752	Sweden	4.15	124	1.59	229
			53 280	West Germany	36.63	116	5.37	209
			55 756	Switzerland	3.52	23	0.72	260

*1974 index = 100

Table 1.6 Sectoral analysis of export markets

SITC	CCCN	Product	UN CC	Country	Demand — Total imports of product into country, Value (£m) 1979	Demand — Index,* 1974–9	Supply — Product exports to country from UK, Value (£m) 1979	Supply — Index,* 1974–9
Sector 3: Low demand/low supply								
745.20	84.19	Packaging machinery	55 756	Switzerland	5.66	199	0.119	98
			21 124	Canada	7.62	190	0.069	35
			11 710	South Africa	6.63	105	0.90	89
716.21	85.01	Electrical machinery	53 300	Greece	0.416	188	0.087	184
			11 710	South Africa	37.1	179	10.5	171
			21 840	USA	1512.0	126	40.5	148
783.10	87.02	Commercial vehicles	57 724	Spain	0.367	163	0.023	68
			55 756	Switzerland	91.3	157	5.16	145
			11 710	South Africa	219.2	146	1.11	67
			33 076	Brazil	0.28	4	0.110	67
278.12	25.02–25.10	Building materials and fabricated components	33 076	Brazil	1.25	83	0.070	13
Sector 4: High demand/low supply								
745.20	84.19	Packaging machinery	53 300	Greece	0.144	283	0.090	176
			57 724	Spain	0.222	223	0.074	176
716.21	85.01	Electrical machinery	57 724	Spain	0.319	359	0.015	125
			21 124	Canada	155.2	236	3.53	90
783.10	87.02	Commercial vehicles	21 124	Canada	222.3	315	0.092	72
			55 752	Sweden	51.46	209	0.962	83
278.12	25.02–25.10	Building materials and fabricated components	21 124	Canada	46.2	281	0.35	64
			21 840	USA	1317.6	266	13.66	155
			53 250	France	17.6	251	1.3	191

*1974 index = 100

17

tries supplying more of the domestic demand; nevertheless, if one or two countries can be identified in sector 4 of the grid—High demand/low supply—the export potential of that product in those markets is very high.

Each of these sectors clearly has different implications for marketing strategy. Products in sector 4, for instance, warrant the most active promotional efforts because exporters have not tapped the large market that exists. Those in the other sectors offer less favourable prospects for increased trade. The products that fall into each of the four sectors can, therefore, be categorized into top-, medium- and low-priority targets, with this breakdown forming the basis of marketing planning.

Of course, it is necessary to take into account in this analysis the general economic situation in both the supplying and the overseas target markets, the particularities of the product, the local supply situation, the structure of sub-markets or market segments in each overseas (importing) country and the impact of inflation on export values and currency fluctuations.

Clearly, what is of value to management is to know in which group of products there are overseas countries with untapped demand, and which groups of countries have similar sales potential for one homogeneous group of products. Once the sector where exports can be increased has been identified, management action in terms of overseas representation, supply capacity, finance, promotion and follow-up can be put on a planned basis. It follows that, where stagnant or declining overseas markets are identified, the action to generate more demand or pull out and devote resources to markets with better potential must be taken (see Tables 1.5 and 1.6). But this strategic appraisal using sectoral analysis clearly must come first, and planning second. In too many companies there is little planning, and sadly deficient strategic analysis, partly because there prevails a short-term view of business overseas, and partly because such techniques as sectoral analysis using trade intelligence are not known or used.

1.3 Multi-country research

Introduction

The applications of research techniques to international markets can be complex, and they require careful design and control. Management must be alert to the following important aspects:

1. validity of data;
2. comparability of results;
3. organization of multi-country research.

Some of the operational problems of implementing multi-country research are indicated by some of the following factors commonly encountered.

1. *Languages and literacy*. The need to verify accuracy and validity of translation.
2. *Patterns of consumption*. Usage rates and product applications can vary widely across countries.

3. *Social organizations.* Decision-making within families and groups can also differ considerably (e.g., the 'head of household' may not have the same social identity).
4. *Cultural values.* Behaviour patterns and attitudes towards products, brands, etc. (e.g., differences in levels of response to questionnaires) need to be understood if multi-country research is to produce comparable results.
5. *Economic and market conditions.* Per capita income, purchasing power and the structure of sub-markets in each country to be researched must be understood.
6. *Sources and quality of information.* Published data (e.g. census statistics, industry sales data) are sparse or, worse, unreliable in some countries.

Of course, not all errors and omissions can be fully resolved in multi-country research, and management must use research results with discrimination, allowing for some of the significant differences outlined above. One analysis[7] sums up this aspect:

> In order to have truly comparable data from multi-national markets, it is not sufficient to attempt to control sources of error. Since such errors will never be completely eliminated, the data, having been collected, have to be adjusted for residual error sources.
>
> However, before such adjustments can be done, much more knowledge is required. Such knowledge is generally obtained at a cost and usually requires some form of experimentation. And here is where one of the major problems arises in the multi-national marketing field. First, the funds for conducting such research may not be readily available, as research budgets are generally controlled at the national level, and at that level the concern about comparability across nations is not as strongly felt. More important, however, is the general nature of the problem—the subject does not lend itself to experimental design.

So multi-country research involves dealing with countries that differ not only in language, but also in economic and social structures, in behaviour and in attitude patterns. It is essential that these differences are taken into account in the formulation of the initial design of a multi-country survey, and they may well necessitate variations in the research methods to be applied in individual countries. To ignore these differences in the interests of a spurious comparability is to commit the cardinal error of many researchers, both national and international: namely, to take a technique rather than a problem-orientated view of their function. After all, the purpose of market research is to help in the solution of marketing problems, and the purpose of multi-country research is to help in the solution of multi-country marketing problems. There are, of course, a number of these problems that can be solved by using exactly the same sample design and asking exactly the same questions in all the countries under investigation; frequently, however, the imposition of a rigid research structure on a number of very different countries may defeat the very objectives that the research is trying to achieve.

Data collection and data interpretation

At this stage, an important distinction should be made between (1) comparability in data collection and (2) comparability in interpretation.

While the achievement of comparability at the data collection stage may be no more than an academic research exercise, comparability at the interpretation stage is absolutely essential to any research that has been set up to provide a basis for international planning. Whether the decision-making is concerned with priorities between countries for a new product introduction, or the advisability of a product modification in a number of existing markets, or the viability of an international advertising campaign, the research must be structured in such a way that the results can be used to make valid comparisons between the countries covered. In other words, a multi-country survey must be able to provide a basis for the solution of marketing problems such as 'How should marketing expenditure be distributed between various countries?' or 'To what extent should the product, or the pack, or the advertising, be varied between one country and another?' Multi-country research can help in the solution of these or similarly international marketing problems only if the results enable us to measure one country against another—in other words, if comparability is achieved at the interpretation stage.

However, this achievement does not necessarily require that the same type of information be collected in each country, or that the information be collected in the same way in each country:[8]

> Research methods might differ considerably but still allow comparability on the indirect or interpretative level . . . [it is possible,] . . . even though utilising varying methods, to provide information comparable in the sense of answering the same marketing questions for all three markets.

So failure to take into account these factors, and in particular some of the important differences across countries, can result in embarrassing and highly misleading conclusions, as in Case example 1.2.

Designing multi-country surveys

Differences in behaviour and attitude patterns, then, may necessitate considerable differences in survey design. In Britain, Germany and Scandinavia, for instance, beer is generally regarded as an alcoholic beverage, and the factors underlying its consumption are similar to those underlying the consumption of other alcoholic beverages; in Greece, Spain or Italy, however, beer is regarded much more like a soft drink, such as Coca Cola or orange squash. A survey designed to help a beer manufacturer determine his marketing strategy in Europe would have to obtain information on behaviour and attitudes in relation to soft drinks in some countries and in relation to alcoholic beverages in others.

There are many other examples of how the design of a multi-country survey can be affected by differences in attitude or behaviour patterns between one country and another. A German housewife, for instance, if asked about her use of bar chocolate for cooking or on sandwiches would—to say the least—be somewhat surprised; however, in France cooking is an important use for bar chocolate, and in Switzerland it is quite common for children to be given a bar of chocolate between two slices of bread to eat during the school break.

Extremes of poverty and wealth in some countries may limit the market—and consequently the usefulness of market research, for a number of products—to a restricted sector of the population. There are many products in the toiletry, cosmetics, packaged food and electrical appliances field for which it would be wasteful to cover all social grades in many of the less affluent countries.

Case example 1.2
A commissioned survey into the purchase and consumption of spaghetti and macaroni was done some years ago in Western Europe.

Among a lot of other information, this survey gave the impression that the consumption of spaghetti and macaroni was significantly higher in France and West Germany than in Italy. The percentages of households buying spaghetti and macaroni for use in the home were:

	Percentage
France	90
West Germany	71
Italy	63
Luxembourg	61
Belgium	45
Netherlands	45

Taken at their face value, these results suggest that popular notions about Italian eating habits are quite mistaken, and that spaghetti is really the national dish of France or West Germany rather than Italy! The trouble was that the relevant question in all countries was concerned with packaged and branded spaghetti, and many Italians buy their spaghetti loose. Subsequent analysis showed that, if the question had been asked in a different way, the result for Italy would have been 98–100 per cent.

There is also the question of different 'universes' to be considered; in market research, the term 'universe' is applied to the total population a particular survey is designed to cover. Completely different circumstances may result in a different universe having to be covered in each country.

While a multi-country survey will, of course, throw light on the differences in attitudes and behaviour between one country and another, few manufacturers have the inclination or the resources to acquire this type of knowledge for its own sake. The objectives of most manufacturers embarking on a multi-country study are normally dictated by several practical considerations, such as evolving a product formulation likely to achieve acceptance in the maximum number of countries, or adapting marketing and advertising strategy to differing local conditions. The purpose of most multi-country surveys is not to obtain information on basic economic and cultural differences: these should constitute the background against which a multi-country survey is planned; in other words, they should have already been understood and appreciated at the planning stage, since they are basic to the formulation of the initial design of such a survey.

Case example 1.3
In an eight-country survey among doctors on an ethical pharmaceutical product, it was found that in the Netherlands general practitioners are very restricted in the drugs they are allowed to prescribe, and there was no possibility of the product under examination being included in the Dutch national insurance list. Interviews were therefore limited to hospitals and specialists. In Belgium, however, general practitioners have considerable freedom in the drugs they prescribe; most of the interviews were, therefore, carried out with this group. The problem was the same in both countries, namely, to establish the acceptability of the product among the medical profession. However, there would have been no point in interviewing general practitioners in the Netherlands, or in concentrating on specialists in Belgium. Comparability at the interpretation stage was achieved in so far as the relative acceptability of the product in the two countries was established, but the methods of data collection were very different.

Organization and control of research activities
These considerations make it clear that multi-country research is a very different type of operation from single-country research. They also have an important bearing on the type of people or organizations that are able to carry out multi-country research. A researcher or research organization that thinks in terms of one country only is unlikely to have the adaptability, knowledge or experience to conduct multi-country research. Researchers or research organizations operating on an international scale not only have to think internationally (and speak a number of languages), but also have to have a considerable experience and knowledge about individual countries and international conditions. They must be constantly prepared to draw on this fund of knowledge or to obtain new information when faced with a specific research problem. Moreover, they must be capable of using this knowledge, as well as their knowledge of research techniques, when designing a multi-country survey. In other words, they must be international marketing men/women as well as market researchers.

Case example 1.4
A questionnaire was administered by a research agency to women in each of seven countries. The questionnaire was concerned with whether the respondent was married or engaged, whether she had received an engagement ring, and the type of engagement ring she had received. The first three questions on the questionnaire used in England were:

(a) Are you married?
       If YES: in what year were you married?
       If NO: are you engaged to be married?

If married or engaged, ask:
(b) Do you own an engagement ring, or did you obtain one or more rings at the time
      of your engagement?

If YES:

(c) What type of ring is it/was it?
      – No stones
      – Single diamond only
      – Several diamonds, no other stones
      – Diamond(s) and other stones
      – Other stones only

This looks like a very simple list of questions, involving no difficulty of direct translation, and yet, if they had been applied as they stood in all seven countries, the results
would have been meaningless.

The question, 'Do you own an engagement ring?' would not have worked in
Germany since many German women receive a plain gold band at the time of engagement which they later transfer to the other hand and use as a wedding ring. Frequently, there is an exchange of rings between the couple at the time of engagement,
and a whole battery of questions was needed to obtain information for West
Germany that was equivalent to that for the other six countries.

Another modification to ensure comparability concerned the list of pre-coded ring
types. Although pearl rings were relatively unimportant in most of the countries
covered, they accounted for a high proportion in France. To include pearl rings as a
separate category in most of the countries would have unnecessarily complicated the
list; however, to exclude them in Japan or France would have resulted not only in a
loss of information but also in confusion arising from the list of ring types being incomplete.

In organizing research activities, particularly as far as co-ordination and control
are concerned, Table 1.7 illustrates some appropriate options in terms of management
organization. Moreover, the determination and application of research techniques
best suited to the multi-country marketing problem to be solved usually involves a
high degree of co-ordination and central control; this is to maintain standards of verification and comparability in both planning and interpretation.[9]

To achieve these objectives, a method often used is to sub-contract local fieldwork
and basic editing, while doing the planning, questionnaire development, analysis and
interpretation centrally; the work of local sub-contractors must be closely supervised
on the spot by executives of the contracting agency.

Table 1.7 Organizational options for international marketing research (*Source*: Simon Majaro, *International Marketing: A Strategic Approach to World Markets* (rev. edn), Allen & Unwin, London, pp. 74–5)

Structure style	Main characteristics	Typical problems and/or strengths	
		Problems	Strengths
'MACROPYRAMID'	1. A central marketing research department is responsible to a central strategic person, e.g. marketing director. 2. Such a department is responsible for total research effort throughout world. It prepares budgets and determines presentation. 3. Marketing research officers located in major foreign units are still responsible to boss in centre. Their relationship to managers in own market is purely functional. 4. Heavy travelling and costs. 5. Extensive use of outside agencies.	– Frequent conflict between the central MR management & local managers as to responsibilities. – Smaller markets often neglected. – Extensive & often superfluous travelling.	– Funds used in a planned fashion. – Priorities identified in a systematic way. – Communication of findings good. – Comparability sought & achieved. – The strategic level has quick & frequent access to information. – Useful opportunities to explore standardization possibilities.
'UMBRELLA'	1. A small marketing research department forms part of central services. Its role is mainly advisory, educational & residual viz. dealing with corporate matters. 2. Marketing research activities are undertaken at local levels & are responsible to local marketing management. Relationship to central MR department is purely functional. 3. Larger foreign subsidiaries have their own MR departments; smaller units will use outside agencies as required. As soon as expenditure rises to a certain level, they tend to have own MR facilities. 4. Aggregate expenditure throughout the world is heavy.	– Inadequate communication of information and findings. – Poor comparability of data. – Heavy total expenditure.	– Adaptability to local needs. – Local MR personnel understand fully market conditions. – Can be a useful source of creative ideas.

The steps undertaken in a typical multi-country survey are as follows.

1. The project is discussed at length with the client.
2. The fieldwork agencies for each country are selected.
3. The questionnaire is developed centrally.
4. The questionnaire is translated locally and the translation is checked centrally.
5. The questionnaire is piloted locally.
6. The questionnaire is finalized centrally.
7. The interviewers are briefed locally by an executive of the central company.
8. The fieldwork is carried out.
9. A coding and editing plan is provided for the local agencies.
10. The edited and coded questionnaires are returned to head office.
11. A coding and editing check is carried out centrally.
12. Computing is carried out centrally.

Co-ordination and control to this degree are usually essential if management is to arrive at and apply the technique that is best suited in each country to the solution of the research problem, and to achieve comparability of quality and of interpretation. And central ownership, or membership of a chain of the local research agencies, cannot in itself be considered the equivalent of central control and co-ordination. Central control and co-ordination mean that one researcher or research group is responsible for a multi-country research project in all the countries covered, much as an international brand manager is responsible for the brands in all his markets. It involves horizontal rather than vertical lines of responsibility. While this can happen in chains of research agencies—and there are certain advantages in belonging to a chain—in a centrally controlled and co-ordinated multi-country research study, it is irrelevant whether the local agencies used for fieldwork belong to the same chain or not.

The earlier part of this section has emphasized the necessity of taking local conditions into account in the planning and execution of multi-country research; the emphasis here is on the need for central control and co-operation. These two aspects may appear to be in contradiction since it may be argued that, if local conditions have so much effect on the research design, the best way of carrying out multi-country research may be to leave the determination of techniques and the interpretation of results in the hands of a separate, locally based company in each of the countries covered. This is in practice what frequently happens in multi-country research.

> International market research is that research undertaken regarding market circumstances in countries additional to or other than the one in which the client company's head office is located, so that relevant decision-taking personnel in that company may be expected to be unfamiliar, to a greater or lesser degree, with the circumstances of the individual country and markets and of those who operate in them.[10]

Excessive anxiety over the problem of dealing with a number of different and alien countries simultaneously can result in using six different research organizations for a six-country study and letting them implement it in their own way, on the basis of local knowledge. Frequently, the main criterion for selecting a local research company is that somebody there speaks English, or whatever is the language of the originators of the research. The selection of local research companies for a multi-country study is a highly skilled task, involving not only considerable research experience but also extensive knowledge of local conditions. Unless local research companies are carefully selected and supervised, a multi-country study is likely to be a failure. For example, the local staff may tend to have a very subjective view of conditions in their country. The acquisition of knowledge of local conditions should not depend exclusively on the views of one company, which may have a vested interest in doing things in a particular way, but rather on a combination of the study of published statistics and previous research findings, and an objective examination of the experience of a number of people involved in marketing and other relevant fields in the country concerned. Moreover, any survey covering a number of countries must be thoroughly piloted in each of the countries covered, not only to deal with problems of language, but also to establish whether the questionnaire and survey techniques are viable in the context of the area in which they are supposed to be applied.

Another hazard of over-fragmentation is that research companies in different countries may differ not only in the quality of their work but also in the techniques they employ. Many research companies have their own favourite techniques, which are not necessarily determined by the particular conditions of the country in which they operate. In fact, the differences—both in approach and in quality—between one research company and another in the same country frequently are greater than the differences between research companies in different countries. While it may well be necessary to vary the research approach from country to country, these variations should certainly not depend on the 'quirks' of individual research companies. Nothing is more hazardous in multi-country research than to have to brief six or more different research companies, each with its own background of experience and its own way of working. It is quite possible that each of these organizations may interpret and execute the brief in a different way. Moreover, it is unlikely that a research organization operating in one country only—and especially in a small country—will have the knowledge and experience of all the research techniques applicable to any particular research problem.

A project director responsible for the survey in all the countries covered is not only more likely to have a deeper overall understanding of the marketing problem to be solved than a research agency in any one of the countries to be covered; he is also much more likely to be experienced in a greater variety of research approaches and techniques. Moreover, he is in a position to assess objectively the value or otherwise of the research methods practised by local research agencies, and frequently he is able to suggest alternative methods to the benefit of both parties involved. Finally, the greatest hazard in fragmenting a multi-country research project between a number of local research agencies is that management has no way of knowing whether the differences that have emerged are genuine differences, or whether they are merely the result of differences between the research approaches, or the research capabilities, of the local market research agencies. Market research can help to solve international marketing problems only if uncertainties of this type are eliminated, and if management has a valid basis for measuring one country against another, so that comparability is achieved at the interpretation stage. And this can be ensured only by central planning, control and interpretation.

1.4 Trade intelligence and information technology

Introduction

This section is concerned with some applications of trade intelligence systems (TISs) to improve analysis, planning and control in international markets; there will also be some assessment of information technology and its impact on competitiveness. First, a TIS is designed to provide remote-access intelligence which is up-to-date, specific and actionable. A flow chart of TIS is contained in Fig. 1.5.

The need for a thorough analysis of TIS is underlined by the haphazard ways in which many companies trading internationally obtain, interpret and act on market data. Despite its long tradition in overseas trade, the UK still lacks a strategically planned approach to overseas markets by companies. Yet it is clear that companies that have access to market data through a TIS are in a better position to identify and measure market opportunities.

There are complex problems in obtaining and processing data about overseas markets and relating them to company resources, particularly finance, marketing and production. The complexity arises because there are over 130 national country markets in the world; added to this is the 'distance'—physical, cultural and commercial—which produces a critical intelligence gap for many companies.

Traditional sources of information such as trade, press and bank reports, feedbacks from agents and export staff are still widely used. Yet these sources, while of some tactical value to companies already operating overseas, provide little in the way of market data that can be used for international planning. Indeed, a planned, strategically based approach to world markets requires the more sophisticated data base that a trade intelligence system can provide. Effective use of a TIS can enable companies to identify and quantify market opportunities and growth prospects.

Two reports have underlined this lack of a systematic approach to world markets by British industry. NEDO, using international statistics, argues:[11]

> Too many British companies treat exporting as a marginal activity; there is a lack of a systematic and researched approach to quantify growth prospects and market opportunities overseas for strategic planning.

Secondly, the Barclays Bank report on industrial and export performance[12] argues that many British companies do not systematically research and quantify foreign market potential; this pertains not just to small- and medium-sized exporters but to '122 British companies that are responsible for about 25 per cent of exports of manufactured goods'. The BBI report goes on to emphasize the need to concentrate on

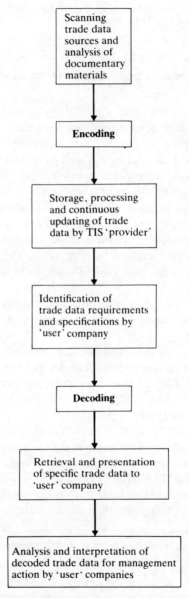

Fig. 1.5   Flow chart of a trade intelligence system (TIS).

Table 1.8 Information sources used by UK companies (%)

Information source	%
Feedback from export sales staff	61
Trade associations and Chambers of Commerce	54
General knowledge	44
Press reports	32
Export departments of banks	29
Local press & journals	20
Test marketing	5
Financial institutions	14
No information base	15

'key' overseas markets; but this presupposes an effective intelligence gathering system to identify them. Indeed, the report found it remarkable how few British companies know where they are strong (e.g. in which geographical area); in those cases where they *could* identify their success areas, managers were frequently surprised at the composition of such a list.

How much use do UK companies make of trade intelligence systems? The answer is, statistically, little. Some further researches in a regional sample of British companies in key industrial export sectors[13] have shown that most companies use published data from trade associations and Chambers of Commerce, and from information received from their overseas offices: 15 per cent of companies have no information base at all for their export operations, 44 per cent use general knowledge, and approximately 30 per cent use trade and financial press and export departments of banks (see Table 1.8). These researches also analysed the most frequently used government services in UK (Table 1.9). Some of these are provided under the British Overseas Trade Board's Export Intelligence Service, which is discussed below.

Table 1.9 Most frequently used government services in the UK

Rank order	Service
1	Specific export opportunities
2	Help with overseas visits
3	Tariffs
4	Finding overseas agent
5	{ Calls for tender / Economic reports
6	{ Status reports / Market reports / Export regulations

According to the British Overseas Trade Board (BOTB), British companies have been losing export business through not subscribing to the Export Intelligence Service (EIS).[14] It is arguable, therefore, that they can substantially enhance the impact, growth and profitability of their international operations by an awareness and cost-effective use of EIS and other trade intelligence systems. Furthermore, management should understand the applications of both TIS and information technology (IT).

Export Intelligence Service (EIS)

The EIS provides subscribing firms with details of specific export opportunities abroad and other items of market and economic intelligence important to exporters. Subscribers receive a tailor-made service in which their information requirements are computer-matched against data received from diplomatic posts. The service has about 7700 subscribing companies (although this is actually fewer than the membership of the London Chamber of Commerce and Industry, which is 8800). The subscription cost is £45 and 150 'notices'. The range of intelligence offered by EIS is comprehensive, and falls under numerous headings, the most important of which are:

1. specific export opportunities;
2. short market pointers to new trade opportunities;
3. market reports;
4. overseas agents seeking British principals;
5. calls for tender (including invitations to pre-qualify);
6. successful bidders and awards of contracts;
7. overseas business visitors to the UK;
8. outward opportunities for co-operation with overseas firms;
9. inward opportunities for co-operation with overseas firms;
10. changes in overseas tariffs and import regulations;
11. aid and loan agreements (international and UK);
12. trade agreements;
13. national and other development plans; general economic reports;
14. lines of credit opened by the Export Credits Guarantee Department (ECGD);
15. notification of overseas trade fairs, exhibitions, missions (inward and outward); store promotions;
16. world economic comments and quarterly overseas trading reports.

The EIS also provides data on geographical classifications (Section 2) and commodity classifications (Section 3, Chapters 1–98). A relatively recent addition is Section 4 (Chapter 99), covering consultancy services, projects, joint ventures, contracting services, plant and equipment, supplies and components, all manufactured to overseas customers' specifications. This part of the EIS classification system covers intelligence that cannot be identified in terms of the individual commodities in Chapters 1–98.

It is not generally appreciated by many British companies that the EIS has recently been substantially improved in both its range of data and its speed of transmission.

More sophisticated data processing enables companies to receive data on more specific opportunities overseas relative to their own production capacity and technical resources. With the new system, the information received from Britain's commercial officers in diplomatic posts around the world is keyed into an ICL 1904S computer using a CMC Sovereign multiple processor keying system. After the computer has identified subscribers' interests, the information is reproduced on continuous stationery by computer-linked high-speed printers. This output is then enveloped by a Kern mark-sensing in-line guillotine inserter ready for mailing to subscribers. The same computer also prints out the master copy of the Daily Gazette, a compendium of each day's information complete with an index. Using this master, copies of the Daily Gazette are reproduced on a Rank Xerox 9200.

Significantly, a number of countries are now storing 'export opportunity' sales leads for their nationals, collected from their embassies abroad on computer data bases. It is clear that British embassies in important markets will soon need to have terminal facilities for the remote searching and updating of these data bases, available to any travelling national who does not have his own terminal and password.

The former Central Policy Review Staff, in the course of a *Review of Overseas Representation*,[15] questioned the value EIS really has, and commissioned a research study[16] to find out how useful subscribers find the EIS notices. This study revealed that only a minority—30 per cent—of the 'notices' received by the sample of subscribers interviewed were considered useful. The majority were seen as 'too late', 'inappropriate to the subscriber's business', etc. Of this 30 per cent minority, only a third, or 10 per cent of the notices received, led to some action being taken in terms of market development. The researchers regard this as a low success rate, although it compares quite favourably with the average response rate experienced in direct mail (about 2 per cent).

The most interesting finding, however, is that the information contained in the 'notices'—whether actionable or not—is, in the view of the sample of subscribers, available elsewhere only in a small minority (under 20 per cent) of the cases. There seems clear evidence that, whatever its quality, efficiency or cost effectiveness, EIS can fairly be regarded as an irreplaceable intelligence medium.

How can the scope and impact of EIS be improved? Clearly, it is essential to make the EIS 1904S computer accessible to British companies by Telex or else by Prestel, the remote access teledata system operated in UK by the Post Office Telecommunications. Export sales leads and market opportunities then can not only be input directly into the computer from foreign posts but can be accessible directly by subscribing companies in their offices. The technology for this exists; indeed, the US Department of Commerce, through its Trade Opportunities Scheme (TOP), and the Italian External Commerce Institute (ICE) are introducing just such a system for their exporters.

With modern data retrieval software, the subscriber can have far more flexible options for enquiry than the rigid pre-keyed coding of 'notices' and 'subscriber-profiles'. Also, with this software the subscriber can communicate back directly to the overseas post which is the source of the original sales lead, requesting further information or other follow-up action on the spot (within minutes of identifying leads that do seem worth following up).

One further point about computerization: at present all foreign import data are held at BOTB in the original; without the use of trade classifications, these data would be unusable, because of the problems of product definition, language and currency movements. It is essential that such data be computerized at an early date so that they become available as trade intelligence on a remote-access basis. The same requirement for computerization applies to the Bill of Entry Section at HM Customs and Excise, where all data on British exports are collated.

Interfile

Interfile was developed by the New York World Trade Center, and offered a computerized TIS to subscribing companies throughout the world through the network of world trade centres. It codified world trade under three main codes: a Function code, a Country code and a Commodity code. (The complete range of the Function code is shown in Table 1.10.) This coding system, developed by the International Marketing Institute of Cambridge, Massachusetts, was employed for the computerized trade intelligence service by the New York World Trade Center.

Interfile had the following operating features.

1. It lent itself easily to automated handling and provided for efficient storage and quick retrieval of data sources.
2. It provided for constant updating to accommodate the frequent changes in world trade regulations, import and export data, economic conditions in various countries and other changes.
3. It provided a cross-reference index so that data related to any subject for any specific commodity and any country or region could be quickly identified.
4. It was adaptable, to provide for the incorporation of new sources and new categories of data.
5. It was compatible with existing international nomenclature and codes in order to facilitate the world-wide interchange of data.
6. The codes were all numerical, avoiding any language difficulties.

Some explanation of the coding system used in Interfile is now required. The Function code provided rapid identification of source material for all major factors relating to world commerce, such as trade statistics, import and export regulations, fiscal policies, financial data and many others. It was a five-digit numerical code with some 220 function sub-codes under 33 major headings. This code was reviewed by a number of leading authorities in international business in the USA and in other countries. Changes and additions were made from time to time, and there was provision for adding new subject headings to the list by leaving unused numbers throughout the code. The Function code of Interfile was also of significance in that it codified every

Table 1.10   Interfile function code

Code	Function	Code	Function
03000	Advertising and sales promotion	51600 Sub-	Policy
03304 Sub-code	Showrooms and display centres	code	Purchasing in international business
		52000	Management consultants
06000	Banking and finance	54210	Market indicators
08000	Channels of distribution		Market factors
09000	Commodity/product information	60000	Port facilities
12000	Documentation	63000	Postal shipments and regulations
15000	Economic, social and political data	69000	Product development and technology
15112 Sub-code	Economic indicators and forecasts	69104 Sub-code	Product design
			Industrial design
18000	Business firms	72000	Public relations
18510 Sub-code	Buyers' guides	75000	Regional trade blocs and economic unions
	Government buyers		
	Purchasing agents	78000	Data sources and services
21000	Foreign trade regulations	80000	International trade and business associations
21600 Sub-code	Import standards and specifications		
		82000	Trade contracts: foreign sources in country
24000	Free trade zones		
27000	Freight forwarding	84000	Trade contacts abroad: overseas offices of country
36000	Insurance		
39000	International organizations	86000	Trade promotion
42000	International business terminology	86104 Sub-code	Trade delegations and missions
45000	Investment opportunities and regulations		Outgoing missions
		90000	Translation services
46000	Investments	92000	Transportation and shipment of commodities
48000	Legal information		
48406 Sub-code	Taxation	94000	Travel and tourism
	Corporate overseas earnings	96000	World weights and measures
51000	Management International business		

activity in trade and manufacturing, including export services, marketing research, advertising and promotional activities and purchasing operations overseas.

The Country code employed in Interfile was based on the United Nations Country Code (UNCC). Certain modifications were made to provide for new economic groups, trade blocs and new nations which emerged since the UNCC was designed. UNCC has several advantages.

1. It is universal in scope, including not only all countries of the world but also all territories, possessions and other entities that constitute significant trading areas.
2. It is compatible with existing international nomenclature, since it is the result of agreement among all members of the United Nations. Thus, it can provide a common basis for the world-wide interchange of trade data based on a common code.
3. It has the flexibility required to provide for political changes which may take place in the future, since the code numbers are spaced at intervals of four.

4. The code provides for efficient computerization. The first two digits identify areas, economic groupings or trade blocs, and the final three digits identify individual countries. In a computerized system, if a search of data sources for a particular country is not successful, the computer can move automatically to the next higher classification such as trade bloc, area or continent.

For coding commodity data, Interfile used the Standard International Trade Classification (SITC) (Revised), which has already been explained.

Interfile was designed for the identification, storage and quick retrieval of data sources covering all aspects of world commerce. Sources were books, directories, trade journals, magazines, documents or other publications, plus other data banks, agencies of government, international organizations or commercial firms that offered consulting or research services. Each source entered in Interfile was coded by function, country and commodity. For printed materials, the name of the publication and a brief abstract of its contents, date, number of pages, price and publisher were included. When the source was an organization or agency, the file entry included a brief description of the services offered, the address and the telephone number. Data sources that covered more than one subject, country or commodity were coded accordingly. A special code letter on the computer printout identified publications that were maintained physically in the data collection. For publications not available at the New York World Trade Center, a special ordering service was provided.

Interfile was the most comprehensive, computerized TIS available for some years. It has recently been superseded by a new, electronic transmission system called 'NETWORK', also developed by the World Trade Center. This has been on-line for two years, and access to NETWORK can now be gained by telephone for companies subscribing to the World Trade Centres Association. Through NETWORK, companies can put offers to sell in an electronic data base, and importers world-wide can call up the offers on their computer screen. Importers can then send messages to exporters' electronic mailboxes, accepting advertised prices or initiating electronic negotiations.

IT and competitiveness

So information technology (IT) enables management to use and benefit from automated information processing in international operations. But IT also has an interesting bearing on competitiveness: an authoritative and well researched paper claims:[17]

> Information technology is changing the way companies operate. It is affecting the entire process by which companies create their products. Furthermore, it is reshaping the product itself: the entire package of physical goods, services and information companies provide to create value for their buyers.

The research cited in this section indicates that IT is also affecting competitiveness, in three ways.

1. It changes industry structure, and in so doing alters the rules of competition.

2. It creates competitive advantage by giving companies new ways to out-perform their rivals.
3. It spawns whole new businesses, often from within a company's existing operations.

In particular, IT can sustain competitive advantage by lowering costs, enhancing differentiation and changing competitive scope.

What is important to management, though, is that IT must be operational; and remotely accessible computers now have much to offer managers when they travel overseas. In countries where the national telecommunications authority does not operate a monopoly over 'message-switching', it is possible to communicate with a computer service, whether the firm's own or a time-sharing system, at less than half the cost of the telex, and through the computer with the home-based office.

Even more useful to management than simply relaying information home is the ability of the mobile executive, equipped with a portable or locally borrowed terminal, to provide his customers or distributors overseas with on-the-spot documentation rather than having to send it on later. Remote access to a well designed text processing system, such as many companies are beginning to install, can provide the executive overseas with an appropriately edited contract draft, technical proposal or specification, amended price list in the local currency or export documentation; all this can be available within hours of a business meeting. Access to a project control system in a remotely accessible computer can also enable a sales engineer abroad to provide his customer with a construction and delivery schedule that is completely up to date (and which may have changed substantially since his departure from UK factory).

Providing the link between the executive overseas and his home base is a feasible, economic and relatively simple task for well designed computer systems; yet insufficient use is made of this technology to date. Clearly, the link stands or falls by the quality of telecommunications available to the traveller, a quality that is adequate between most European countries and North America. Moreover, the company can set up the same link for its distributors, customers and agents abroad, and thereby can reduce the amount of time spent abroad problem-solving, and increase the selling potential of its own staff by the time saved.

Two new types of data technology are also available. 'Intelpost' is operated by the British Post Office and offers a new international facsimile transmission service by satellite. This means that facsimiles of commercial contracts, advertising copy, promotional designs and statistical analyses can be studied within hours by the company's associates overseas; the first link between London and Toronto is now open.

Second, with the development of Prestel, the opportunity exists of instantaneous 'view data', showing export information by country, product or other classification on the TV screen, for the personal use of export management. Prestel was the first system of its kind in the world; it links an adapted television set with a computer via the public telephone system, at home or at work, and now provides a wealth of information from latest share prices to airline schedules, advertisements and economic data. The user dials one of the new regional computers which store continuously updated data provided now by over 130 organizations such as the Central Office of Information, Reuters and the Stock Exchange. Already over 150 000 pages of information are available from such 'information providers', although access to specialized information is restricted to closed user-groups. It is estimated that there are more than 500 000 receivers meeting the needs of approximately one million users. For managers, the advantages of Prestel are visual attraction, ease of use and lower costs; they can have a small black and white receiver on their desks, with an alphanumeric keypad. Users will be guided on how to extract detailed, specific information by simple instructions and 'prompts' on the screen directing them to the required pages.

References

1. Statistical Abstracts and Bulletins of International Monetary Fund (IMF) and US Department of Commerce.
2. World Bank Atlas and Hudson Institute, Paris.
3. OECD, Paris and World Bank Atlas, New York.
4. T. J. Gordon, Changing Technology and the Future of Marketing, Conference Board Record, New York, December 1984.
5. C. G. Alexandrides and G. P. Moschis, *Export Marketing Management*, Praeger, New York, 1977, pp. 24–5.
6. B. Ancel, 'Analysing your Export Efforts', *ITC International Trade Forum*, October/ December 1978.
7. C. Mayer, 'The Lessons of Multi-national Marketing Research', *Business Horizons*, December 1978.
8. R. Day, 'The Meaning of Comparability in Multi-country Research and How to Achieve It', *Proceedings of ESOMAR Congress*, 1965.
9. J. Jenkins and J. Kendall, 'Formulating Quantified Objectives and Evaluating Progress without Profit or Sales Data', *Proceedings of ESOMAR/WAPOR Congress*, 1969.
10. C. K. Squires, 'International Industrial Market Research—Some Aspects', *Proceedings of ESOMAR/WAPOR Congress*, 1969.
11. D. Connell, 'UK Performance in International Markets—Some Evidence from International Trade Data', National Economic Development Office (NEDO), London, 1980.
12. 'Factors in International Success—Report on Export Development in France, West Germany & UK', *ITI Research*, Barclays Bank International, 1979.
13. D. W. Bromley, 'Survey of Information Requirements of Exporters', MA thesis, Sheffield University, 1976; T. Pointon, 'Economics of Government Export Promotion', PhD thesis, Cranfield, 1977.
14. *Journal of the Institute of Export*, **43**, 6, 1980.
15. *Review of Overseas Representation*. Report of Central Policy Review Staff, London, HMSO, 1977.
16. Market Opinion and Research International (MORI), London, 1979.
17. M. E. Porter and V. E. Millar, 'How Information Gives You Competitive Advantage', *Harvard Business Review*, **63**, 4, 1985.

2

Directing international marketing policies

2.1 Strategy, environment and planning

Introduction

International strategy must be designed to meet clear objectives. The strategic planning process starts and finishes with stakeholders such as shareholders, customers, managers and other staff, creditors, suppliers, bankers and distributors. Corporate objectives represent a statement as to what the company will achieve over a known time in terms of asset management, return on investment, market positions and development of key business sectors in all countries of operation. These objectives must be expressed precisely (see Fig. 2.1).

Thus, if the corporate objectives prescribe building market share(s) the marketing department must plan how to achieve this *into its own strategy*. So the planning process becomes the operational means by which strategy is implemented. Of course, in all marketing-oriented companies, marketing management will be involved in, and will influence the setting up of, strategy at both corporate and functional levels. This sequence can be described as follows.

1. Develop long-term strategy.
2. Determine objectives and timing.
3. Design and develop plans to meet these objectives.
4. Allocate resources for plans, and agree costs.
5. Implement plans.
6. Control, progress review and amend (within agreed limits).
7. Evaluate the effectiveness of plans in implementing strategy.

Long-term plans

There are certain key factors that management must take into account in setting and developing marketing strategy in the company's international operations.

- *Demand*: elasticities of demand; developments in taste, usage patterns, consumption; movement of economic indicators; demand stimulation and forecasting as an integral part of the marketing programme
- *Demographic factors*: changes in profile by age, socioeconomic status, population density and geographical locations of new business/industrial zones

Fig. 2.1 Development of strategy.

- *Technology*: impact of microcomputers on purchasing and production methods; reformulation of products and impact on life-cycles of products of new manufacturing processes
- *Competition*: new forms of direct or indirect competition; competitive strengths and weaknesses in product development; creativity in promotion, service provision
- *Distribution*: changes in channels; growth of direct mail, changes in customer uses of channels; purchasing and bargaining powers of key sectors of distribution system
- *Finance*: profit implications of alternative marketing strategies; profit improvement projects; high turnover/low profit versus high profit business/low turnover and the movement of margins; key financial ratios in alternative pricing decisions; control of direct marketing costs
- *Environment*: legal, cultural and political codes; standards and effect of regulatory laws/inspectorates

So long-term plans, also known as corporate or strategic planning, endeavour to assess future developments in the international environment and the marketing policies required to exploit them. The importance of this approach has been stressed by a leading management writer:[1]

> The international marketing programme will be, increasingly, the framework of progress and growth, and of more far-reaching improvements, such as diversification, overseas expansion, or management development . . . Knowing products and potential markets available to it, the firm selects those opportunities which will enable it to afford the best possible supply and service to customers at optimum profit-levels for itself; it recognises the channels of trading for this supply whether at home or abroad, and sets thereby guidelines to the organisation for all selling and sales promotion efforts; strategic guidelines take account of the economic, technological and social environment within which the trading activities will be carried on; they take account also of the financial resources and physical facilities available to the firm, as the basis for determining the scale and range of its operations.

The long-term plans of the company should be established and appraised on the following criteria.

1. *A precise understanding of the end purpose of the business.* This refers to the ultimate aim of the company, its scope, potential and character. If a company says that it makes breakfast foods, it limits its market; if it says it makes convenience goods, it enlarges its market; if it says it makes foods, it expands its potential still further. What can the company do better than other companies; what has it got, individually, that no other company can copy?
2. *The possession or acquisition of the means by which the company hopes to attain its objectives.* This embraces money, management, production facilities, distribution system—the international product/service offer. It means above all the recruitment and retention of the right calibre of management at all levels.
3. *The organization and management structure necessary to achieve company aims.* Of course, if the right people have joined the company, the correct organization and management structure will be developed by them.
4. *The ability to evolve operational controls required by the management.* This means, among other things, the ability to recognize, isolate and eliminate limiting factors, whatever they may be; in a management situation, limiting factors are usually directly concerned with personnel.

Management must, therefore, postulate its own long-term plans, since each company has its own characteristics. Common to all companies operating internationally, however, should be the following aims:

1. profit growth to give increased resources for investment for international operations;
2. increased earnings per share to attract new capital from international sources;
3. a higher, or more successful, achievement of certain management ratios, particularly
   (a) net profit to net sales (this indicates the competitive standing of the company, and is a most important marketing indicator, especially in relation to competitors, if this can be seen from inter-firm comparison figures);
   (b) net profit to tangible net worth (this shows the return of money invested in the business: if the figure is low, it can mean the money is invested in a stagnant or dying industry—what diversification steps should then be considered?);
   (c) turnover rate of capital employed (a slow rate of turnover can mean that the company impact is small, its penetration of the market weak: too much money has been invested in plant and not enough money in marketing);
4. growth in sales, and growth in market shares overseas;
5. growth in reputation and in impact and influence on overseas markets.

Strategy, while essential to future growth, is not enough on its own. It requires

– programming, so that a commitment to the international operational aspects is assured; and
– an action plan, so that implementation and control are assured too across the spectrum of markets.

The marketing programme

To the managing director, the international marketing programme is a tool for the exercise of his leadership in the effective management of the firm's affairs; all policies for planning and control should derive from this. Thus, the marketing programme forms the co-ordinating framework within which all the managers in the team exercise their delegated responsibilities. (How and when the programme is implemented depends on the mechanics of management of individual firms.) There will be some cases, of course, where the managing director has drawn up the programme unaided, but this is likely to occur only with very small enterprises or with new firms at an early stage of development.

There are three distinct stages that management should follow in setting up and implementing marketing strategy in international markets:

1. strategy formulation;
2. programming;
3. action/implementation.

Evaluation

The following check-list of questions can be used to evaluate the strategy of the company across all its markets.

1. Is the strategy identifiable, and has it been made clear either in words or in practice?
2. Does the strategy fully exploit the domestic and international market opportunities?
3. Is the strategy consistent with corporate competence, resources and products, both present and projected?
4. Does the strategy contain realistic and specific objectives stating how and when they will be achieved?
5. Are the major provisions of the strategy and the programme of major policies of which it is comprised internally consistent?
6. Is the chosen level of risk feasible in economic and personnel terms?
7. Is the strategy appropriate to the values and aspirations of the key managers?
8. Is the strategy appropriate to the desired level of contribution to society?
9. Is the strategy reflected in an appropriate organizational structure?

Programming

The next stage of the corporate strategic process depends on effective programming and control of international marketing. The best plan in the world will come to nothing if this is not carried out effectively.

This leads to an analysis of marketing objectives in international markets. The generation of cash must be considered throughout any such analysis, particularly in the selection of 'product/market portfolios'. There are, however, other objectives that may be pursued in determining such portfolios in various international markets. One may be the gathering of strategic information about the evolution of consumer needs, competitive moves or technological developments in leading markets. Different product innovations occur in different countries, and there are clear advantages for a firm to be present in these markets, as in the case of Gillette for disposable lighters. In the motor car industry, experience in front-wheel drive technology, originated by Citroen, was gained in Europe by Ford and Chrysler before being exploited in the US market.

Another objective in entering a market may be to prevent competition from gaining cost advantages arising from unchallenged world expansion, and thus indirectly to protect other international markets. Also, the development of a good relationship with local government can be an important part of marketing policy. This may lead to some specific actions, such as keeping a product that does not meet the firm's profitability norms, product adaptations, local production facilities or exports to a country that was not considered in the international marketing strategy of the firm—as in the case of Ford, which accepted delivery of cars from Argentina to Cuba following a 'desideratum' expressed by the Argentinean government. In all these instances, it is clear that considering a wide range of objectives can result in marketing strategies different to those generated purely by an analysis of the international product/market portfolio.

Working out a strategy (product/market structuring) is a task that will grow in importance as markets and environments become less stable and competition increases. The sensible application of product portfolio techniques constitutes a powerful tool for general and marketing management to guide and direct operations.

The management of product portfolios is increasingly important and is analysed in Section 2.2 below. It is essential to realize that different types of leadership and management skills are often required to handle products at different stages of their life-cycle. Product portfolio analysis can be useful not only in assessing and planning the company's product range, but also as a check on available managerial skills. For example, a company that decides on a strategy of new product introduction must ensure that the right type of manager (the 'thrusting' type) is available to handle successful market launches.

Figure 2.2 shows the important relationship between strategy and planning;[2] as the strategic options are narrowed down by management, so the selection of a particular strategy sets the foundation for the development of operational objectives, and the expansion of operational plans. The link between strategy and planning is therefore of special significance in international marketing, since the strategy on which it is based represents management's commitment to international operations to develop the business. This means that there must be a clear, articulated strategy to guide both the company's entry into overseas markets and its mode of international operations. Both of these latter aspects are dealt with at length in the following chapter. Often it is the failure to develop long-range international objectives, together with an under-estimation of difficult and different operating conditions, that can lead to abortive

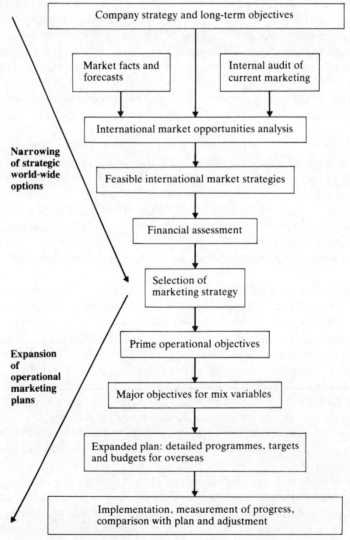

Fig. 2.2 The link between strategy and planning (*Source*: adapted from L. Fisher, *Industrial Marketing*, Business Books, 1976)

and unprofitable marketing policies. Case example 2.1 illustrates the point that the lack of a strategic approach by management can be the root cause of poor international performance.[3]

Case example 2.1
In a large pharmaceutical firm, senior executives still held the opinion that foreign investment projects were inherently riskier than domestic ones. They therefore favoured domestic investment projects over their international counterparts. Every year, the firm's international division was allocated a certain percentage of the total funds available for new investments, so that, according to one senior executive, 'safer' domestic investments did not have to compete against 'glamorous' but 'riskier' international projects. Furthermore, the international division lacked a clear-cut policy to guide allocation of its funding between projects for expanding existing facilities and those for entering new (overseas) markets. Thus, decisions concerning the allocation of corporate resources within the international division were reached primarily through 'negotiations' among various interest groups. One executive, noting the inadequacy of this method, commented: 'We take a great pride in being an international company, but we are far from achieving optimum allocation of resources on a global basis.'

The international marketing environment

While international marketing operations must be soundly based on strategy and planning, it is the heterogeneous environment in which the firm operates that requires both analysis and responsiveness: it is this environment that typically requires the firm to set its strategy so that, operationally, marketing components such as the communications mix, the product portfolio and market coverage/concentration are modified for specific regions of the world to achieve the best possible 'fit'. Indeed, the critical distinction between international and domestic operations derives from the fact that the differentiated international marketing environment makes it likely that some heterogeneous strategies will be required to achieve and hold substantial market shares. Most mistakes that have occurred in international operations derive from

- the lack of a clear strategy (already discussed). and
- attempts to 'transport' a marketing strategy that proved successful in one country, 'intact', to another country.

In addition, there are special factors relating to trade barriers which can frustrate the implementation of an international strategy; these barriers directly affect access to markets, and require as much analysis and interpretation as research into demand factors such as sales potential. These research aspects have already been discussed in Chapter 1, but they repay further attention because of the diversity of barriers to access—economic, cultural, political, competitive, technical and legal. In this chapter, the options available to management in tackling these environmental factors will be analysed. For example, the international company can come to assume increasing control of distribution operations as it moves from exporting through joint ventures/ licensing to owning subsidiaries and manufacturing plants overseas. Whether such increased control is worth the higher initial investment costs will depend on such factors as sales potential, market access, the nature of the product, the resources of the company, competitors' policies and, of course, the long-term strategic objectives of the company itself.

The key question to be answered in evaluating management's strategy and operations is, What factors can be identified which particularly influence the level of success likely to be achieved in international operations? A recent research report[4] investigated both marketing practice and management attitudes, with particular reference to increasingly complex international trading conditions. Perhaps the most striking feature to emerge from this report is that, despite facing difficult trading conditions in recent years, top marketing executives are generally optimistic about future business prospects. While the adverse economic climate clearly had major negative impacts on nearly all sectors of industry and commerce, there appear also to have been unexpectedly positive outcomes. Many executives report that improvements in organizational flexibility and market orientation have been generated by recent economic circumstances.

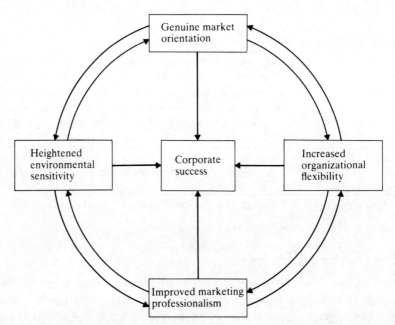

Fig. 2.3 The 'virtuous circle' of best marketing practice (*Source*: *Marketing in UK: Current Practice and Performance*, University of Bradford, Institute of Marketing and Industrial Market Research, 1984)

The high performers

Despite these conditions, some companies have fared considerably better than others, and it is possible to isolate certain key features that characterize the high performers. These features, which are summarized diagrammatically in Fig. 2.3, provide important guidelines for improved marketing effectiveness. The best companies and the most successful managers combine an unwavering commitment to classic marketing principles with a significantly heightened sensitivity and responsiveness to environmental signals.

Case example 2.2

Clark's is a leading construction machinery company. Thirty per cent of the company's sales were outside its home country in 1983, through 15 subsidiaries and 33 licensees manufacturing Clark products at 51 plants in 23 countries. This company showed a history of development over 25 years in accordance with the classical pattern. Initially, international sales were strictly a corporate responsibility; but as international sales grew, so subsidiaries and licensees became companies in their own right, properly equipped to take more of their own product line and promotional decisions. Clarks recognized that subsidiaries were not just branches, but separate legal entities, subject to the laws and practices of their own countries, and so it developed a largely decentralized policy in regard to the development of marketing programmes capable of implementation across diverse markets. Nevertheless, corporate headquarters adopted a co-ordinating role and developed uniform advertising programmes, patterned after the Clark corporate image, which were adaptable to the several construction machinery products throughout the world. The Clark corporate image programme both recognized the importance of individual product names, and also hammered home the advantages of the overall strength of the company. This was further supported by collateral media, such as brochures, and the importance of Clark's international operations, printed in several languages and released worldwide. Finally, Clark succeeded in deeply involving distributors in Clark marketing programmes, and this played a large part in increasing market penetration, opening new markets and introducing new product improvements world-wide.

The key elements of the flow diagrams in Fig. 2.3 are as follows.

1. *Genuine market orientation.* This study demonstrates the unquestionable strategic value of a sound grasp of fundamental marketing principles. For, while the environment has undergone radical changes in recent years, the need for marketing has in no way diminished; the research suggests that the converse is true. Indeed, any attempt to profile the high performers in the survey confirms that effectiveness and success are still rooted in the skilful and professional application of basic marketing perspectives. The key to marketing success lies in the development and maintenance of a clear-cut and competitively defensible market position. This involves the recognition that most markets are composed of segments which differ

considerably in terms of needs, size, growth trends, level of competitive threat and inherent profitability. Equally, it is necessary to recognize that most companies have a distinctive profile of skills and capabilities. The core of good marketing is to isolate a market segment or segments where the organization's distinctive competences find a profitable match with unsatisfied customer needs. In pursuit of this goal, the best performing companies demonstrate an unwavering focus upon the market-place and relate all their major operating decisions to the dictates of customer needs.

2. *Research*. Significantly, this kind of marketing orientation is not possible without the genuine understanding of the market-place which is derived from sound market research. The survey suggests that many organizations that claim to be market-oriented neglect this fundamental truth. It is no coincidence that the weaker performers often show a low level of reduced commitment to market research, allowing short-run financial pressures to obscure the centrality of the need for updated market information. The study suggests that considerable room for improvement exists in the acquisition and use of market research by companies. In particular, the survey indicates an over-reliance on internally generated data (such as sales-force reports, etc.) at the expense of primary, externally sourced, data. There was also a reluctance to seek skilled, specialist, outside advice. Genuine market orientation demands a commitment to sound research. A systematic and periodic review of the extent, professionalism and use made of market research is an integral element in corporate marketing success.

3. *Heightened environmental sensitivity*. The development of a genuine market orientation is a demanding task in a stable environment; it becomes even more difficult when the environment internationally is subject to significant change. The survey suggests that the impact of change on today's business is more complex, more rapid and more unpredictable than ever before. Thus, while the task of monitoring, scanning and assessing the implications of change upon the organization has never been harder, it has never been more essential. The survey confirms that the best performers are highly sensitive to change and attempt to realign their activities to movements in the market-place. They move as the environment moves. Conversely, the failure to sense and respond to change is the most common reason for poor or mediocre performance. If an organization is to keep in step with its environment, it is essential to adopt planning approaches that incorporate effective external scanning systems. The high performers clearly recognize that sound information is the basis for effective decision-making and that the provision of good data in a shifting environment is a process that must be carefully managed. Heightened environmental sensitivity is a hallmark of effective performance in modern markets.

4. *Organizational flexibility and adaptability*. A striking finding from the survey concerns the predominance of markets assessed by executives to be in maturity or decline. This sobering assessment suggests several vital strategic imperatives. First, it would seem that an essential prerequisite for corporate success in complex and

turbulent markets is a high level of flexibility and adaptability in an organization's systems, attitudes and structures. There is an overriding need to avoid over-dependence on too narrow or rigid a trading base. The more successful companies have taken steps to spread risk by attempting to ensure that healthy new ventures are developed in sufficient time to come on-stream at the first signs of decay in older, declining markets. Second, the constant shifts in the relative value of products and markets necessitate the setting of clear priorities in resource allocation. Management must ensure that it has a structured basis for deciding on the merits of conflicting claims on limited resources. A balanced portfolio of products or services is necessary if organizations are to have the required spread of cash generators and cash users. Third, organization structures must be designed which can accommodate strategic flexibility. Strategy can be successfully implemented only if an appropriate structure exists within the organization. If strategy changes in response to the market-place, then the continued adequacy of organizational structure must also be reviewed. Flexibility and adaptability are not simply related to attitude and systems: they are a function of sound organizational design.

5. *Increased marketing professionalism.* A recurring theme in the survey is the importance of skilled, professionally trained personnel with a good grasp of modern marketing techniques. The best organizations show a commitment to the training of their people and a willingness to experiment with new ideas and concepts. Higher levels of training tend to be associated with better levels of performance. Conversely, the weaker performers reveal either a reluctance to use sophisticated techniques or, more seriously, a lack of awareness that they exist. This tendency is particularly marked in the areas of new developments in strategic marketing planning and the analysis of complex multivariate data. A recognition that better marketing performance can come only from professionals who are trained and retrained is the hallmark of the successful operation.

Considerations of strategy and the impact of the environment, highlighted in the above mentioned report, underline the need for research and planning—in particular, the implications in operational terms of any strategy that involves, progressively, increases in international market entries and operations. It is essential, therefore, to rank the potential foreign markets surveyed in some order of priority, adjusted to allow for differences in competitive conditions. The real or potential threat of actions by competitors in certain overseas markets may force management to consider changing the priority among potential markets whenever, for example, there is a danger that the first entrant into a specific foreign market can effectively block the subsequent entry of others. Furthermore, even when a strategy of new market entry has been agreed, management is typically preoccupied with finalizing commercial agreements, assessing social and political trends and negotiating financial terms with its overseas partners or agencies, and so vital aspects of market development and prospects tend to be put aside, even ignored, under the pressures of short-term commercial dealings. These aspects include competitive strengths, distribution networks, product policies and the capital requirements of new ventures. All these are essential parts of the marketing planning process, and need to be resolved as far as possible before international operations begin.

Environment management

Reference has already been made to some aspects of the total environment (economic, cultural, social, political, geographical, etc.) within which the international firm operates. Clearly, this environment has profound implications for the ways in which marketing policies/programmes are designed and implemented. And the traditional concept is of the company deploying the four elements of the marketing mix (price, promotion, product and place) designated the 'controllables' within an 'uncontrollable' market environment (involving cultural, legal, economic, political, etc., factors), requiring the management continually to adapt the mix to the requirements of this environment. This concept has, in recent years, proved to be increasingly facile (and unsatisfying conceptually) and, in an international context, increasingly unrealistic operationally. The reasoning behind this change is as follows.

1. The market environment is, of course, dynamic, not fixed, and as it develops new market opportunities arise.
2. Identification of effective demand in the market cannot be actioned unless and until market access is secured by some reduction, if not removal, of obstacles to trade.
3. The concept of 'uncontrollable' environment implies that the company must operate within fixed parameters which management can do nothing to influence or change, and this is often fallacious in an international context.

What has emerged, therefore, to change this traditional concept is the principle of 'environment management'. This is an approach to the environment that recognizes the need on the part of management to influence and bring about improvements in trading conditions and market access which will benefit both company and customers. Of course, this is a long-term process, and one that often requires a 'consortium' approach to improve market access overseas (e.g. by joint government/industry missions, trade and industry associations acting on behalf of small- and medium-sized firms). In short, the traditional concept of the 'mix' postulates a largely re-active role by management, while environment management demands a pro-active role in all phases of the marketing process, from market entry to direct investment operations overseas. This is the only way now to open up access for products in difficult markets, where import restrictions, 'invisible' tariffs and 'gatekeepers' otherwise bar market entry for high-quality products but for which there is effective demand among consumers. Clearly, the company's management often cannot achieve all this on its own: embassy staff may have to be used to tackle or bypass 'gatekeepers' and advise on negotiating positions; trade missions can be used to open up particular industry sectors of the market; ministerial pressure in the manufacturer's home country may have to be applied to ministerial counterparts on official overseas visits; and so on.

One foremost writer on marketing[5] characterizes the scenario illustrated in Fig. 2.4 as 'mega-marketing', defined as

> the application of economic, psychological, political and PR skills to gain the cooperation of a number of parties in order to enter and/or operate successfully in a given (overseas) market . . . Megamarketing expands the idea of who the marketing targets are—they may include government officials, public interest groups, news media—and the marketing mix tools.

Interestingly, early work on communications effectiveness has also shown that personal influence and recommendation, and group pressure on individual opinions/

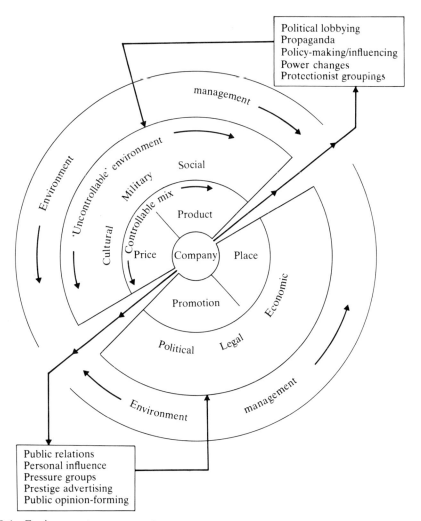

Fig. 2.4   Environment management.

attitudes, particularly when combined with some media exposure, are most likely to bring about changes in behaviour sought by the communicator.

Case example 2.3 illustrates some aspects of environment management.

Case example 2.3

Some years ago Air Canada was faced with a problem. This was before the 'satellite' modernization of Gatwick airport or the construction of Terminal 4 at Heathrow. The Department of Trade and Industry (DTI), which controls civil aviation through the CAA, was concerned that increasing usage of Heathrow by the world's airlines was causing congestion. In order to relieve this problem at Heathrow, DTI instructed several airlines, including Air Canada, to move their operations to Gatwick within a specified time limit. The management of Air Canada was very concerned that moving to Gatwick would have, overall, a serious and adverse effect on the airline in terms of operating competitiveness, back-up services, image and route coverage. Accordingly, the management determined to oppose the move, and appointed a small but respected firm of PR consultants to act for it, specifying a detailed brief, the objective being to remain at Heathrow. Over the following two-year period, this PR firm undertook skilful and persistent lobbying of ministers, politicians and other 'influencers' as part of a campaign to keep Air Canada at Heathrow. (No doubt at some point reciprocity of services for British Airways in Canada was mentioned.) The outcome of this two-year campaign was successful: DTI relented, and Air Canada did not have to move to Gatwick.

So environment management involves influencing external conditions to bring about improved market access, representation and performance; it is also concerned with the pro-active role of management in stimulating demand, or at least reducing obstacles to demand satisfaction; this latter aspect is discussed in detail in Section 2.3 below. Clearly, companies are concerned to know what strategies can be adopted to implement environment management: the most authoritative analysis of strategic options has been published by the American Marketing Association (AMA) in a paper that groups the options under three main headings:[6]

1. Independent strategies
   (a) Competitive aggression: company exploits a distinctive competence or improves internal efficiency of resources for competitive advantage, e.g. product differentiation, comparative advertising.
   (b) Competitive pacification: company takes independent actions to improve relations with competitors, e.g. helping competitors find raw material.
   (c) Public relations: company attempts to establish and maintain favourable images in the minds of those making up the environment, e.g. corporate advertising to opinion-formers.
   (d) Voluntary action: company tries to manage and becomes committed to vari-

ous special interest groups, causes and social problems, e.g. 3M's energy conservation programme.

(e) Dependence development: company aims to create or modify relationships with external groups so they become dependent on the company, e.g. production of critical defence-related commodities, providing vital information to regulators.

(f) Legal action: company engages in private legal battle with competitor or antitrust, deceptive advertising, trademark infringement or other grounds.

(g) Political action: company tries to influence elected representatives to create a more favourable business environment or limit competition, e.g. corporate constituency programmes, direct lobbying.

(h) Smoothing: company attempts to resolve irregular demand; e.g., telephone company lowers weekend rates, airline offers inexpensive fares during off-peak times.

(i) Demarketing: firm attempts to discourage customers in general or a certain class of customers in particular, on either a temporary or a permanent basis.

2. Co-ooperative strategies

(a) Implicit co-operation: firm adopts patterned, predictable and co-ordinated behaviours, e.g. price leadership.

(b) Contracting: company negotiates an agreement with another group to exchange goods, services, information, patents, etc., e.g. contractual vertical and horizontal marketing systems.

(c) Co-optation: firm absorbs new elements into its leadership or policy-making structure as a means of averting threats to its stability or existence, e.g. consumer representatives, women and bankers on boards of directors.

(d) Coalition: two or more groups coalesce and act jointly with respect to some set of issues for some period of time, e.g. industry associations, political initiatives of the Business Roundtable.

3. Strategic manoeuvring

(a) Domain selection: firm enters industries or markets with limited competition or regulation and ample suppliers and customers, or enters high-growth markets, e.g. IBM's entry into the personal computer market and Miller Brewing Co.'s entry into US 'lite' beer market.

(b) Diversification: company invests in different types of businesses, manufactures different types of products, integrates vertically or expands geographically to reduce dependence on a single product, service, market or technology.

(c) Merger and acquisition: two or more firms form a single enterprise or one company gains possession of another, e.g. the merger between Pan American and National Airlines, or Phillip Morris's acquisition of Miller Brewing Co.

Given the diverse and rapidly changing conditions overseas and the risks inherent in international ventures, the need for marketing strategy is self-evident: without it there can be no effective marketing planning or control of operations and market tactics, which are dealt with later in this section. Management must recognize that attractive-ness of market opportunities overseas varies widely among industries as well as among individual firms: any strategy must therefore take account not only of corpor-ate resources and industry prospects but of differences in levels of industrial activity and economic growth rates of overseas markets. There is also, of course, a wide vari-ation in the capacities of individual firms to exploit foreign markets successfully. In setting up a strategy for international operations, therefore, management must

1. assess opportunities in international markets for its products and technology as well as the potential risks associated with these opportunities;
2. examine the degree to which the firm can develop potential opportunities abroad in the light of its own organizational and managerial competence.

Where research and analysis (discussed in Chapter 1) reveal prospects of long-term market development and/or short-term sales opportunities, management must then determine the extent to which the company has the real or potential capacity to capitalize on these opportunities, and must set up the appropriate strategy for doing so. Clearly, this must take account of the fact that, in all international operations, the managerial task must be performed in diverse economic, cultural, political, techno-logical and legal systems. Distant foreign affiliates must be continuously supported by the financial, technological and human resources of the corporate headquarters.

Strategy implementation

It is at this point, particularly in the light of the critical assessment outlined in 1 and 2 above, that putting the strategy into actionable form by marketing planning becomes the priority for management. Earlier in this section, the relationships between strat-egy, planning and programming were explained. Now, it is appropriate to consider the planning process as it applies in international operations. The consequences to the firm of a lack of overall planning can be serious. Failure at the planning stage can re-sult in sub-optimum deployment of corporate resources overseas and a consequent loss of the potential benefits of international operations. Lack of planning also frus-trates a vital aspect of operations—timing. To exploit market and investment oppor-tunities overseas, the timing of entry, negotiations, promotion and any acquisitions must be judged carefully, in a planned sequence. For instance, unless a firm can plan and time its entry into foreign markets with precision, it may be excluded from certain promising markets permanently, because the first firm that undertakes local produc-tion overseas can often negotiate with the host government for preferred treatment and special concessions, including a provision to make subsequent entry into the market by competitors extremely difficult, if not impossible. Even without these nego-tiated benefits, the first entrant can often enjoy decided advantages over competitors because of the need for a long lead time to plan a foreign venture and to build a viable position in the market.

Two further points. First, a lack of planning tends to restrict the flexibility of a firm's subsequent operations: initial agreements relating to licensing or exclusive distributorships entered into for short-term sales advantage are often found seriously to hamper subsequent overseas expansion. Some firms have found it impossible to establish their own production facilities in certain markets to take advantage of rapidly growing opportunities because of exclusive agreements made earlier without any planning or examination of the consequences. Second, ill-planned market entry is likely to lead to numerous operating problems after the foreign venture gets under way; lacking a plan to guide its moves overseas, a firm may postpone the decision to enter a given market until the last moment, thereby creating further problems.

All these aspects point to the need for management to initiate and implement the marketing plan as the operational focus for all the overseas markets. And it is logical that the analysis of the planning process should follow both Chapter 1, on research and analysis, and the earlier discussion in this chapter of strategy and environment management.

The research function and the planning function are to this extent inseparable. Accordingly, product, consumer, advertising and sales research are prerequisites to the formulation and implementation of the marketing plan, in all its phases of object-ives, programming and operations, and in all key sectors of international markets where the company is already active, or is planning entry.

Aspects of the marketing planning process are illustrated in Fig. 2.5.

From the foregoing considerations, the managing director and his top management can now consolidate their objectives and intentions into a plan for action—the profit plan, or the marketing programme, or, in more conventional language, the sales budget. Their time framework is, say, two years, with the first year spelled out in de-tail and the second year in outline terms of main features of trading targets, concen-trating on new product items and the market growth points.

The first year's plan or programme is an operating document, a tool of manage-ment action. Accordingly, it is laid out in relation to the firm's main divisions or departments, with the targets and control standards in line with the delegated centres of responsibility and accountability. Within the divisions, appropriate sub-sections again line up with operating activities, according to accountability for control: the production division does this by processing and finishing departments or sections, providing also for stores, packaging and transport; factory services are budgeted in standards of expenditure related to the planned volume of manufacture, and so too is provision for other overheads in supervision and production management. On the sales side, the sub-division is a cross-pattern of territories and product groups, such that each selling team or section knows what volume and turnover targets have been set for it in product-mix and in periods over the year; similarly, sales expenses and overheads are aligned in the budget, and the sales manager has his corresponding pro-gramme and budget for publicity and sales promotion. Provision is made for new product development activities, for research and development, and for the overhead expenses of managing and administering the firm, including such special activities as personnel services and the management development programme. All through, costs and expenses are budgeted in terms of standards for the planned pattern of trading

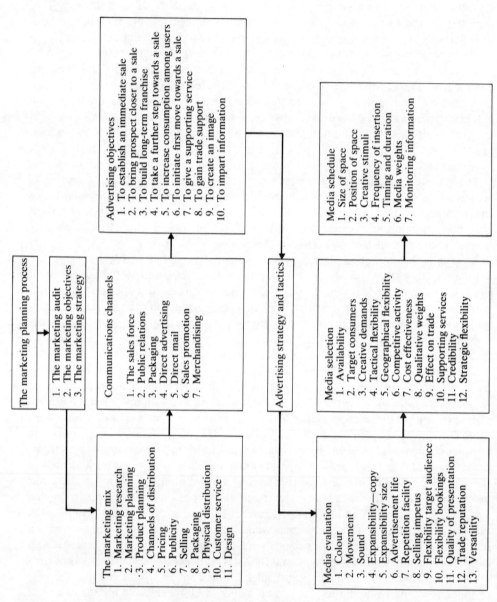

The marketing planning process

1. The marketing audit
2. The marketing objectives
3. The marketing strategy

The marketing mix
1. Marketing research
2. Marketing planning
3. Product planning
4. Channels of distribution
5. Pricing
6. Publicity
7. Selling
8. Packaging
9. Physical distribution
10. Customer service
11. Design

Communications channels
1. The sales force
2. Public relations
3. Packaging
4. Direct advertising
5. Direct mail
6. Sales promotion
7. Merchandising

Advertising objectives
1. To establish an immediate sale
2. To bring prospect closer to a sale
3. To build long-term franchise
4. To take a further step towards a sale
5. To increase consumption among users
6. To initiate first move towards a sale
7. To give a supporting service
8. To gain trade support
9. To create an image
10. To impart information

Advertising strategy and tactics

Media evaluation
1. Colour
2. Movement
3. Sound
4. Expansibility—copy
5. Expansibility size
6. Advertisement life
7. Repetition facility
8. Selling impetus
9. Flexibility target audience
10. Flexibility bookings
11. Quality of presentation
12. Trade reputation
13. Versatility

Media selection
1. Availability
2. Target consumers
3. Creative demands
4. Tactical flexibility
5. Geographical flexibility
6. Competitive activity
7. Cost effectiveness
8. Qualitative weights
9. Effect on trade
10. Supporting services
11. Credibility
12. Strategic flexibility

Media schedule
1. Size of space
2. Position of space
3. Creative stimuli
4. Frequency of insertion
5. Timing and duration
6. Media weights
7. Monitoring information

Fig. 2.5 Marketing planning process (*Source:* International Trade Centre UNCTAD/GATT, Geneva)

activity, so that the 'variances' can be thrown into relief in the control statements. The profit targets feature prominently in the main trading plan, and associated statements forecast the capital requirements and the expected cash flow.

As an instrument of management, the international marketing programme has this same two-way application throughout the firm: it is the basis for briefing through executive instructions, because it sets out the objectives and the targets within a plan of action; and it is the basis of effective control, because it makes possible the comparison of what is actually happening against what was planned. In terms of documents and procedures, the marketing programme is the framework of the management information system, by means of which control is attained: the periodic operating and financial statements are the sectional portrayal of what is happening, set against the targets, plans and standards in the programme. This is, perhaps, an argument in favour of the alternative term, the 'profit plan', which would emphasize the profit objectives towards which the firm is working and in terms of which the plans have been formed. In his periodic control meetings, the managing director uses as his instrument of control the feedback of 'actual' attainment in comparison with the planned targets in the detail of the programme, both ways round: positively, in terms of sales turnover achieved and profits earned, and negatively, in terms of excess cost or expenditure incurred above standards budgeted. Review of performance is thus meaningful, the control of operations is effective, and both are supported by a single integrated management information system. Above all, warning signals can indicate potential dangers, be they in sales trends, advertising effectiveness, adverse price and cost movements, processing deficiencies or cash flow, and in which markets.

But top management must direct the business and provide the resources so that the company's international markets become the touchstone of company policy.

Commitment to marketing by top management means in practice that it has become a 'marketing-led' business. The implications of this have been thoroughly explored in this section: in short, the company's business begins and ends with the customers. The company must understand their real and perceived needs better than any other companies, and must then set out to serve those needs better than any other companies. The whole organization should be geared to the achievement of these goals.

So once marketing staff have identified market opportunities overseas, top management's task is to direct the business, long-term, to offering a comprehensive product and service to cover the profitable and growing segments of the world market. Of course, marketing staff must use large-scale data continually to interpret market trends, as described above, as a basis for management action, and must design the marketing plan and subsequently execute that plan accordingly.

Case example 2.4 illustrates an effective approach by management towards marketing planning adopted by a rubber manufacturing company.[7]

Case example 2.4

Marketing plans are prepared annually, and in recent years have become more closely tied to the company's strategic plan objectives.

Marketing planning is preceded by the establishment of strategic objectives for each marketing division. Senior executives representing marketing, manufacturing and administrative services meet in formal planning sessions to consider progress against past objectives, the changing competitive and business environment within which the company operates, and forecasts relating to markets served. Updated and revised strategic objectives are arrived at, giving consideration to the following:

(a) profitability history of marketing units measured by net profit to sales, manufacturing costs trends and return on investment;
(b) market position history—an assessment of each marketing operation's current share position relative to competitors and progress against share objectives;
(c) long-range market growth prospects;
(d) product cost review—consideration of significant design or process improvement plants;
(e) manufacturing capacity—current and projected.

From these deliberations, strategic objectives are set stating sales growth, market share, and profit goals for each marketing unit. Sales divisions then prepare marketing plans designed to meet the targets stated in the strategic objectives. These plans do not follow a set format, but all include most of the elements listed below. Plans are prepared by the manager directly accountable for the sales operations covered by the plan. They generally include

(a) a restatement of strategic objectives;
(b) analysis of these objectives' potential effect on future profits;
(c) a presentation of elements of the marketing plan: these vary depending upon the characteristics of the markets for which each sales operation is responsible, but may include
    – training—special training plans for field sales personnel and/or customers
    – pricing plans
    – identification of target markets or customers: these may be industries or individual accounts where improved sales penetration is required to meet objectives
    – field sales programmes—identification of planned advertising and promotional programmes
    – promotion programmes—identification of planned advertising and promotional programmes
    – product plans, including new products: these include product design changes, product deletions and planned new introductions;
(d) a presentation in greater detail of selected key elements in the marketing plans;

(e) presentation and discussion of next year's sales budget, with some product detail and consideration of its fit to the strategic objective.

Marketing plans are presented in person to senior executives annually. Agendas for these market planning sessions include all marketing units, and are restricted to a consideration of each marketing operation's plan and its fit to strategic objectives. A summary of decisions made and actions required is prepared at the conclusion of the meetings.

Adaptations

While management has the responsibility of formulating the marketing plan in accordance with agreed, overall strategic objectives of the company, there are some important adaptations, both in management style and in plan implementation, that have to be made to take account of the diversity of conditions found in operating across political boundaries. Further complicating the marketing plan is the multiplicity of different types of marketing organization that may be used simultaneously by the same international firm. The conventional planning sequence, therefore, used in mainly domestic marketing—resources audit, objective selling, demand and financial analysis, programming operations, review, evaluation and control—while valid in principle, requires differing applications for international operations in order to cope with different levels of uncertainty and diverse operating environments across foreign markets. Some of these special factors in planning for international operations might include the following.

1. *Regional specialization.* Priorities among major economic regions must be determined in the light of exploitable market opportunities and the firm's own resources to operate globally.
2. *Timing and risk analysis.* Decisions in the plan have to be reached regarding both the timing of market entry to some foreign countries, and the time-scale of operations in other countries where the 'pay-back' periods have to be estimated against some analysis of risks, both commercial and political.
3. *Nature and extent of foreign commitments.* This refers to what is probably the most important aspect of the international marketing plan: management's decision to plan for 'market concentration' *v.* 'market-spreading', depending on its assessment of commercial trends/prospects in different regions and the resources of the firm to 'cover' a given number of markets effectively. There is available an interesting analysis of this 'dilemma' and how to resolve it for the purposes of planning.[8]
4. *Degree of operating flexibility.* In planning the development of the firm's overseas markets, management must assess the extent to which the firm's designs, product specifications, technical services and brand images should be changed to satisfy the requirements of different markets. This operating flexibility has to be built into the plan so that marketing programmes appropriate to each market can be resourced, implemented, controlled and evaluated effectively.

In incorporating all four of these essential elements into the international plan, management must pay particular attention to an analysis of the foreign operating environment, including an assessment of risk and evaluation of competition, both local and international. In Chapter 1, various aspects of research and analysis were discussed, and these must be consolidated as a data base on which management can construct the plan. Subsequently, in Chapter 3 various modes of market entry and operations will be analysed, and these must be viewed in their totality as the implementation of the plan, with the broad objective of developing the firm's overseas business cost-effectively and competitively. The assessment of risk is emphasized because this is an essential part of planning, as opposed to 'intuitive' management, which is still prevalent in many firms (particularly in industrial goods sectors), and which copes with crises and difficulties simply as and when they occur. While not all eventualities (e.g. retrospective import quotas suddenly imposed by a foreign government) can be foreseen, operational risk assessment can be and should be included in the plan; risks arise from certain inadequacies in indigenous technological and institutional systems, and from the scarcity of essential resources needed for the effective running of an industrial enterprise. While some political risks derive from minor bureaucratic harassment to outright expropriation, economic risks can take the form of unstable currency, poor foreign exchange position, severe inflationary trends or uncertain government economic policy.

The essential point for marketing management is that, with a sufficient data base, many of these risks can be assessed in the plan, and, more importantly, minimized/ reduced by action in the plan relating to, for instance, negotiations with government agencies and other organizations prior to market entry, or prior to any major new investment in foreign markets where the firm is already operating. Therefore, while much research has been done on the complexities of international marketing planning,[9] it is clear that these complexities arise mainly because the firm is operating in widely differing commercial environments and is adopting different modes of operation (such as direct exporting, contract manufacturing, etc.) to suit the requirements of foreign markets at differing stages of economic and industrial development.

The overall objectives of the international plan, therefore, must be:

1. to design programmes for national markets in order that the marketing mix will enable the company to adapt to each environment in such a way that its goals are achieved; and
2. to integrate all of these marketing operations into an effective world-wide corporate effort.

Interactive marketing planning

The actual implementation of marketing planning, particularly managing both international communications and product portfolios, is discussed in depth in subsequent sections of this chapter; particular attention is also paid to the 'matrix' approach to products and markets.

There remains the question of whether there is any optimal form of organization for the setting up and implementation of marketing planning across national markets; in short, who is to do it? Certainly, it is arguable that lack of adequate information in many markets, particularly concerning customer motivations and attitudes, makes some marketing planning a subjective task that is best left to those more closely in touch with local consumer needs and trends; one leading analyst[10] has maintained that, because of this, 'responsibility for marketing planning must be carried out by those overseas executives who are most familiar with the local environment'; and, furthermore, in order to facilitate an understanding of locally prepared marketing plans, headquarters should merely develop standard definitions and formats of presentation, at the same time supplying local management with important information at the macro level, such as oil and chemical prices and trends in other world markets.

This approach to planning implementation world-wide has been supported by some other research.[11] The major advantage of this co-ordinating role by headquarters is that it enables top management to isolate markets offering opportunities for product and market rationalization and extension. And the approach itself has been characterized as 'interactive' marketing planning and, as such, superior to either centralized or totally decentralized planning. Headquarters still bears the major responsibility for searching out similar characteristics and unifying influences that provide opportunities for standardizing elements of the global marketing plan such as product development and advertising programmes.

An international company planning and operating on this basis has some advantages over a company that allows its national managers complete freedom to plan and exploit their own local environments.

1. Within the global plan, such programme transfers enable a company to exploit successful practices, such as tried and tested promotional ideas, on a wider basis.
2. System transfers, such as planning budgeting and research systems, increase the efficiency of local operations and help top management to understand and react more accurately to the needs of local management.
3. Specialists, particularly in analysis and planning, can be assigned across national boundaries.
4. Headquarters management can ensure that no one national plan or policy will adversely affect another as for example in the case of a large customer who spans more than one market.

The interactive approach to international marketing planning can, therefore, combine inputs from both the global and the local perspective, thus achieving a balance that approximates the objective of global optimization as opposed to national sub-optimization. In the research just quoted, one international company in particular is cited in support of this approach (see Case example 2.5).

Case example 2.5

In ITT Corporation, headquarters staff develop plans for 400 operating units in 60 countries by first setting basic quantitative objectives and then reviewing the plans submitted by operating managers. Thus, central management does not make the plans: it merely reviews and co-ordinates them against basic quantitative parameters, and acts as a resource centre. This method is not without its problems, which arise principally because factors such as financial incentives, free competition, consistency of government policy, management skills, availability of market data and so on vary considerably from country to country.

There is some empirical evidence, as well as research, that this interactive approach to international marketing planning offers the optimal organizational and operational framework. In theory, headquarters staff would attempt to assess opportunities on the basis of world trends and then to break them down on a country-by-country basis, with an indication of sales and earnings expectations for each. Within the framework of such guidance from headquarters, subsidiaries would then search for programmes that would achieve the specified expectations. These national plans would then be agreed with headquarters and integrated into the country-wide plan. Thus, headquarters would be responsible for strategic planning and would decide what resources to allocate, as well as co-ordinating and rationalizing product design and the advertising, pricing and distribution activities of each subsidiary. The major advantage of this approach is that it recognizes not only the major differences in the world's national markets, but also the similarities and common denominators.

These theoretical advantages can manifest themselves in the following ways. First, certain marketing information variables can be standardized in order to allow a comparison of performances in the planning process. Second, headquarters staff can present a market study in one country as a result of similar study in another, or can suggest a new use for a product in one country based on experience in another, or can pass on any kind of useful knowledge gained in comparable markets. Third, a skilful manager with successful experience of problems in one country can assist in formulating plans to tackle similar problems in another market. Fourth, marketing plans and programmes can be tested in various forms in different markets. Finally, cost savings can result from developing intranational promotional programmes and product adaptations; for example, it may be possible to standardize product and promotional programmes for certain similar areas rather than allowing fifty separate developments to take place.

So this concept appears to offer the ideal solution to the problem of planning at headquarters; and the research cited goes some way towards showing that headquarters can play an extremely valuable role in the planning process, and that it is possible to realize synergistic benefits in an integrated international company.

Other important aspects of corporate organization and management development for international operations are explored in Chapter 4 (Section 4.2).

Corporate marketing direction check-list

1. Setting and using corporate marketing objectives
   (a) Is there a detailed up-to-date analysis of what business(es) we are in?
   (b) Are there clear profit and profitability objectives, broken down into goals for each component part of the business?
   (c) Have growth rates been defined, and is there an optimum rate and/or size beyond which we should not expand?
   (d) Are the objectives practical, specific, where possible quantitative, timed, competitively advantageous and limited enough to ensure commitment?
2. Selecting corporate marketing strategies
   (a) Have the four major categories of strategy—market penetration, market development, product development and diversification—been investigated in turn and thoroughly?
   (b) Have the selected strategies been evaluated to ensure their relevance to the market-place, the corporate objectives and resources, the marketing activity and the competitive situation?
   (c) Have our strategies been checked and integrated into a cohesive approach which in turn could lead to a redefinition or extension of our objectives?
   (d) Do we have an effective mechanism for considering and deciding our corporate marketing direction?

2.2 The product portfolio

Introduction

The process of developing and managing a product portfolio for international markets is increasingly complex. The strategic question to be resolved is, How far should a standard product portfolio be marketed world-wide, and how far should different portfolios be adopted for trading regions at different stages of market development? There are tactical decisions to be made: targeting product lines in countries where the product life-cycle is operating at different stages, and developing brands and brand images to exploit short-term market opportunities, while at the same time investing in longer-term brand development across national frontiers. Then there are substantial economies of scale to be derived from volume sales of world brands. But how are such volumes to be sustained by Western manufacturers in a world where low-cost volume manufacturing is increasingly moving eastwards to the 'Pacific Rim' countries of South-east Asia; and is the pursuit of 'niche' product marketing on a world-wide basis likely to provide a viable alternative strategy? These and other important aspects of managing the product portfolio will be addressed in this section.

Product life-cycle

By far the most significant factor for management to consider at the outset is the product life-cycle. While the concept is not, of course, new, it has special applications in international product management. In the first place, there is a link between the life-cycle and international trade: management needs insights into the overseas sales potential of its products as well as predictors of which products are most likely to be threatened by import competition. Nevertheless, macroeconomic theories abound. The theory of 'comparative advantage' states that, ideally, every country will market those products that use the country's most abundant production factors. As such theories have been found to have only limited use at the micro level, increasingly, research has concentrated on managerial applications of the trade cycle, and its relationship to the product life-cycle. According to one early study of US industry, the trade cycle concept means that many products typically follow a pattern that can be divided into four stages.[12]

1. Export strength is based on heavy investment in manufacturing and a large body of high-income consumers.
2. Foreign production starts as demand builds up overseas and volume sales bring down manufacturing costs in countries formerly importing.
3. Foreign production becomes competitive in overseas markets as unit labour costs undercut those of original manufacturers.
4. Import competition begins as foreign manufacturers optimize mass production based on home and overseas markets, further lower their unit costs, and capitalize on newer plant.

These stages at the macro level correspond to the four stages of the product life (the micro level), which, of course, are: introduction, growth, maturity/saturation, and decline. So this trade cycle infers that many products too go through a cycle during which high-income, mass-consumption countries are initially exporters, then lose their export markets, and finally become importers of the product; other industrializing countries also make corresponding changes from importing to exporting, and this pattern is followed in the final stage by the developing countries.

In principle, therefore, management must ensure that its product portfolio is soundly based for international markets; that it is developed at stages of the life-cycle to exploit the 'macro-market' factors already referred to. Indeed, at different phases in the trade cycle there must be variations in the makeup of the product portfolio. Apart from the implications of profit planning through the 'building up' of the portfolio (referred to later), life-cycle analysis can also identify the critical stages through which a product is passing, thereby indicating some appropriate options for strategy.

Further research[13] has also indicated some hypotheses about the elasticity of several marketing variables at each major stage of the life-cycle, as shown in Fig. 2.6. While there is little doubt that, in different marketing environments world-wide, different elasticities will apply, the analysis highlighted in this research is of importance in setting up marketing strategy. It is interesting to observe here how the elasticity of product quality (q) has the major impact on sales in the introductory stages of the life-cycle, where the X-axis represents sales responsiveness and the Y-axis increasing marketing costs. In the stages representing growth and maturity, sales become much more inelastic to improved quality. And by the saturation stage, there emerges the factor that this research cites as 'quasi-quality' (such as packaging changes), which has some effect, but much less than the original force of quality, and the responsiveness of sales to all marketing variables becomes consistently more inelastic as the cycle progresses.

These applications of demand elasticities to the stages of the life-cycle clearly have important implications for international markets. Because of differences in the levels and quality of consumer spending, and in the stages of industrialization and urbanization, similar products, world-wide, are likely to be at very different stages of the life-cycle. These considerations apply more, today, to industrial and technical goods than to consumer goods: the latter are increasingly subject to world-wide branding, and will be discussed later. Clearly, although there are many industrializing and developing countries where relatively low unit labour costs and proximity to supply sources combine to keep low unit medium-technology products in the maturity and saturation stages, in the most advanced industrial countries these products have long since gone into the decline stage, to be replaced by high-technology products in the growth stage.

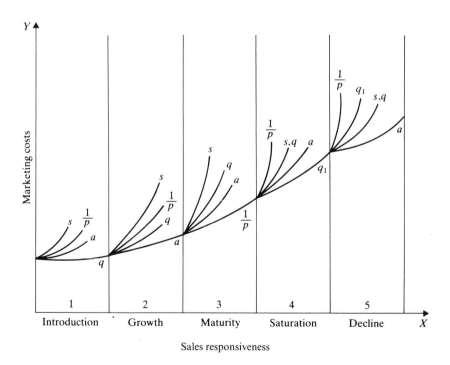

a — advertising; q — quality; q_1 — quasi-quality; s — service; $1/p$ — price inverted

Fig. 2.6 Elasticity of marketing variables at each stage of the product life-cycle (*Source*: G. Mickwitz, *Marketing and Competition*, Central Cyckeriet, Helsingfors, Finland, 1959)

Referring to Fig. 2.6, it is clear that, in developing and managing a portfolio of products, sales become more volume-sensitive, in that increasing inelasticity means that proportionately higher sales costs are incurred to bring in incremental sales revenue. The precise levels of elasticity will, of course, vary at each stage of the life-cycle in different national markets. This highlights the need for management to assess the positions of products within its portfolio in different markets and to compare the costs of maintaining sales by marketing expenditures: this will reveal in which markets the portfolio can be maintained at its most profitable position. The development and extension of the portfolio in terms of profit enhancement will also be discussed later (see Case example 2.6). It is sufficient to note, at this stage, that the relationship between total sales volume and net profits varies among different markets in the course of the life-cycle. The peak of net profits is usually reached much earlier than the peak of total sales volume; this is because, from a certain point onwards, additional sales can be realized only through a reduction in the selling price and/or through additional, but less cost-effective, expenditures on marketing, as is clear from Fig. 2.6.

Case example 2.6
A West German printing and packaging machine manufacturer, with world-wide sales, did an analysis of the positions of different grades of machines on the life-cycles in its major trading regions. At issue was the extent to which the firm should continue manufacturing/marketing low unit value machines when, to retain its competitive lead in industrialized markets, the development of high unit value machines was essential. The life-cycle concept was applied to the entire range of machines, and while many low unit value ones were in the decline phase in industrialized markets, two salient features emerged.

(a) These low unit value machines were still bringing in volume sales revenue in the maturity phase in less industrialized countries.

(b) In the highly industrialized markets, replacements of these older machines by high unit value machines in the growth phase need to be built into the marketing planning process.

While some rationalization in the range of machines became necessary so as to increase manufacturing efficiency, this application of the life-cycle concept enabled management to apply a world-wide marketing strategy based on segmentation of markets by stages of the cycle. This has proved an effective strategy against low-cost competitors as well as ensuring competitiveness by innovation at the high-technology end.

Further research has also been undertaken on the analysis of the life-cycle as an indicator of specific global marketing policies, taking into account some of the basic assets of the business (capital, people, etc.) and adapting these to changes in demand and market structure at each stage of the cycle.[14] The results of this research for the first three phases are summarized in Table 2.1.

Table 2.1 Product portfolio through the life-cycle (*Source*: adapted from J. de la Torre, 'Product Life-cycle as a Determinant of Global Marketing Strategies', *Atlanta Economic Review*, **25**, Sept./Oct. 1975)

Characteristics	Introduction	Growth	Maturity/saturation
Technology	Rapidly changing and adapting to consumer preferences	Few product variations of importance with various degrees of refinement; process innovations critical	Both product and process stable; no major design innovations of importance
	Closely held by innovating firm; no licensing or sale	Patent variations decrease monopoly of technology; some diffusion and licensing	Readily available and transferable
Production	Product-centred	Shifting to process	Process-centred
	Short runs; proto-type manufacturing	Larger runs; mass production introduced although techniques may differ	Long runs; stable processes
Capital	Low use of capital; multi-purpose equipment	Increased utilization	High investment in specialized equipment
Industry structure	Innovating firm leads, with others entering field to capitalize on success	Large number of firms; many casualties and mergers; growing integration	Number of firms declining with lower margins
	Know-how principal barrier to entry	Financial resources critical for growth	Established marketing position principal barrier to entry
Human inputs	High scientific engineering and marketing skills	Financial and production management necessary to reduce costs	Unskilled and semi-skilled labour; marketing
Marketing and demand structure	Sellers' market	Balanced market	Buyers' market
	High introductory marketing effort in communication and awareness	Beginning product differentiation; distribution critical	High brand and product differentiation may appear through various means
	High monopoly prices	Increased competition reducing prices	Lower prices and margins

Table 2.2 International consumer product 'generations' (*Source*: International Trade Centre UNCTAD/GATT, Geneva)

Washing powder	Coffee	Prepared foods
1. 'Conventional' soap powder (granulated, chips, etc.) Synthetic detergents: simple	1. Conventional ground coffee	1. 'Straight' canned
	2. Soluble coffee powder: metal can	2. Mixed canned
		3. Fully prepared and frozen
2. Synthetic with additives: bleaching/blueing	3. Soluble coffee powder: glass jar, vac. pack	4. Pre-cooked and frozen
	4. Soluble coffee powder: concentrated (spray dried)	5. Freeze-dried
3. 'Low-sudsing' for washing machines		6. 'Microwave' preparations/ formulations
	5. Soluble coffee powder: expresso, sanka	
4. Cold and hot water synthetic detergents	6. Soluble coffee powder: freeze-dried granules	7. High-concentrated ('space-food')
5. 'Bio-degradable' synthetic detergents	7. Soluble coffee powder: freeze-dried cubes or bags	
6. 'Bio-active' synthetic detergents		

The term 'product generations' is closely related to life-cycles: many products sold internationally evolve as a result of changes in manufacturing or processing brought in by competitors, or changes in taste, fashion and habits across national boundaries, the impact of new mass media, etc. Initially, 'generations' have been associated with high-technology products such as aircraft, machine tools, equipment and computers; but the analysis in Table 2.2 shows that the concept has been just as significant among consumer products.

Indeed, in many consumer goods industries, more than half the products sold world-wide today did not exist 10–15 fifteen years ago, and most of the products that will be sold 20 years hence have not been invented. For instance, Turkish and Greek tobaccos dominated the market in Western Europe until 1945: since then, American-type tobaccos have almost completely taken over, with dramatic effects on the Turkish economy. And in the electronics industry, the development of transistors, printed circuits, microchips and fibre optics has completely changed the structure of the industry and accelerated the rate of change in product portfolios over the last 15–20 years.

The international product portfolio

What is defined as a company's 'optimal' international product portfolio is very much determined by the company's basic objectives.

1. If the basic objective is profit maximization, then the optimal product portfolio has

been achieved when no addition, deletion or changes will lead to increased total profits.
2. If the basic objective is world-wide sales growth, the product portfolio is optimal whenever any change will lead to a lower rate of growth of total sales.
3. If the basic objective is stability and security for the company, then the optimal portfolio guarantees stable sales volume, cost levels, profits and cash flow.

In practice, it is more useful and realistic to seek situations and conditions in world markets that indicate that the product portfolio is less than optimal, rather than to seek standards/criteria for the ideal situation, which will be difficult to achieve. Typical indications that the product portfolio is not optimal include the following.

1. There are wide variations in utilization of manufacturing capacity supplying important overseas markets, over a set period.
2. A small proportion of the portfolio has a very high share of the company's world-wide sales and/or profits.
3. The company's overseas marketing and sales organizations are not fully occupied with the existing portfolio.
4. The markets serviced by the company are expanding into product types not currently marketed but for which production capacity could be adapted.
5. Sales volumes and profits relating to a significant part of the portfolio are steadily declining.

In international operations, most companies now recognize that their survival and financial security depend on growth; it is only through growth that sales volume and profits will increase steadily. The development and extension of the product portfolio is essential to growth in this highly competitive international environment. Case examples 2.7 and 2.8 illustrate this aspect. The first of these, on Stride Rite, shows how developing the range can strengthen a company's overall market position;[15] the next case takes it further and shows how corporate profits can be substantially increased by a complete re-think and overhaul of the portfolio by management.

Case example 2.7
The US Stride Rite Corporation recently extended its product range. The company has long been respected as a high performer in selling quality children's shoes; it is customer-oriented and has maintained a strong brand name recognition in markets. But recent market trends have been increased competition from imported brands (which by 1984 had 60 per cent of all US shoe sales), and the effect of declining birth rates in the 1970s on demand in the 1980s. Consequently, the product range has been extended to include shoes for other markets, while retaining the emphasis on brand name recognition; so Stride Rite is going after adults in suburbs and cities who want boots for weekend life-styles with its 'Herman' boots. There has also been expansion into women's casual footwear, and more recently into quality athletic shoes with 'Pro-Ked'.

Case example 2.8

Back in 1975, Dunhill Co. had annual sales with a retail value of about £35 million, of which three-quarters was cigarette lighters (most of these being sold in Japan). Today, Dunhill sells a portfolio of branded luxury products, from pipes and pipe tobacco to watches, pens, menswear and women's wear, with a retail sales value in 1985 of £450 million (with profits rising from £5.9 million in 1983 to £15 million in 1985). Dunhill's management has shown how to drive up corporate profits by exploiting a portfolio of products under a luxury brand name. While other companies have done it with individual brands (e.g. Cartier and Gucci), only Dunhill has assembled a portfolio of products in a holding company structure. This has been done on the basis of exploiting the Dunhill name with a wider portfolio, and using the company's cash balances to fund expansion; at the same time, some other companies have been bought out to 'round out' the portfolio with the addition of new brand names: Lane (US pipe tobacco), Montblanc-Simplo (West German quality pens) and Chloe (French luxury women's wear and perfumeries). Most recently, the 'Varsity' clothing range has been promoted. All this portfolio development has also been combined with rationalization in pipe manufacturing, thus also sharply improving return on capital employed.

Clearly, a product portfolio must be developed to produce a specified rate of return while at the same time minimizing risks in world-wide operations. Widely accepted managerial approaches to this use are

- portfolio analysis, and
- development of 'global' brands.

Portfolio analysis

The computation of rate of return and risk is complex because of the difficulties in estimating the expected rate of return for each product. So portfolio analysis is concerned with the relationship between risk and return, and the products in a company's portfolio will therefore have varying degrees of risk and return associated with them. Four possible combinations are attainable, and these are depicted in Fig. 2.7. It

		Return	
		High	Low
Risk	High	1	2
	Low	3	4

1: High risk, high return
2: High risk, low return
3: Low risk, high return
4: Low risk, low return

Fig. 2.7 Product portfolio analysis.

should be possible to represent a product mix on such a matrix (using the four co-ordinates against 'risk' and 'return'), thus ensuring that the performance of the product portfolio is continually monitored.

Indeed, product portfolio analysis can also be used to develop profiles of different products in terms of their suitability for global marketing, which is to be discussed shortly. For the assumptions underlying all global product marketing are that the investment costs in promotion and 'education' world-wide, and in manufacturing world-wide, are all justified by researched evidence of demand/sales potential. In this analysis, the competitive position and strength overseas of the product portfolio, and the extent and strength of significant market differences (economic, social, cultural, etc.), are two significant factors to be taken into account. Much will depend on the nature of the product: some consumer products are heavily branded world-wide to the same specifications and appeal to an international taste (for example, the global campaign for Camel cigarettes); but specialized industrial products are by definition severely limited in their scope for global marketing, since they are designed to meet specific technical requirements in different markets. One interesting and topical analysis of the spectrum of 'opportunities and risks' shows how different product portfolios can be assessed by management.[16] This analysis goes on to explain some significant differences (see Fig. 2.8):

> A major difference between companies in quadrants I and II is that those in I typically have a competitive attractiveness that is based on both product and marketing communications superiority, whereas those in quadrant II might rely more on marketing communications superiority only. Companies in quadrant III sell, for example, standardized products in the maturity phase. From a marketing point of view these products are difficult in all markets . . . Companies in quadrant IV expose themselves to large risks; they do not have any real competitive advantage and they are perceived to be different from what the market is used to . . . these are innovative companies . . . and companies which have made unrealistic evaluations of resources needed, competitive pressure, and consumers' willingness to adopt differences in foreign markets.

Figure 2.8 illustrates some recent approaches to the analysis of the product portfolio in terms of competitiveness, risk, return and adaptability to global marketing conditions. Management must ensure that this sort of analytical approach is used, particularly in evaluating global aspects of product development and branding.

The development of 'global' brands

While the concept of global branding of products has been recently widely documented, in practice it is not in all cases an appropriate marketing strategy; indeed, it should be seen as only one of a number of options, among which is the development of regional or national brands as distinct from global brands. In evaluating these options a useful classification for management has been proposed (see Table 2.3).[17] This classification leads further to an assessment of characteristics to identify global brands. The assessment is quoted in full from the study cited:

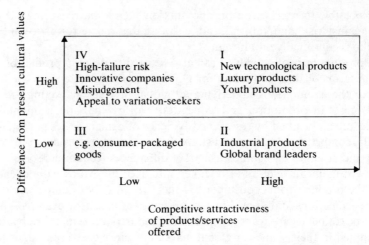

Fig. 2.8 Analytical model of product opportunities and risks in foreign markets (*Source*: R. Martenson, 'Future Competition in a Cross-cultural Environment', *European Management Journal*, 4, 3, 1986)

Table 2.3 A classification of international branding options (*Source*: A. E. Pitcher, 'The Role of Branding in International Advertising', *International Journal of Advertising*, no. 4, 1985. Copyright © 1985, Cassell Educational Ltd.)

	Product	Current positioning (*point A*)	Desired positioning (*point B*)	Strategy	Execution
Global product	Must be same	Not applicable	Not applicable	Not applicable	Not applicable
World brand	Must be same	Optimally same	Must be same	Optimally same	Optimally same, including name and packaging
Regional brand	Same or different by region	Reflects existing consumer perceptions	Different by country	Usually different	Usually different
National brand	Same or different by country	Reflects existing consumer perceptions	Different by country	Usually different	Usually different

1. How widely available is the product under consideration?
   - Are distribution channels common around the world?
   - Are the pricing structure and the margins similar?
   - Are there differing legal constraints on the product—ingredients, attributes, etc.?
2. What is the competitive climate, country by country?
   - How many brands compete?
   - What is their ranking?
   - Are there strong local entries?
   - Is the brand in the same product life-cycle stage around the world?
3. What consumer usage segments support the brand?
   - For what reasons?
   - What are their attitudes towards the category? the brand?
   - How is the brand used by consumers?
   - Are consumer segments consistent on life-styles and values across borders?
4. What is the brand's advertising history around the world?
   - Are there any commonalities of strategy, execution, etc.?
   - What has been the role of advertising in promoting the brand?
   - What media are used?
   - What is the competitive advertising activity?
5. What is the advertisers' organizational structure, and can it 'support' world brand orchestration?
   - Centralized v. decentralized?
   - Recent history of (world-wide) growth?
   - Sophistication of temperament to deal with the exigencies of international marketing?

While this assessment is clearly of value to management at the micro level, there are other macro aspects of global branding which must form part of the overall analysis of options. These 'macro' aspects essentially concern long-term market trends world-wide, rather than short-term market prospects; so they are on the one hand negative, and on the other, positive. Negative factors can be overcome by manufacturers seeking to market global brands, but they require increasingly heavy investment in new manufacturing technology, distribution and brand promotion; they include

1. the growing influence of the retailer in many parts of the world, bringing a diversion of marketing funds to the retailer and away from the consumer;
2. depressed or static economies, creating increased competition for market share;
3. continuing pressure from low-price or generic brands in many basic packaged goods categories;
4. product quality converging with increasing technological parity among major marketing companies;
5. continuing government restrictions on brand marketing, including regulation of advertising copy and media;

Table 2.4 Value of international brand franchise (*Source*: AGB, SAMI)

| | Market share (%) | | | |
| | UK | | USA | |
	1979	*1982*	*1978*	*1982*
No. 1 brand	31.3	32.6	29.5	31.4
Other manufacturers' brands	53.2	46.7	51.8	44.8
Retailer brands	15.5	20.7	18.7	23.8

6. growing marketing expenses as manufacturers respond to the ever higher costs of reaching the consumer.

Against these, of course, must be set some significant and positive factors which favour the development of global brands. Foremost among these is the value of a brand franchise. Recent research has shown that leading global brands, backed by consistent investment in promotion, advertising and any other 'image-strengthening', not only hold their own, but actually benefit from the weakening position of the lesser brands. This is especially noteworthy in view of the growth internationally of retailer brands (see Table 2.4).

Certainly another significant point is that consumer convergence in demography, habits and culture is increasingly leading manufacturers to a 'consumer-driven' rather than a 'geography driven' view of global markets for products. Demographic convergence is the single most important factor in brand development in industrialized markets: it derives from such factors as ageing populations, falling birth rates and increased female employment. On the economic front, too, many of the 'negative' factors already referred to have actually underlined the economic logic of world brands; continuing cost inflation, and the competitive intensity of maturing packaged goods markets have reinforced management's opportunities for international economies of scale as the basis of long-term strategic market development and security: indeed, the continuing competitiveness of a global brand depends critically on skilful management of these economic aspects.

The final component that management has to consider, therefore, in developing brands as part of a world-wide product portfolio is the measurement and enhancement of 'brand character'. (Brand 'image' and brand 'personality' are other widely used terms to denote this concept.) Measuring brand character world-wide can be hazardous, owing to differences of local customs, language, media availability, etc.; nevertheless, four basic components of brand character can be identified:

1. functional attributes (such as cleaning and decay prevention for dentifrices);
2. emotional attributes (such as 'confidence-inspiring', 'old-fashioned and reliable', 'modern', 'cheerful', etc.);
3. market status (is the brand perceived as the outstanding leader in its field, one of a number of acceptable choices, or 'out of the running'?);

4. 'badge' status (what kind of people use the brand, and what does it say about them?).

Some assessment of these factors is essential for the management of global brands.

Saatchi & Saatchi, among the world's leading advertising agencies, have recently developed the Brand Character Index (BCI) on the basis of research initiated in their New York agency. BCI provides a structure that allows management to assess decisively the extent to which any particular brand lives up to the company's chosen central positioning strategy for that brand; this research means that the apparently ephemeral subject of brand character can be managed by objectives in the same way as most other aspects of an efficient company's business. So BCI would enable a multinational company to measure the extent to which a brand's character differs across national boundaries: the key point of reference in the development of an international measure of 'brand character' is the clear definition of the desired character for the brand. So there is a two-way interaction, between the actual position of the brand's character as revealed by market research, and management's perception of where the brand's character should be, even if the product is not quite perceived in those terms by the consumer. So BCI measures the gap between actual and optimum brand character.

Case examples 2.9, 2.10 and 2.11 illustrate the potential, in penetration and power, of developing clear and consistent brand personalities.

Case example 2.9
One of the leading European manufacturers of electrical domestic appliances is the Italian company Zanussi, which as IAZ International has been trading in UK for many years. A few years ago, this company was among the first successfully to develop a new clear brand personality encompassing its complete range of appliances. Two points are noteworthy: first, the 'personality' comprised the concept of 'modern scientific man' utilizing the very latest technology, made available (of course) by the Zanussi company; this was a radical departure from the mundane 'kitchen-centred' brand advertising being adopted by its competitors. Second, this 'personality' was consistently and clearly projected in the company's TV advertising by skilful use of 'impact' camera work showing the sudden appearance of the newest machine in the range, with the smart slogan reinforcing the concept: 'Zanussi—the appliance of science'. Research in the UK has shown that this strong 'scientific' personality has made a longer-lasting impact on European consumers than the more pedestrian images of Zanussi's competitors.

Case example 2.10
The Coca Cola company adopted a novel approach to find a new 'personality' to promote 'new' Coke to younger buyers who were increasingly drinking Pepsi. This

personality is 'Max Headroom', a computer-generated television image (created by a British video company) with his own 'chat show'. Backed by Coca Cola's $25 million advertising campaign, 'Max' has become a full media star, with the release of two books, a rock record, a video, etc. Research has shown that the adolescent age group relate very closely to 'Max' both emotionally and psychologically. On this basis, Coca Cola has launched not only TV spots but billboards, T-shirts and even 50 'video vans' featuring Max Headroom tapes. To date, the results have been dramatic: advertising research shows one of the highest all-time 'retention rates', and overall sales of Coke are now growing faster than Pepsi. To sustain this 'personality', the company is planning TV ads in Europe and Australia and 'Max Zones' in North America to promote books and a 'home video biography' of Max.

Case example 2.11

Suntory Co. is Japan's leading distiller, but it is a relative newcomer in the Japanese beer market; its market share remained at about 6 per cent, and the company had difficulty in achieving distribution in the face of competition by the established market leader, Kirin, which had 70 per cent market share. Suntory initially focused on improving the formulation of its product by concentrating on canned beer for home consumption, and on 'authenticity/purity' in non-pasteurized or draught beer, both aimed at young drinkers. Management's next step was to devise a 'character-based' campaign to attract older drinkers and their families. Utilizing the initial appeal of an existing commercial with dancing penguins, the company made three animated penguin commercials based on well-known movies: *Casablanca*, *Rocky*, and *Brief Encounter*, all with a romantic and sentimental theme. Not only did Suntory beer sales move ahead in the 'low' autumn season, but 'penguin cans' became an integral part of brand marketing, with the symbol appearing on cans, and a hit song and an animated film reinforcing the penguin character. Suntory's market share has already doubled. Moreover, research has shown that 90 per cent of all sectors of the population, irrespective of age and sex, are enthusiastic about penguins, and therefore that this 'characterization' has achieved remarkable 'across-the-board' appeal.

In conclusion, management should seek to develop a product portfolio that includes, where scale economies permit, regional as well as global brands. In some companies, country managers and their local advertising agencies are required to implement standard programmes for each company's global brands, while these managers retain full responsibility for the marketing programmes of their locally distributed brands. Companies can motivate their country managers to stay interested in the global brands by allocating development funds to support local marketing efforts on these brands and by circulating monthly reports that summarize market performance data by brand and country.

2.3   The communications mix

Introduction

The management of an international company has special responsibilities for developing effective communications with important sectors of each country in which the company has business interests. Foremost among such sectors are consumers/customers (depending on the nature of the product or service). Much of the communications mix directed at these will be media advertising and other forms of promotion (these aspects will be discussed later, and in particular the impact of new technology); personal influence is also an important factor. But the first step for management, before any detailed planning of media advertising is done, is to determine the direction and development of the communications mix, in its totality, in regions of operation.

Different forms of communication must be used to develop relationships with the major 'publics' involved with the company's operations. These sectors, with some of the appropriate communications methods, can be summarized as follows, together with expectations/requirements as perceived by both company and stakeholder.

1. *Customers* (consumer and/or industrial): expect quality, value, service, satisfaction, reassurance, reliability; in return, the company expects goodwill, loyalty, satisfaction, favour. Communications modes: advertising, sales promotion, personal selling, trade fairs and missions.
2. *Suppliers*: expect reliability and efficiency, fair credit treatment, financial dependability; in return, the company expects service, value, reliability and loyalty. Communications modes: personal communications and some promotion/public relations.
3. *Government*: expect fostering job provision, legal operations, productivity, public spiritedness; in return, the company expects understanding of business needs, favourable business climate, infrastructure. Communications modes: personal communications, public relations, public opinion forming, political lobbying, corporate advertising, trade missions.
4. *Employees*: expect fairness, rewards, job satisfaction/security, being kept informed; in return, the company expects loyalty, honesty, effort. Communications modes: internal promotion, personal relationships, training programmes.
5. *Trade/distributors*: expect product quality, service, profits, value, marketing skills; in return, the company expects trade support, goodwill, loyalty stockholding, customer access. Communications modes: trade promotion, personal contacts, selling, trade symposia, fairs.
6. *Local community*: expects employment, clean environment, social activities, trading prosperity; in return, the company expects local infrastructure, labour provision, social support. Communications modes: personal contacts, public relations, open days, sponsorships, training.
7. *Bankers and creditors*: expect sound management of markets and assets, credit-

worthiness, realism in risk analysis; in return, the company expects financial support and expertise, understanding of company's business, trust. Communications modes: regular personal contacts, corporate advertising.

8. *Media organizations*: expect openness, professional briefing and de-briefing, information and planning on marketing policies; in return, the company expects integrity, expertise, reliability, favourable coverage/comment and effective control. Communications modes: briefings, presentations prior to and during media campaigns to selected markets.

9. *Shareholders*: expect sound financial management, integrity, profits, corporate growth; in return, the company expects support, trust, satisfaction, increasing investment and recommendation. Communications modes: direct mail, presentations, personal contacts, public relations particularly regarding institutional shareholders, corporate advertising.

The management of the total communications mix entails a continuous and complex set of tasks leading to the establishment of an overall communications strategy, so that the component parts of the mix can be both integrated to serve that strategy, and targeted to meet specific objectives for each of these major market sectors. Clearly, certain parts of the mix are directly concerned with the marketing of goods and services to customers in different national markets, particularly sales and sales management and media advertising. These two aspects of the mix will be discussed specifically later in this chapter; at this stage, two significant points must be noted by management.

1. There is a close link in both concept and implementation between the total communications mix and 'environment management'; the latter was explained at length in Section 2.1 above, together with the role of management in using specific parts of the mix (e.g. political pressure, public opinion forming) to manage or at least influence the company's trading environment.

2. The planning and implementing of those parts of the mix that are the responsibility of marketing management, particularly selling and media advertising, must be done in the context of an agreed strategy for the company's total communications mix, as outlined above. This approach is essential to ensure consistency and quality in all communications with these major sectors: public relations, public opinion forming and corporate image building, for example, should all be directed to maintaining favourable attitudes to the company and a favourable business climate in which selling and advertising themselves can work most productively.

Both of these aspects are touched on in Case example 2.12.

Case example 2.12

The Esso Petroleum Co. in South America (which became Exxon in North America) was faced with a difficult situation. The assets of the company had been expropriated in Peru, and management had to decide what stance the company should adopt in other South American countries. Rather than embark on divestment and 'damage limitation', the company adopted a strong, positive profile. In particular, it contrived to project a better image in Colombia by organizing a comprehensive collection of Colombian art and sponsoring its presentation in the USA. The acclaim this received created a better understanding of South American culture, and led to the company being awarded the Colombian government's highest decoration. This initiative helped the company to secure its market position as well as creating a favourable public image throughout South America.

Overseas representation

The management of the communications mix is closely bound up with the quality and consistency of the company's overseas representation. (A detailed analysis of market entry and operations is contained in Chapter 3.) How effectively a company operates overseas clearly depends heavily on planning and on the quality of the company's communications. Sales and sales management, for example, are the operational means by which products find customers, and so a large part of the communications process is to create and sustain demand. And indeed, the various methods of ensuring effective representation overseas are by no means mutually exclusive. Many companies find, for example, that the overseas agent can be made more effective in sales coverage and promotional impact if supported by some form of direct sales organization. As mentioned earlier, many firms conclude that, as sales develop, it is time to establish their own sales office in the market; there are two main reasons for this.

1. Companies relying heavily on agents risk losing control of the selling process; agents often prove less flexible than direct sales staff in coping with competition and are relatively expensive in areas where sales volume is high.
2. Productivity and performance of agent's staff are generally lower than company's own staff in terms of obtaining orders, handling customer problems/complaints, product knowledge and technical support and demonstrations.

So on-the-spot company sales representation can make the agency system work more effectively for the manufacturer selling overseas: the agent ensures specific expertise in knowledge of the language, local competitors, trade regulations and contracts in the localities, while the company representative promotes the firm's sole interests, ensures that the agent is giving priority to its products, and provides local agency training.

Case example 2.13
An Italian paint manufacturer with world-wide sales treats its agents as an extension of its own sales force. Sales offices abroad and agents alike are expected to submit monthly progress reports, which are put into a computer for analysis, and a video display system enables the company's management to check what stocks key customers

have bought and the price paid; if an agent's sales fall off, management can quickly identify the problem area and send one of its senior staff to investigate, and support the local agent.

Companies in industrial sectors particularly favour direct selling internationally, especially where market growth is slow or where negotiating with key clients is a necessary part of the sales process. Advantages claimed by companies doing this include

1. close relationship with customers who prefer to deal direct with manufacturers;
2. increased confidence in the supplier where technical problems can be sorted out directly with technical sales staff;
3. sounder base for longer-term market development and sales planning;
4. more accurate and fuller reporting back to the company of price levels, competition and changes in specifications or buyers' organizations.

In many countries, personal selling takes on special importance where restrictions on advertising and lack of media availability restrict advertising; again, low wages in other countries enable the company to hire a much larger local sales force than at home. Although there is no substitute for the trained and experienced home-based sales representative, a local force of sales assistants *can* cover a local market effectively; this is the sales organization favoured by some major cigarette manufacturers in developing countries. Depending on the type of product, sales support staff are often drawn from nationals of the overseas country. Some manufacturers use national representatives in each of its markets; whereas in the case of sales to large retail or wholesaling organizations, which handle their own important arrangements, it is common for the manufacturer's sales representative to sell across national boundaries. However, if it is the company's policy to have local sales assistants who are nationals working under the overall direction of senior home-based sales staff, either directly or through an agent, the management of such a force will have to be largely decentralized to each national market, with home-based staff acting as sales trainers and advisers to national operations, contributing guidance and direction because of their special product knowledge and experience.

Sales profile analysis

In setting up and running an international sales force, the company's management should undertake a sales profile analysis of the market (and should update it as appropriate); this should include the following:

Environment   Extent and topography of area to be covered
Requirements of distributors as to sales support
Expectations and attitudes of key customers to selling methods
Language

Competition	Competitor sales audit
	Key points of effectiveness of competitors
	Competitor information on market prospects including strengths and weaknesses
Institutions	Organizations that support and/or recognize the value of salesmanship
	Contract/task sales forces
	Study of purchasing institutions
	Training (e.g. languages) institutions
Legal System	Laws relating to selling practices and transfer of goods and services
Economic	Market growth rates and other business indicators (e.g. stock levels)
	Credit terms; expected levels of trade solvency
Technology	Applications of microcomputers; extent of 'remote-access' buying; communications levels

This sales profile analysis is a vital, yet often ignored, step in establishing (and updating) realistic views of the sales potential (growth prospects, competition levels) of an overseas market. While it will not answer all problems, and in particular lacks the sophistication of demand forecasting techniques now used (usually with computer applications) by many multinational corporations, it does at least guide management as to the most relevant and effective sales organization required by a particular market.

In managing an overseas sales force, two problems can arise.

1. Selling is a low-status occupation in some countries, and therefore quality of training and competitive pay are vital in attracting high-quality sales recruits.
2. Finding people with the requisite educational and technical (and social) accomplishments is often difficult and time-consuming for management.

Differences of culture, environment, status and economics have similar impacts on management's methods of remunerating, motivating and controlling the sales force overseas. Clearly, non-monetary rewards such as status, foreign travel and recognition will have greater pull in some countries than in others. (Philip Morris of Venezuela publicizes the achievements of its best sales staff.) A mix of monetary (salary and/or commission) and non-monetary rewards appropriate to each overseas market must be set which will take account of these local values or 'norms'. Further, where the sales profile analysis is carried out, and other well proved sales management ratios used, and updated for each market, comparative evaluation of the performance of each overseas sales force becomes standard practice (the comparisons must be among groups of similar countries); and performance can be improved overall (particularly where some innovation is put in hand) by learning from experiences in the company's other markets.

Case example 2.14

NCR Company has been in Japan for over seventy years, but only in the past two decades has it been able to recruit college graduates; selling was considered low-prestige. Today, however, 80 per cent of its sales force are college graduates, as a result of targeted, planned promotion of the company in higher education, and the design of management training programmes linked to career development plans.

Case example 2.15

A joint venture between 3M Company and Sumitomo has developed a sales training programme that has drawn much interest from Japanese firms. This programme involves initial training, dealer training, marketing seminars, training for experienced sales staff, sales manuals and national sales meetings. New sales recruits from Japanese universities have two months' intensive training, followed by ten months more of general marketing and field training.

All such programmes (for agents and sometimes for licensees) must, of course, be part of the company's planned communications programmes, usually supported by a home-based resource team. Indeed, as the company finds new product applications, or enters new market segments, the sales tasks will have to be changed or sharpened, especially in such sectors as computers, chemicals and technical equipment. Much will depend on management's assessment of the competitiveness of the company's sales operations; and this will depend on factors such as the productivity of sales representatives and agents. Overall, the development of a plan for this sales component of the mix requires attention to the following:

1. key markets and key customers overseas, to be targeted in the light of research and analysis;
2. task force selling in appropriate markets where strength of competition requires it; this means supporting all sales staff with technical, design and financial expertise to negotiate and develop sales from key customers;
3. constant review of productivity of overseas sales operations in terms of unit values/profits and levels and quality of manpower.

Advertising and promotion

The effectiveness of international sales operations is determined by the quality of management, and by the impact and organization of the company's advertising and promotion; these must be targeted in overseas markets and must create and sustain the demand which sales can then exploit. Particularly important, therefore, are the links between media advertising, sales promotion, publicity and public relations.

As has been pointed out, the scope of the communications mix is wide, requiring the planning and implementation of many interlinked activities; these include (apart from sales and media advertising) promotional activities such as trade fairs, trade missions, store promotions, trade symposia, sponsorship and endorsements, and marketing weeks in trade centres. Reference should also be made to those other aspects of communications discussed in Section 2.1 above, including influencing opinion formers, political lobbying and other forms of PR. All these parts of the communications mix have objectives that, tactically, are by no means the same as sales operations (to obtain contracts/orders): they are designed and planned in the context of

1. long-term market development;
2. creating a favourable international image of a company;
3. setting up conditions conducive to business deals/contracts;
4. communicating with key sectors of business and governments overseas about the benefits of the product or service.

So, while public relations is concerned with creating and maintaining favourable relationships between an organization and its 'publics', media advertising encompasses persuasive communications paid for by the advertiser and transmitted through one or more media, designed to secure purchases or other behaviour by customers favourable to the advertiser. Media advertising therefore occupies a central role in the total communications mix, and in terms of investment represents one of the major sets of decision in international marketing planning. The first steps in planning advertising, therefore, are to undertake

1. Advertising profile analysis:

Environment	Culture; literacy levels; readership details; response to symbolism; general attitude to advertising; details of buyer, decider; influencer patterns; market segments; demography
Competition	Identification of competitive advertising practices; their expenditure and ratio to sales over a period
	Research into strengths and weaknesses of competitors' advertising policies
Institutions	Total advertising expenditure in country; media available and growth in expenditure patterns; technical facilities (e.g. colour)
	Media details—circulation, readership and segments, media costs, frequency; code of advertising
Legal System	Trade description legislation; special rules pertaining to various products (e.g. cigarettes, drugs, fertilizers)
	Law limiting expenditure
Economics	Levels of consumption; disposable incomes; ownership of radios, TVs, etc.; readership of newspapers, magazines; socioeconomic class structure
	Degree of social mobility
Language	Translation and 'back-translation' of copy, etc.

Technology   Availability of satellite/cable communications etc. and levels/ organization of research methodologies; microcomputer applications

2. Setting up advertising objectives in relation to market opportunities and company resources (see Fig. 2.9).

The next steps are, of course, concerned with the actual implementation of advertising plans through media campaigns. These involve the appointment, briefing of, and establishment of working relationships with advertising agencies in overseas markets, or the co-ordination of an international advertising campaign by one agency headquarters through subsidiary/associated companies in the countries concerned. Operations involve creative work—origination and design—to agreed briefs; media planning, buying and scheduling, control and evaluation of media campaigns; and financial aspects.

In briefing and evaluating the advertising agency, management can refer to the following useful set of guidelines.[18]

1. *Market coverage*: does the particular agency or package of agencies cover all the relevant markets?
2. *Quality of coverage*: how good a job does this package of agencies do in preparing advertising in each market?
3. *Market research, public relations, and other marketing services*: if the firm needs these services in world markets, in addition to advertising work, how do the different agencies compare on their offerings of these facilities?
4. *Relative roles of company advertising department and agency*: some firms have a large staff that does much of the work of preparing advertising campaigns. These firms require less of an agency than do companies that rely on the agency for almost everything relating to advertising. Thus, a weak company advertising department needs strong agency, and vice versa.
5. *Communication and control*: if the firm wants frequent communication with agencies in foreign markets and wishes to oversee their efforts, it will be inclined to tie up with the domestic agency that has overseas offices. The internal communications system of this agency network would facilitate communications for international arrangement.
6. *International co-ordination*: does the firm wish to have advertising tailor-made to each national market? Or does it desire co-ordination of national advertising with that done in other markets, and/or with the domestic programme? One of the major differences between agency groups will be their ability to aid the advertiser in attaining international co-ordination.
7. *Size of company's international business*: the smaller the firm's international advertising expenditures, the less its ability to divide its expenditures up among many different agencies. The firm's advertising volume may determine agency choice to ensure some minimum level of service. A small volume multiplied by a

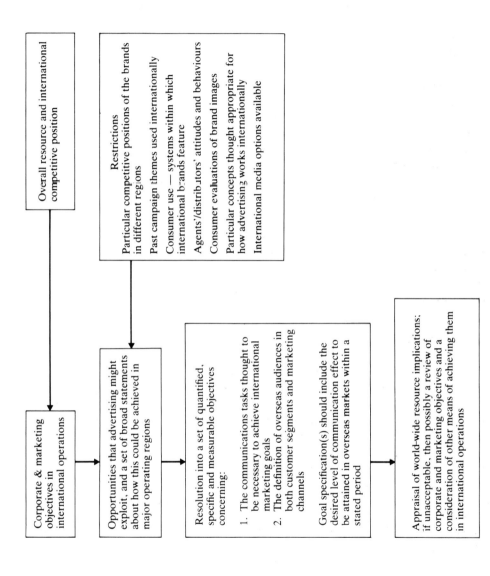

Fig. 2.9 The development of international advertising objectives.

Overall resource and international competitive position

Corporate & marketing objectives in international operations

Opportunities that advertising might exploit, and a set of broad statements about how this could be achieved in major operating regions

Restrictions

Particular competitive positions of the brands in different regions

Past campaign themes used internationally

Consumer use — systems within which international brands feature

Agents'/distributors' attitudes and behaviours

Consumer evaluations of brand images

Particular concepts thought appropriate for how advertising works internationally

International media options available

Resolution into a set of quantified, specific and measurable objectives concerning:

1. The communications tasks thought to be necessary to achieve international marketing goals
2. The definition of overseas audiences in both customer segments and marketing channels

Goal specification(s) should include the desired level of communication effect to be attained in overseas markets within a stated period

Appraisal of world-wide resource implications; if unacceptable, then possibly a review of corporate and marketing objectives and a consideration of other means of achieving them in international operations

83

number of markets could be of interest to an international agency even if it is of no interest to an agency in any one market.

8. *Image*: does the firm want a national or international image? Desire for local identification and good local citizenship might indicate that the firm should choose national agencies rather than an international one. This is the practice of IBM, for example.

9. *Company organization*: companies that are very decentralized, with national profit centres, might wish to leave agency selection to the local subsidiary.

10. *Level of involvement*: in joint-venture arrangements, the international firm shares decision-making. The national partner may have preferences and/or experience with national agency, which could be the decisive factor. In licensing agreements, advertising is largely in the hands of the licensee. Selling through distributors can also reduce the control of the international company, though sometimes the firm may have a regenerative advertising programme with distributors; of course, where the firm has a 50–50 co-operative programme with its distributors, it may also have some say in agency selection.

The advertising profile analysis can highlight significant differences in the organization of advertising media in overseas markets, and in the types and levels of tastes, attitudes, spending habits, consumption, styles, etc., of consumers. These differences should be noted by advertisers when selecting media and evaluating impact, and are aptly illustrated in Case example 2.16.

Case example 2.16

Italy has by far the largest cinema attendances in Europe; Portugal has the highest level of commercial TV advertising; Sweden has the highest consumption per head of 'glossy' magazines; and West Germany has the highest readership of trade and industry journals. Householders in Belgium and Holland receive more pieces of direct mail per head than anywhere else in Europe; Belgium boasts the highest expenditure per head on posters/outdoor advertising; TV is more controlled in France, and some products such as textiles, books and furniture cannot be advertised. The UK has the largest network and readership of national newspapers (and regional newspapers alone account for about one-third of all UK advertising expenditure). Commercial radio and cinema advertising have relatively more impact in countries such as India and Nigeria than in Europe. In the USA there are typically about 10 local and national TV networks to choose from in the localities (e.g. CBS, ABC, PBS, NBC, etc.) and as many cable TV channels (e.g. WGN, USA, HBO, WOR, Cinemax, Showtime, etc.).

Cable networks and multinational advertising

The single most important new development affecting advertising—and, indeed, touching all aspects of the communications mix—is the new technology, particularly

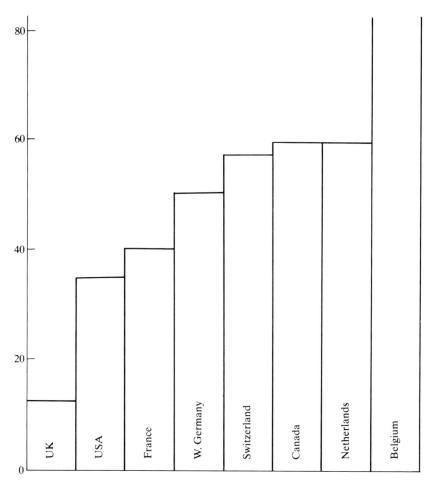

Fig. 2.10 World cable networks: percentages of TV-owning households with Cable TV, 1980
(*Source*: AGB, Media World)

cable and satellite (see Fig. 2.10). European cable channels facilitate pan-European advertising campaigns on a scale that would have been impossible up to now (Table 2.5). Before the advent of cable networks, for example, West German air time had to. be bought a year in advance, while Norway would take no advertising at all. Substantial parts of the USA and Europe are already wired up for the reception of multi-channel cable networks. In Japan a successful 'wired city' experiment has shown the viability of fully interactive cable-based technology, which provides not only entertainment, but also a complete communications service between schools, offices and homes.

Table 2.5 National cable penetration in Europe, 1986 (*Source*: ADMAP, 1986)

	%
Australia	12
Belgium	83
Denmark*	5
Finland	15
France	1
Greece	0
Ireland	26
Italy	0
Netherlands	56
Norway	26
Portugal	0
Spain	0
Sweden	7
Switzerland	56
United Kingdom	1
West Germany	9

* Definitions vary. Around 50 per cent of Danish homes belong to communal aerial feed systems, which are sometimes categorized as 'cable'.

The USA has 30 million cable-receiving households compared with only 3 million five years ago, and over half of the 90 million American households will be linked to cable in the next ten years. Cable has already begun to erode the US networks' share of the national television audience—down from 93 to 90 per cent. As more cable stations start to carry advertising (70 per cent of systems do already), they take more of the network share of advertising revenue, as well.

Internally, much of cable's promise as an advertising medium stems from its ability to attract audiences through selective programming aimed at more clearly defined groups than the mass audiences of the major networks. Multinational advertisers with a specific target audience in each country will be able to reach their target segment through a cable channel concentrating on its specific interest.

At the same time, mass advertising itself is increasingly becoming multinational. In Europe, two pan-European satellite channels, 'Sky' (News International) and (Music Box' (Thorn EMI), have advertised brands such as Mars Bars and Mattel to multi-country audiences. These channels are funded partly by subscriptions and partly by advertising revenue: the penetration of homes is currently around 10 million by 'Sky' and 7 million by 'Music Box'. Whether the pool of pan-European advertising will be large enough to fund all the Euro channels, both operational and planned, is doubtful at this stage, although there are forecasts that, while pan-European advertising cur-

Table 2.6 European satellite stations supported by advertising, 1986
(*Source*: ADMAP, 1986)

	Household universe (*m*)
English language 'Pan European'	
Sky	9.4
Super Channel	8.1
MTV (Aug. 1987 launch)	1.3 (plus)
The Children's Channel	0.3
CNN	0.1
German language 'Pan-German'	
RTL Plus	2.5
SAT 1	2.4
KMP Musicbox	2.1
Eureka	1.5
French language 'Pan-French'	
Canal 1	*

* Negligible.

rently accounts for 1 per cent of TV advertising revenue, this proportion should rise
to 10 per cent within a decade (see Table 2.6).

The other development in new technology is Direct Broadcasting by Satellite
(DBS). Since its launch in 1978, the European Orbital Test Satellite (OTS) has completed many tests such as the 'Eurikon' experiment, in which the European Broadcasting Union (EBU) beams an international selection of television programmes,
simultaneously translated both into teletext and the spoken word, which is received
by 'dish' aerials. Also, Satellite TV, a UK company, has introduced the first commercial European satellite network, broadcasting to Finland, Norway, Switzerland and
Malta. This 'super-station' went into orbit in 1987, and European counterparts are
pressing ahead with DBSs, of their own, the output of which will soon be beamed to
the UK via high-powered satellite. France, Germany, Italy, Luxembourg, Switzerland and the Nordic countries have 'L-SAT' projects, and already have some multi-
channel satellites transmitting. The French TDF system, for example (the first to go
into orbit), has been devised as a five-channel, two-satellite format: two of these channels are to be allocated to the existing national television networks, and a third is to be
leased to Radio Tele Luxembourg to beam German-language programmes over much
of West Germany.

Needless to say, there will be a high degree of overspill of transmissions from the
new 'super stations' of these European countries; indeed, the phenomenon of 'media
overlap' with existing networks has made Belgium for some years the 'test market' of
Europe. Case examples 2.17 and 2.18 concern pan-European advertising campaigns
using TV networks. Furthermore, the appeal of foreign-language programmes whose
satellite 'footprint' passes over the boundaries of other nations will be increased by

the advent of multiple audio channels to accompany each video channel, making it possible to provide a choice of languages on any satellite channel.

Case example 2.17

The Martini Rossi Co. for some years ran a European TV campaign for Martini with the slogan 'The right one' (German translation, 'Dabei mit'). The basic advertising concept was the presentation of the brand as a pleasant, refreshing and smart drink for the young professional classes. These people have an active, socializing life-style, and the brand is promoted as being 'just right' in that context. While this concept was put across consistently and clearly, the actual visuals used in the commercials were specially designed for German, UK and Italian audiences: car racing scenes were filmed in Italy as the backdrop to a young couple drinking Martini and watching the race (reflecting the popularity of the sport in Italy). Germany consumers typically like to know more about the product and how it can best be used, so mountain ski scenes were used to show how Martini is an especially refreshing drink for skiers. In the UK, TV viewers have become more accustomed to complex visual images, and so 'fantasy' sequences are popular and are increasingly used by advertisers: in this case, ballooning sequences over castles in mid-summer followed by a drinks party for the balloonists were used. Interestingly, the advertising in France was initially unsuccessful and had to be changed: the first visuals showed a hunting scene with riders enjoying Martini 'après la chasse'. This proved unacceptably 'exclusif' as a concept, connoting 'le snobisme'; the visuals were changed to show young people enjoying Martini in a fishing village. These campaigns were successful in terms of both increasing sales revenue and establishing a clear advertising concept for the brand.

Case example 2.18

Rank Xerox undertook a European advertising campaign for a new model of office photocopier some years ago. A new typeface was designed (common to all countries) to illustrate the clarity and quality of copy and visuals in newspaper and TV advertisements. Again, different visuals, or variations on a basic picture, were used in press advertisements throughout Europe. In West Germany a photograph of a child was used to appeal to the executive secretary in German companies (usually female) who would make or influence the decision to buy. In the UK the appeal was to a traditional game: a group of footballers! In another series of advertisements the concept was problem-solving and office efficiency: two office products (including the new photocopier) were pictured, together with a teapot for UK customers, with the copy, 'These three products solve all office problems: Rank Xerox make two of them.' Coffee pots replaced teapots in France and Benelux countries (though even here the designs of pot differed); but these were considered too flippant for the practical Swiss and German markets, so a telephone was substituted. This pan-European campaign soon established the product as the best-selling office copier throughout Europe.

mráɨn

Convergence in brand advertising

The success of these pan-European campaigns, and now the impact of new communications technology already discussed, highlight a critical development: the drive towards cultural and economic 'convergence' or 'conformity' in world-wide brand advertising. This is the most significant policy question facing management over the next decade, and it requires full explanation; indeed, the analysis is further developed in the context of 'global' marketing in the first part of the next section. Here, the concern is with advertising.

Consumer convergence in demography, habits and culture have been leading manufacturers increasingly to a 'consumer-driven' rather than a 'geography-driven' view of international markets. Some media advertising has accordingly been oriented towards audiences that share demographic rather than geographical commonality. Trends of significance to consumer advertising such as ageing populations, falling birth rates and increasing female employment are common to many countries of the industrialized world. These mean that management must change its attitudes towards communicating with consumer groups such as the family, which no longer conforms to the home-centred stereotype of years ago: changes to the composition of the household have been dramatic, and there are now fewer children per family and a declining proportion of households that conform to the two adults/two children patterns (see Fig. 2.11).

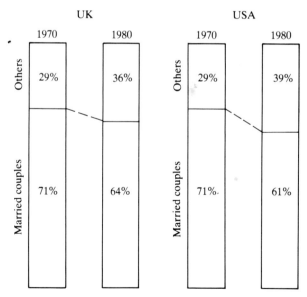

Fig. 2.11 The changing composition of households (*Source*: CSO, *US Annual Abstract of Statistics*)

Table 2.7 Static populations (*Source*: World Development Report)

| | Population growth per annum (%) | |
	1960–70	*1980–2000* *(estimate)*
Australia	2.0	0.8
Canada	1.8	0.8
USA	1.3	0.7
Spain	1.1	0.7
Japan	1.0	0.6
France	1.0	0.4
Italy	0.6	0.3
UK	0.5	0.2
Germany	0.9	0.1

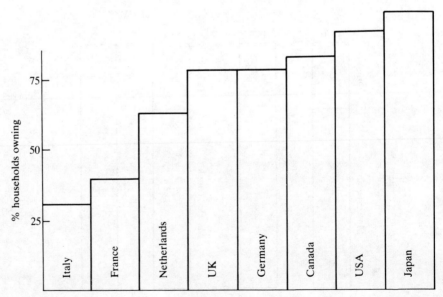

Fig. 2.12 Penetration of colour television, 1980 (*Source*: Consumer Europe, Advertising Forum)

Table 2.8 Profile of advertising expenditure, 1981 (*Source*: IAA)

	Expenditure (US £b)	*Share of total (%)*
USA	61.3	48.3
Japan	12.4	9.8
UK	7.4	5.8
Germany	6.3	5.0
France	5.0	3.9
Italy	4.6	3.6
Canada	3.4	2.7
Netherlands	2.8	2.2
Australia	2.8	2.2
Brazil	1.8	1.4
Spain	1.5	1.2
Others	17.8	13.9
Total	127.1	100

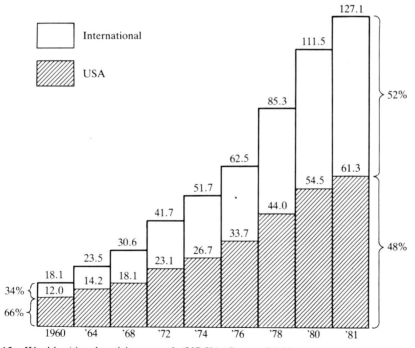

Fig. 2.13 World-wide advertising growth (US $b) (*Source*: IAA)

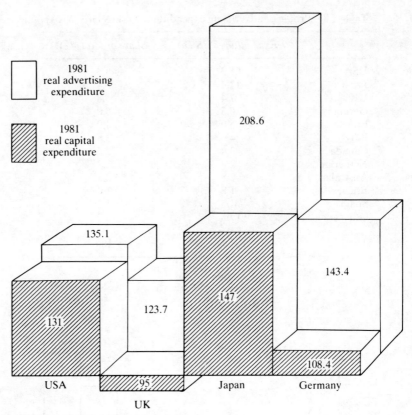

Fig. 2.14 Growth of advertising and capital expenditures (1971 = 100) (*Source*: Phillips and Drew, IAA)

Even within static populations (see Table 2.7), common trends are emerging which are of importance to international advertisers: the over-65s are a growing group relative to 25–65 age group, and that group is growing relative to the '14 and unders'. With improved health and pension funding, older age groups are becoming a significant, economically active, section of the population.

And, of course, as demographical factors are converging, the impact of this communications technology is creating elements of shared culture; and cultural convergence has facilitated the establishment of multinational brand characters. (Some of these were analysed in the previous section.) The world-wide proliferation of Marlborough cigarettes, for example, would not have been possible without TV, cinema and poster advertising about the virile, rugged character of the American West and the American cowboy—helped by increasing colour penetration in most countries (Fig. 2.12).

As further evidence of social and cultural convergence, research by some media owners has shown that a class of 'international executive' has emerged over the past three decades. The profile is increasingly precise: he/she will have attended a management development programme; works for an international company; and has a lifestyle, in terms of car and house ownership, pattern of holidays and leisure, that is increasingly shared by his/her counterparts in other countries. More pertinently, he/she typically reads a common selection of journals/papers, including *Newsweek*, *Time*, *Financial Times*, *The Economist* and a limited number of international management journals. Typically, he/she travels by air extensively (usually business/club class), speaks English plus one or two other Romance languages or an oriental language, stays in a certain type of hotel, and even buys similar brands of shoes, luggage and other leatherwear. All these developments are reducing cultural barriers as countries exchange their media output through satellite networks, for the first time allowing viewers freer access to international television advertising without the barrier of language. The significance of this 'profile' is shown in recent British Airways advertisements aimed at the business travellers.

In the industrialized economies, international advertising has come to be regarded by management as protection for the largest single asset of major companies (except that it does not appear in their balance sheets): the brand franchise. This, with the 'convergence' factors mentioned, is reflected in advertising policies: recently Fiat and Philips NV among others, have consolidated their world-wide advertising into a single agency (which bills all expenditures world-wide). Their objectives are to make each product's advertising more consistent around the world and to make it easier to transfer ideas and information among local agency offices, country organizations and headquarters.

Research in several countries after the recession in the 1970s showed that those companies that maintained their advertising investment have been rewarded by short-term and long-term sales growth significantly in excess of those companies that looked for immediate returns by reducing their international expenditures. Indeed, in the industrialized economies, management is increasingly viewing marketing expenditure and capital expenditure as forms of corporate investment. Although these forms of 'investment' receive very different accounting treatment in corporate balance sheets, advertisers have increasingly sustained the link between their investment in advertising and their investment in new technology (see Figs 2.13 and 2.14).

This section concludes with a selection of advertising concepts used by international airlines (in journals referred to earlier as typically read by executives/professionals) (Table 2.9), and a case example (2.19) demonstrating how all the elements of the communications mix can be effectively controlled to implement a specific marketing policy.[18]

Table 2.9 Selected international advertising concepts
An analysis of airline advertisements over recent years in international journals such as *Time* and *The Economist* shows the following concepts stressed:

Advertiser carrier	Theme	Concept
KLM	'Brilliant tradition' (father-to-son diamond polishing) Rembrandt Tax-free shopping Museum guide Windmill and water power Smiling welcome	Holland's standard attractions
Pan AM	'The world's most exclusive place to dine . . .' (first-class dining room upstairs in a 747)	Distinction
Kenya Airways	Africa's mountains Wildlife and game reserves Pearl-white beaches Fishing	Kenya's standard attractions
TWA	Food and drink (3 international entrées) 8 audio tracks Friendly service Contour seats Speed through customs	Flight's key attractions
Japan Air Lines	'Happi' coat (clothes less crumpled) Japanese or European cuisine 1000-year tradition of hospitality Hot towels	Exotic, millennial Orient
Singapore Airlines	Gentle hostess All-Boeing fleet 300 flights per week	Oriental charm Technical competence • Wide coverage
KLM	Extra fast check-in Special seat selection Quiet for businessman Special cabin service Special baggage handling Special office attention	Value for money Special treatment
Lufthansa	'Flights made in Germany' 273 offices, on all continents	German quality World-wide coverage
SAS	Arrival in Japan Sunday morning	Overcome 'jet lag'

Table 2.9 continued

Advertiser carrier	Theme	Concept
Pan AM	World's largest fleet of 747s Comfortable seats First-class dining room More space Films and music	Flight comfort
British Airways	Direct from London to 11 North American destinations Cool, calm and collected crew	Wide choice of destinations British character
Avianca	The people who know South America best since 1919	South American specialists
SAS	Fast Way West Polar experience Wide-body jets	Go West in comfort
Thai Airways	'Beyond Bangkok' 'Beautiful Thai'	The other Thailand Thai women
South African	International coverage 'Where no one's a stranger'	Big-hearted growth

Case example 2.19

The Timex Corporation designed and implemented a marketing policy in West Germany by co-ordinating the mix as follows.

(a) *Products.* The company studied the competitive situation and found existing producers selling primarily high- and medium-priced watches—as status items. There were also sales of low-priced, low-quality watches, sold without guarantee and with the initial repair costing more than the price of the watch. The company felt that its products filled a gap between these two segments, as to both price and quality.

(b) *Service.* To beat the low-priced competition and to meet the high-priced competition, Timex provided service arrangements at moderate cost. Service was free during the guarantee period. After that, a new movement could be purchased for one-half to one-fourth the price of the new watch. This helped upgrade the image of the inexpensive or 'cheap' watch.

(c) *Guarantee.* The company offered the first inexpensive watch with a guarantee. In fact, the guarantee was as liberal as those on high-priced watches, with free service or repairs during the first year. This was important in persuading a sceptical public about the quality of the inexpensive watch.

(d) *Price*. Timex stressed its low prices but at the same time emphasized the quality and the guarantee. The company's prices were generally a step above the low-priced competition, but well below most of the high-priced competition. Other pricing decisions were to maintain price levels and to give retailers the same margins as on high-priced watches (33 per cent).

(e) *Distribution*. Distribution strategy was one of the major elements in the Timex programme in Germany. Since jewellers sold 75 per cent of the watches, Timex needed that channel. However, the company also felt it necessary to use the large department stores and mail-order houses. Others who had tried this earlier had been boycotted by the jewellers. Timex was successful in persuading jewellers that its business was too profitable to ignore. The elements of persuasion were:

- giving the same margin as on expensive watches;
- saving repair work by having the watches sent to the Timex factory in France, while giving the dealer 25 per cent commission on the charges to the customer;
- a heavy publicity and advertising campaign (more than twice what all German competition spent): this made Timex the best-known watch in Germany.

(f) *Promotion*. A heavy advertising campaign, double the total competitive outlays, initiated the 'hard sell' approach. Dramatic 'torture tests' were used as the advertisements. Competitors called these undignified, but later on some began to imitate them. Eighty per cent of the marketing budget went on television because of its coverage and dramatic effect. In a separate promotional effort, a missionary selling force toured Germany, explaining to retailers the advantages of handling Timex.

2.4 Corporate promotion

Introduction

The preceding section contained a detailed analysis of the communications mix. This section is, in effect, a sequel, which develops specific aspects from the viewpoint of the multinational corporation (MNC).

Corporate promotion is basically concerned with the communication of positive and consistent messages about the MNC to both internal and external audiences, and particularly to opinion formers. It is very much related to corporate image and identity, and to the effective projection of policies and actions by the company consistent with that image. It encompasses arts and sports sponsorship, publicity and public relations, internal promotion and any targeted communications to those 'stakeholders' defined in Section 2.3 above. The essential question, of course, is what to communicate: corporate promotion can work effectively only if the company has at least some clear corporate objectives. With regard to the examples that follow, management should not consider adopting all, but only those that are internally consistent and accord with overall strategy:[19]

1. to be world-wide in scope; not just to sell in every country in the world, which, through distributors, the company is already doing, but to think internationally, to consider operations in any country, and to arrange the organization and activities of the company on a basis where there is no distinction between home and foreign operations;
2. to increase profitability and earnings per share each year by improving the company's added value, not only as a proportion of sales income but also in terms of the average amount generated by each employee;
3. to be an integrated producer: not only will the company seek control over the manufacture of its products, but it will progressively arrange for the manufacture of components at such locations world-wide as will give the company real flexibility in sourcing or assembling finished products at points where costs, tariffs and demand may dictate. This is to be a prime factor in the company's strategy, and the means of regulating total corporate activities;
4. to be flexible and not to depend too much on any one product, customer or market sector; to continue to broaden the base of the trading activities of the company world-wide; and to maintain an efficient research and development policy so that opportunities can be quickly recognized and exploited;
5. to remain an independent public company with a distinctive management style; to give executives the maximum freedom of action, and to encourage them to make the fullest use of it, so that they can personally influence profits;
6. to pay the best wages and salary rates that the company can afford, and to ensure job satisfaction for all employees through enlightened management. To improve working conditions in all countries of operation, and to take appropriate steps to ensure the health and safety of all employees. To promote the best possible human relations and a situation in which people really enjoy working for the company;
7. to continue to encourage employee participation in the ownership of the company (the group profit-sharing scheme is an important step in this direction);
8. to benefit the local community in every country of operation whenever and wherever the company can afford to do so, and to preserve the quality of life and of the environment (see Case example 2.20).

Case example 2.20

The Esso Petroleum Company, part of Exxon Group, USA, recently took the initiative to promote woodland conservation as part of the European Year of the Environment. Esso has joined with the Nature Conservancy Council (NCC) to launch, in the UK, the Ancient Woodlands Project to halt the cutting down of mediaeval woodlands. (Since 1945 in UK 10 per cent of the remaining 500 000 hectares has been cut down.) This sponsorship by Esso has been featured in national newspaper advertisements under one caption, 'On guard', with the Esso logo shown underneath with the other caption, 'Quality at work for Britain'. This corporate promotion is clearly intended to project the image of a successful international company, aware of and acting on its responsibilities to protect the environment.

Corporate communications are therefore a means to an end, and not an end in themselves; with clear objectives, they can be used to best effect to promote the interests of the company. Indeed, the growth in the communications industry in the last few years indicates the importance that MNCs are now attaching to their image; management is increasingly using identity, corporate culture and reputation as a means of improving profitability (as some of the case examples in this section show). The way an organization is perceived by its customers, shareholders and analysts, financiers and the media will directly affect both its market position and prospects, and its profitability. This is the company's external market-place, and it must be communicated with effectively, professionally and regularly. But there is also the internal market-place (e.g. employees, distributors, etc.) which requires attention, and where the objectives of the company need to be spelt out just as clearly as to the external stakeholders.

Case example 2.21
The Paints Division of Imperial Chemical Industries (ICI) has recently shown how corporate promotion can be used effectively both to demonstrate positive concern to reduce atmospheric pollution, and to generate profits. Car painting operations are thought to be one of the many contributors to the growing amount of volatile compounds discharged into the atmosphere. (In the process of painting one car, some 12–15 litres of organic solvents are released.) This is a matter of concern for motor manufacturers because the quality of the car finish has become a major selling feature. This presented ICI, as a paint supplier, with a technical problem, and at the same time an opportunity for corporate promotion and profits. The outcome of lengthy research was a waterborne paint, 'Aquabase' (wherein the solvents had been replaced by water), which, while maintaining the quality and appearance of existing paint finishes, reduces very substantially the overall emissions. ICI has also developed an emission-free protective material, 'Tempro', to replace traditional wax car finish (which emitted up to 3 litres of solvent per car).

Corporate promotion in this case example has proved to have had a high impact both on perceptions of ICI as a technically innovative and environmentally sensitive company among industry and the trade. It has also opened lucrative new market sectors for the Paints Division (e.g. camouflage coatings, and temporary road and construction markings using Tempro coatings).

Case example 2.22
H. J. Heinz Co. Ltd have a policy of promotion through sponsorship which is by no means always linked to the promotion of a product, although the benefit the company derives from public esteem and increased sales is, of course, most apparent when the support the company gives an event is related to a specific promotion. But the company's support is often given for reasons of 'good citizenship' or 'social responsibil-

ity', provided there is some relevance to the company's business. So the company's recent support for the World Wildlife Fund (WWF) through its 'Guardian of the Countryside' programme reflects the company's concern to improve the quality of life for the community.

But both this theme and its timing were relevant to the company in 1986. Management was then considering how to follow up a series of successful charity promotions and to enhance its reputation of a caring company. Also, 1986 was the centenary of the first Heinz sale in Britain, and WWF sponsorship provided an ideal opportunity to mark this anniversary. (The Guardian of the Countryside programme encourages adults and children to become involved in a whole range of activities designed to increase their awareness of environmental and conservation issues.)

The key questions remain. What should the company be projecting/communicating to society, and to customers? How is the company perceived by outsiders and stakeholders? Is the management's self-perception in terms of the company's market position, etc., realistic? All these have a significant bearing on corporate promotion (see Case example 2.23). Management must realize the importance of fulfilling promises made in advertising, for example, and must understand how corporate endorsement can be used to strengthen brand image. If an advertising promise is unfulfilled, a company can, in the extreme, actually become a hostage to its own advertising slogan.

Case example 2.23
Three years ago, General Motors Corporation of the USA (GM) undertook a research survey into public perceptions of and attitudes towards its corporate identity in the UK. The aim of this research was to establish how far GM corporate identity was related to, and of benefit to, the market position and sales of the GM brands, and to assess the quality and standing of the GM corporate logo in relation to other major car manufacturers. The survey showed that, while the corporate identity of GM was generally clearly recognized and esteemed, there was a very low comprehension of which were the major GM brands. (Vauxhall, for example, was still perceived by many UK respondents as just another British car!)

As a result of these survey findings, GM management sharpened up the GM corporate logo, but specifically highlighted the main GM brands such as Vauxhall and Opel as part of that logo with the caption, 'Backed by the world-wide resources of General Motors'. Subsequent surveys showed that, not only did public awareness of GM brands improve, but brand sales appreciably increased as a result over the following two-year period.

Corporate culture and corporate image

Two terms of special note, already mentioned, now require definition and analysis in the context of corporate promotion.

1. *Corporate culture*. This has been defined as[20]

> the pattern of habits, goals, concepts, ideas and behaviour that are found within a company. It is strongly influenced by the formulas which management develops to the benefit of the company. In a successful enterprise, the culture reflects the market situation ... Thus, the corporate culture should harmonise with the commercial environment. When this changes, the culture has to change as well, if the company is to survive.

This analysis is significant in that it was done in the context of the airline business. The management of a leading European airline realized that, in order to meet demands in an increasingly competitive environment, the company needed to develop a new organizational culture in terms of attitudes and work practices, allowing for greater flexibility and responsibility for decision-making at lower levels of management, and involving more decisions by 'front-line personnel'. Of course, this was not implemented without considerable investment in both internal and external communications (videotapes, brochures, symposia, etc.), and it will take time to reach fulfilment. It is also significant that 'culture changes' of precisely this sort have now been tried in companies in other sectors, with (so far) beneficial effects on morale, planning and market operations. Furthermore, corporate promotion has a role to play in fostering this cultural change.

2. *Image*. This concerns the identity or 'corporate personality' and reputation of the company as it is perceived by customers and others, in terms of their expectations of the company. Corporate identity has been defined as:[21]

> more than an outward picture (or symbol); it must show inner values and convictions, because only then can it achieve its most important objective: to encourage people to direct positive attention towards the company and its products; only that creates a lasting image which in turn is a good basis for a favourable buying decision.

Image and culture, therefore, largely determine what sort of corporate identity is communicated to customers and to the community. Perceptions of this identity, combined with the record of service and quality typically delivered by the company, make up the reputation of the company in its major markets. Case examples 2.24 and 2.25 illustrate the importance of this image-building.[22]

Case example 2.24

International Telephone and Telegraph Corporation (ITT), headquartered in New York, faced a serious image problem in the early 1970s. A majority of the public was unaware of the firm and its variety of business activities. Furthermore, many of those who were aware of ITT had a rather blurred image of the firm, primarily because of confusion between the ITT and AT&T (American Telephone and Telegraph) names.

In 1974 ITT began a multi-year, multi-million-dollar advertising campaign aimed at building a distinct and favourable image for itself in the eyes of the public. The campaign involved a series of television and print ads that employed very creative approaches to convey memorable messages and slogans, such as 'The best ideas are the ideas that help people.' ITT's campaign won praise from advertising critics and received numerous awards and honours over the years (including the CLIO and EFFIE awards). By 1982, ITT was spending over $10 million per year on its corporate image-building campaign.

To assess the potential impact of the advertising campaign on the public, ITT retained the services of Yankelovich, Skelly and White, Inc., a marketing research firm well known for its expertise in conducting public opinion polls. Yankelovich, Skelly and White conducted a 'benchmark' survey in 1974 to assess the public's views just before the start of the advertising campaign. The survey involved telephone interviews of a national sample of 1500 respondents. Similar surveys, using fresh random samples of respondents, were conducted at least once a year thereafter in order to monitor changes, if any, in the public's perceptions about ITT. A summary of the findings from the surveys showed, for instance, that, while only 68 per cent of the respondents in the January 1974 survey felt that ITT was one of the largest companies, 85 per cent of the respondents in the November 1978 survey felt so; other responses also reflected a change to more positive attitudes towards ITT on the part of the public as a result of this campaign.

Case example 2.25

The Prudential Insurance Co. launched its new corporate logo on the basis of a public relations programme with coverage spanning the financial, design and marketing press. The search for this new corporate identity was prompted by research which showed an alarming and growing gap between what the company actually did (the spectrum of financial services, from pension plans to unit trusts), and what the public thought it did ('Man from the Pru', collecting weekly subscriptions for life insurance). With competition in financial services intensifying from every quarter, it was essential for management to find a clear, visual identity under which to group the company's services. It chose the face of 'Dame Prudence'.

Although it is too soon to say whether, in the longer term, this £1 million PR investment will pay off, the new logo is now being used extensively throughout estate agents acquired by the Prudential, and this will undoubtedly raise the public perception of the company, which now claims to have the largest estate agency in the UK.

All these aspects require positive attitudes and planning on the part of management, and consistent investment in communication, particularly promotion, to convey clearly to the community the developing nature of the company's activities. And indeed, the topicality of these aspects is borne out by the increasing attention to designing new, sharper corporate 'logos', and consistent graphic designs which they represent.

And much of this activity in corporate promotion is based on experiential and survey data. Many MNCs have shown that corporate image-building over many years has sustained their strong market positions and has aided sales. Basic research has shown that:

1. 7 out of 10 of the general public believe that a company that has a good reputation would not sell poor-quality products (whether they are right or not, that is their perception);
2. a company's reputation does influence a consumer's propensity to try new products: women, for instance, are more likely to try a new frozen food product from Heinz than from a large unspecified food company;
3. over half the British public think that 'old established companies make the best products', and 4 people in 10 believe that they 'never buy products made by companies they've never heard of' (this is probably quite untrue, but it is their perception).

So in setting up any policy or plan of corporate promotion, management of a large corporation or MNC would be well advised, on the basis of the analysis and experience offered in this section, to adopt the following steps, in logical order.

1. Establish which public sectors are of importance to the company, in which countries, and why.
2. Assess the perceptions, attitudes and behaviour of these key sectors *vis à vis* the company, by verifiable, valid research methods.
3. Set corporate communications objectives, and criteria by which promotional impact can be judged.
4. Assess what changes or improvements are needed in the way the business is run.
5. Do an audit of the company's current reputation, and determine whether steps 3 and 4 are reinforcing the reputation that management seeks.
6. Choose communications methods, and ensure, as far as possible, that they are appropriate to steps 1, 3, 4 and 5 above.

On the basis of the above, then, corporate promotion can be put effectively into action to: increase awareness, project truths, correct false impressions, establish favourable business climate, develop influence and enhance morale. In terms of effective action, reference should also be made to Section 2.1 above, particularly the aspect of environment management.

2.5 The matrix approach to products and markets

Introduction

While there have been strong trends towards the 'globalization' of markets in recent years, it is not certain how far the concept will be universally adopted by companies operating across country markets. Some trends towards the globalization of brands and markets have already been referred to in Section 2.3 above. Here, the concept is explored on the basis of marketing strategy and, in particular, the management response of the 'matrix' approach to products and markets in a global context. Indeed, the 'matrix' approach is at least partly a response by companies concerned that operating and marketing 'globally', that is, minimizing national market divisions, may not be the optimal corporate strategy in all situations. And the global approach does pose some problems of resourcing, control, cross-country brand promotion, communications and operations which may not sustain a competitive position on a geographical region-by-region basis. On the other hand, global marketing can yield benefits: standardizing products can lower operating costs, and effective co-ordination can exploit a company's best product and marketing ideas.

The automative industry, for example, has become increasingly a global one. The concept of the 'world car' globally marketed is now a reality. There can no longer be a future for cars built purely for the domestic market: those individual markets will no longer support the economies of scale, volume and manufacture necessary to achieve profitable output in the industry. One of the most recent successes, on the global scale, has been the Korean car company which made successful inroads into the Canadian market; indeed, by the 1990s it is likely that Ford will be importing small cars from Taiwan, Indonesia or South America into the USA.

Applying the global concept

The concept of global marketing should not be viewed simply as one end of a spectrum, with the other being complete localization of marketing policy and control. A managerial approach to globalization can fall anywhere along that spectrum, from full standardization of brand promotion and advertising to a market-by-market programme of differentiated promotion and product adaptation. Understanding the concept is one thing: applying it flexibly in international operations is the basis of much of the 'matrix' approach, where industry growth prospects and the company's competitive position can differ significantly from one country and one sector to another.

In applying the global concept and making it work, some adaptations to regional market conditions are essential. Managers need to tailor the approach they use to each part of the company's overall plan and marketing policy. For example, a manufacturer might market the same product under different brand names in different countries, or might market the same brands using different product formulas or advertising visuals. Also, the extent to which a decentralized multinational corporation will wish to pursue 'global' marketing will often vary from country to country. Much will depend upon the company's competitive strengths and management organization in markets of different sizes and types. Large markets with strong local managements are usually less willing to accept global programmes. It is arguable that, as these markets probably account for most of the company's investment, any completely standardized marketing programmes reflect the needs of large rather than small markets. Indeed, managements in the smaller markets depend more on headquarters assistance than those in large markets; and because any standardized marketing programme is superior in scope and quality to what the local executives, even with the benefit of local market knowledge, can develop themselves, they may welcome it, particularly if it requires resourcing beyond the means of the local organization.

If global marketing is to be implemented effectively, it requires a planned appraisal of market priorities across the world in terms of industry attractiveness and competitive strengths; for the reality is that, whether or not some businesses decide to adopt a global strategy, many of their competitors will. This is because some companies view globalization as not only a concept but also an opportunity: the cultural and economic convergences discussed in the last section have led to huge expanding markets for the same or similar products, to new opportunities for economies of scale and reductions in costs and prices, and for regional or standardized brand promotion and advertising programmes. Companies, therefore, that find themselves in the forefront of global competition are those that have products that are similar across borders, have low transportation costs, offer economies of scale in production and marketing, and have long lead times and concentrated distribution.

Companies operating a global marketing policy are likely to have certain key characteristics, such as being technologically advanced, having significant economies of scale in manufacturing, having significant marketing skills, and producing at least one major world-wide selling brand backed by heavy, consistent investment. Furthermore, such a global marketing company is also likely to be capital-intensive and financially strong. (For example, the costs of designing a new aircraft exceed $1 billion; the introductory advertising budgets for Player's cigarettes and Diet Coke were over $30 million and $50 million, respectively.) Indeed, many companies selling on a region-by-region, or sector-by-sector, basis must increasingly compete with global marketing companies in order to survive in their domestic markets. Large imports of energy, advanced technology, products promoted globally to satisfy increasingly sophisticated consumer demand—all have to be met by successful operations on foreign markets. Economies of scale in production as well as in research and development in many industries require world markets for full exploitation, and world marketing requires skilful management. So a reduction in the obstacles to standardization puts additional pressure on companies that do not participate in world-wide marketing programmes.

Furthermore, there are strong forces in the business environment today, driving more and more towards global marketing policies:

1. demographic, cultural and economic convergence among consumer markets, and increasing homogeneity in the requirements of world-wide industrial customers (e.g. machine tools, plant construction);
2. the increasing investment in research needed to ensure long-term competitiveness, increasing lead times involved to bring products to commercialization, and the growing pay-back needed for this process;
3. increasingly significant economies of scale on the supply side (purchasing, manufacturing and distribution and access to resources); also, the impact of technology on manufacturing;
4. macroeconomic changes in regional economic co-operation, leading to freer movements of goods, labour services and capital (particularly for capital to invest in world-wide operations and market development); impact of technology on transportation and distribution;

5. the 'deregulation' of national markets in airline transportation, banking and financial services, and the increasing signs of 'de-nationalizing' of major industrial markets in the supply of telecommunications, power generation and transportation plant and equipment (especially in the USA and EEC).

The matrix approach

In the light of these developments, the matrix approach to products and markets has become more significant in managing and developing international markets. The concept is not new, but it needs to be applied specifically and in a planned way if it is to prove of value operationally. Some example of specific applications by companies will follow shortly, but in general terms, the matrix approach must be set up in two stages:

1. global situation analysis;
2. establishing the product/market matrix.

These are illustrated in Figs 2.15 and 2.16.

The advantages to management of adopting the matrix approach can be summed up as follows.

1. It provides a framework for 'prioritizing' key product sectors for development across global markets.
2. It permits the identification of major growth sectors where additional investment can substantially increase profits and market share.
3. It promotes better understanding and analysis of data needed for overall product/market planning.
4. It provokes greater sensitivity to the impact of external factors, particularly competition, on the success of marketing policies.
5. It permits the identification of products that are generating substantial cash in the short term, but are in long-term market decline, requiring 'harvest' or 'divestment' decisions by management.
6. It provides a framework for formulating both international policies and objectives by market sector/country.

In Fig. 2.15, the matrix approach is developed in stages, beginning with an analysis of industry and market trends, and continuing with an evaluation of market attractiveness and competitive position. In Fig. 2.16 these factors are ranked on a three-by-three matrix relating to growth, earnings and cash.

Understanding the matrix concept and the general benefits to be derived by management in using it is one thing, however; making it operational and specific in the context of a company's international marketing policies is another. And further reappraisal of the concept, as exemplified in the portfolio analysis of the Boston Consulting Group (BCG), has indicated that in international operations there are problems of definition and application. For example, a product globally evaluated as a 'dog' in BCG may have a position as a 'star' in a developing sector of the market. Moreover, as explained in Section 2.2, products can be at different stages of the life-

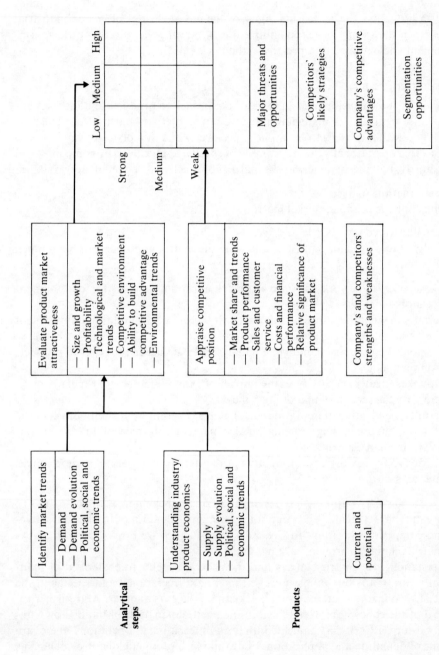

Fig. 2.15 Global situation analysis (*Source*: Session paper on 'Corporate Analysis', European School of Management Studies (EAP), 1984)

106

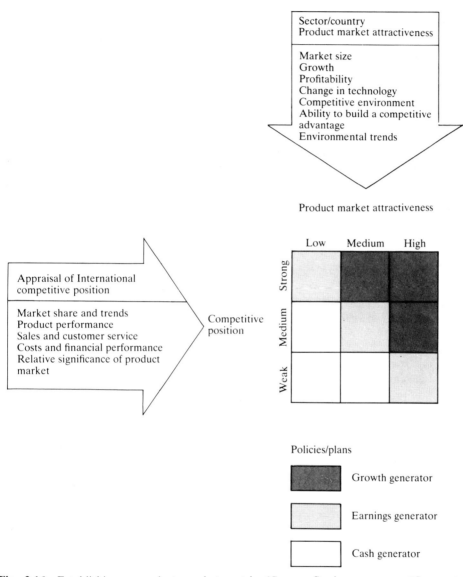

Fig. 2.16 Establishing a product market matrix (*Source*: Session paper on 'Corporate Analysis', European School of Management Studies (EAP), Oxford, 1985)

cycle internationally, and sector/market growth rates will also vary; so international applications will generally lead to considerations of multiple market entries/ operations for a given product, and these are not readily accommodated in the traditional BCG format. There are also difficulties of application brought about by differing levels of competitor strengths across global market sectors, and some wide variations in cost structures of operating in different sectors, which may have similar market shapes and growth prospects, but where profit levels are significantly different.

A recent analysis of global factors in managing multi-country markets[23] demonstrates clearly how a matrix approach that breaks out of this stereotyped model can provide useful policy guidelines. In Fig. 2.17 the matrix is designed to weigh the strength of globalizing market factors and the advantages of globalization against the advantages of local market adaptation. A four-cell matrix emerges.

1. Businesses where strong local adaptation is inappropriate and globalizing forces can be exploited to great advantage. These are global marketing companies: computers and consumer electronics belong in this cell.
2. Businesses that require some degree of local adaptation and where globalization of all functions offers no decisive competitive advantage, such as electrical equipment today. The world market for such multinational businesses is divided into several regions with different customer characteristics. Many of today's global businesses started with this polycentric structure—e.g., automobile and motorcycle manufacture, consumer electronics and production automation.
3. Businesses in which both the globalizing factors and the need for local adaptation are strong. This group consists mainly of businesses that would be global from a purely economic point of view if they were not constrained by law or government purchasing policies to adapt their products. Regional telephone networks and sectors of the armaments industry are typical examples of such 'blocked' global businesses.
4. Businesses such as food processing and basic chemicals, in which strong local adaptation is decisive for success and/or there are no major arguments in favour of globalization. These are the true local businesses.

Further specific applications of the matrix approach have been developed by an increasing number of companies with global product/market businesses.

General Electric Company has developed a nine-cell 'Business Screen'. This is illustrated in Fig. 2.18. Here the vertical axis is based upon a series of factors (each given a weighting) which represent the commercial attractiveness of each industry/market. The horizontal axis represents business strength or competitiveness. The area of the circles shows the size of the industry in which the business or product compete, with the shaded segments showing the company share. Both 'grids' give additional and useful focus to management decision on marketing objectives and policies.

Seagram Distillers Company, adapting the BCG concept, has developed a growth share matrix applied to the portfolio of branded spirits.[24] This is illustrated in Fig.

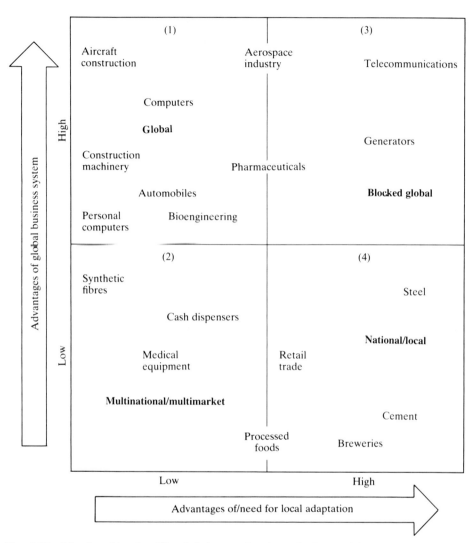

Fig. 2.17 Matrix of 'trade-off'—global *v.* national marketing policies by major industry sectors (*Source*: H. Henzler and W. Rall, 'Facing Up to the Globalization Challenge', *The McKinsey Quarterly*, Winter 1986)

2.19 and would seem to indicate that the brand portfolio is in need of upgrading. Since, on the matrix, the industry growth rate appears to be the same for all brands, the product class definition of the relevant market is used. Five Seagram brands are growing faster than their market segment as in sector 3; moreover, using segment growth in place of product class, growth in the growth/share matrix (sector 4) reveals

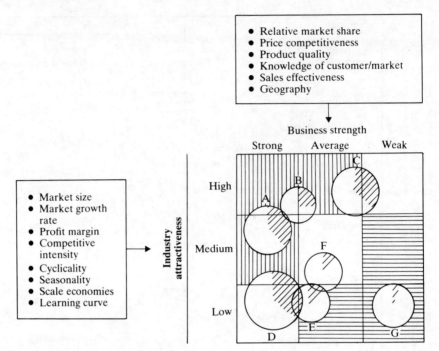

Fig. 2.18   General Electric's Nine-cell Business Screen (*Source*: R. J. Allio and M. W. Pennington (eds), *Corporate Planning Techniques and Applications*, AMACOM (a division of American Management Associates), New York, 1979)

that six brands are leaders in their market segments (of these, five are cash cows and one is a star).

Shell International Chemical Company has developed a portfolio analysis approach to help top management decide which product/market sectors they should be in and which ones ought to be phased out. Shell believes that the development of an optimum corporate strategy demands some structural and preferably quantifiable method of analysis. Its tool for achieving this is called the Directional Policy Matrix (DPM) and is shown in Fig. 2.20.

In this figure, the horizontal axis shows the prospects for profitable operation within the particular sector under investigation, while the vertical measures the company's present competitive position against other companies. The matrix is then divided into a series of boxes and, depending on its position on each axis, each product is categorized.

DPM is considered to be more widely applicable than the Boston Matrix, since criteria can be chosen for different industry sectors and situations where market share is not of paramount importance. The technique developed by Shell for deciding how to place products within the DPM uses a system of stars and grading.

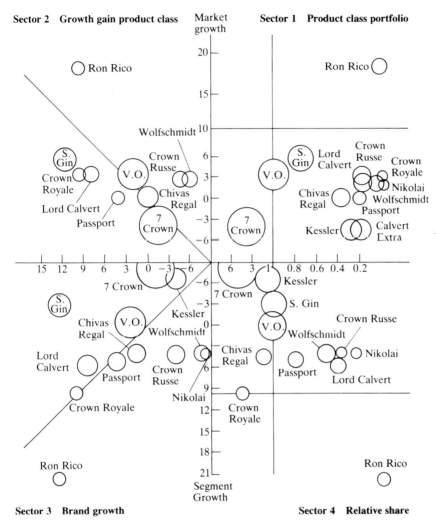

Fig. 2.19 Seagram's brand/market portfolio analysis (*Source*: O. Gur-Arie and J. R. Taylor, 'Portfolio Analysis of the Brand Level', *Proceedings of 9th International Research Symposium*, IAE, Aix-Provence, France, 1982)

In chemicals, Shell has decided that there are four main criteria which need to be used to place products on the horizontal axis:

1. market growth rate;
2. market quality;
3. feed stock;
4. environmental aspects.

Under growth rate, a product will be accorded from one to five stars. Thus, if it is a product for which demand will grow only as fast as the chemical industry average, it will attract three stars, with more stars (up to a maximum of five) for a faster growth rate and less for a slower one.

Under market quality, the ability of new products to achieve a consistently higher or more stable level of profitability than in other sectors is assessed. For example, the analysis will cover whether margins can be maintained at a time of excess capacity, susceptibility to commodity price behaviour, availability of technology to competitors, the number of market suppliers, the power of customers and the risk of substitution by other products.

The availability of feed stock and the likelihood of environmental restrictions on the manufacture, transportation and marketing of a new product are also considered, and stars similarly awarded.

The stars are then converted into points and totalled so that the position of the new product along one arm of the axis can be determined.

In the analysis of the company's competitive position in a particular sector, three criteria are used:

1. market position;
2. production capability;
3. product research and development.

If a company is in a pre-eminent position in a particular market (likely to be followed by others in pricing) and with acknowledged technical leadership, it will probably award itself five stars. If, however, it is one of a number of major producers, it may mark itself down to four; if only a minor producer, it may mark itself two. In assessing production capability, factors such as whether the process used is modern, whether the plant is big enough for market share to be maintained, the degree of security from breakdowns or industrial action, and logistics to principal markets are considered. The research and development assessment will take into account product range and quality, technical service and applicational development.

When the points under each heading (on a 0–4 scale to correspond with the 1–5 stars) have been added together, the position on the other axis becomes clear, and by cross reference to the horizontal axis the position of the product on the matrix can be obtained.

Within the matrix, the boxes have been given labels to indicate the significance of the position in which products find themselves. If a product is in the 'leader' box, it will have scored five points on each axis, and the implication is that the company should give priority to its development, devoting all the necessary resources. The 'try harder' label is meant to suggest that, with the right allocation of resources, the company could build on a number 2 position in which the product finds itself. The 'double or quit' zone is seen as the area from which products that are destined to become future bright prospects should be selected. Elsewhere in the matrix, the 'custodial' position—the zone where most of any company's products are likely to fall at any one

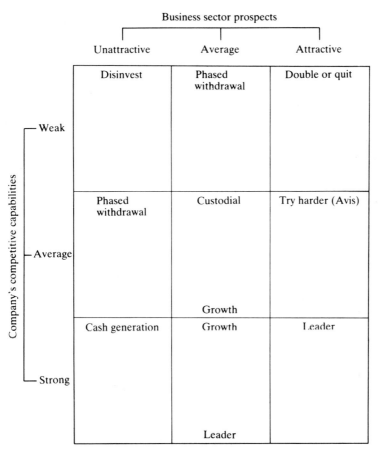

Business sector prospects

	Unattractive	Average	Attractive
Weak	Disinvest	Phased withdrawal	Double or quit
Average	Phased withdrawal	Custodial Growth	Try harder (Avis)
Strong	Cash generation	Growth Leader	Leader

Company's competitive capabilities

Fig. 2.20 Shell directional policy matrix (DPM) (*Source*: Shell International Chemical Company, London)

time—suggests a strategy of maximizing cash generation without further major commitment of resources. Where products are in the 'growth' position, the indicated strategy is to allocate resources sufficient to enable the product (which will probably be generating the funds itself) to grow with the market.

The products in the left-hand column will be those with poor prospects, where perhaps a new product is taking over. It remains possible, however, for companies with a strong position in this sector to earn satisfactory profits which can be used to finance faster growing areas. In the 'disinvest' sector, products will probably already be losing money and the correct strategy is probably to dispose of the assets as quickly as possible.

There are now examples of the DPM being applied to companies such as Rolls Royce, the National Freight Corporation and Arthur Guinness & Co. It has been found that the concepts of market growth, quality and supply are generally applicable, although certain specific criteria have to be changed for particular businesses. The competitive concepts of market share, supply and support raise problems, particularly that of market share, which underlie the Boston Matrix. The criteria chosen for the competitive axis do become more widely applicable if the concept of 'market leadership' is used, and this includes viable and minor producers, as well as leaders and majors.

Some analysts see great value in the use of DPM as a behavioural technique, in that it encourages analysis, helping managers to think as a group about their international markets, the competition and the relative strategic value of particular portfolios to the company as a whole. Finally, it provides a useful way of communicating strategic guidelines to different business units.

In the objective appraisal of alternative markets and products, management should assure itself not only that there is some synergy of marketing, production, technological or other expertise which can be utilized for successful entry, but also that it has the general creative capability and capacity to manage the new business, particularly if unforeseen problems occur at a time when there is pressure on the existing enterprise. The greatest shortage will commonly be in competent management.

In reviewing the range of basic strategies, which is best done by starting with market penetration possibilities, followed in order by market development, product development, and finally diversification potential, it will often occur that, for example, new products or methods developed to penetrate more deeply existing markets can also be used to lead the company into new markets. Whatever the strategies or combinations of strategies selected, management should carefully review them to check if they are implemented successfully.

1. They must satisfy the needs of the various precise target groups at which they are aimed—consumers, distributors, customers, etc.
2. They must achieve the corporate marketing, financial and growth objectives.
3. They must give direction to the various elements of the marketing activity—products, prices, distribution, promotion.
4. They must be congruent with each other, and the fulfilment of one strategy must not adversely affect the achievement of others.
5. They must capitalize on the corporate strengths and minimize the effect of any weaknesses.
6. They must give a competitive advantage which is difficult to match or surpass.
7. They must be within the competence and resources of the company.

In conclusion, the 'matrix' approach to products and markets reflects management's need to respond to increasingly complex and competitive international markets. And in assessing the resources required for existing product/market policies as against resources needed to originate and develop products, a matrix approach more complex than BCG is increasingly required. Priorities must be determined, for example, for investment in resources that ensure intermediate and long-term growth, market penetration and technical develòpment, so that product/market prospects can be exploited to maximize price–earnings ratios of the business. Hence the importance of 'prioritizing' market prospects and product development by sectors, and for this the matrix approach is proving to be a powerful planning and control mechanism.

References

1. E. F. L. Brech, *Managing for Revival*. Management Publications, 1982, Chapter 3.
2. Adapted from L. Fisher, *Industrial Marketing*. London: Business Books, 1976.
3. M. Yoshino, 'Marketing Orientation in International Business', *Business Topics*, **13**, 1, 1973.
4. *Marketing in the 1980s and Beyond: A Survey of Management Practice and Performance*. University of Bradford/Institute of Marketing, 1982.
5. P. Kotler, 'Rethink the Marketing Concept', *American Marketing Association News*, **18**, 19, 1984.
6. C. P. Zeithaml and V. A. Zeithaml, 'Environmental Management: Revising the Marketing Perspective', *AMA Journal of Marketing*, **48**, 2, 1984.
7. D. S. Hopkins, *The Marketing Plan*. New York: Conference Board, 1981; cited in D. W. Cravens and R. B. Woodruff, *Marketing*. Reading, Mass.: Addison-Wesley, 1986, p. 635.
8. N. Piercy, *Export Strategy: Markets and Competition*. London: George Allen and Unwin, 1982, Chapter 6.
9. W. J. Keegan, 'Conceptual Framework for Multinational Marketing', *Columbia Journal of World Business*, November 1971.
10. M. M. Pryor, 'Planning in a Worldwide Business', *Harvard Business Review*, **43**, 4, 1965.
11. W. W. Cain, 'International Planning: Mission Impossible?' *Columbia Journal of World Business*, July/August 1970.
12. L. T. Wells, 'A Product Life-cycle for International Trade?' *Journal of Marketing*, **32**, July 1968.
13. G. Mickwitz, *Marketing and Competition*. Helsingfors, Finland: Central Cyckeriet, 1959.
14. J. de la Torre, 'Product Life-cycle as a Determinant of Global Marketing Strategies', *Atlanta Economic Review*, **25**, Sept./Oct. 1975.
15. J. L. Roberts, 'By concentrating on Marketing, Stride Rite does well despite slump for shoe makers' *Wall Street Journal*, 23 February, 1983.
16. R. Martenson, 'Future Competition in a Cross-cultural Environment', *European Management Journal*, **4**, 3, 1986.
17. A. E. Pitcher, 'The Role of Branding in International Advertising', *International Journal of Advertising*, no. 4, 1985. Copyright © Cassell Educational Ltd.
18. Adapted from Vern Terpstra, *International Marketing Management* (3rd edn), Part Two: 'International Promotion: Advertising and other Factors'. Eastbourne: Holt Saunders International, pp. 416–17 and 476–7.
19. 'Promotion of Industry: Caring for the Environment', *Journal of the Royal Society of Arts*, **135**, February 1987.
20. O. Stiwenius, 'Planning for a Rapidly Changing Environment in SAS', *Long Range Planning*, **18**, 2, April 1985.
21. J. Neumann, 'Audivision: Vorsprung Durch Technik', *European Management Journal*, **3**, 2, 1985.
22. A. Parasutaman, *Marketing Research*. Reading, Mass.: Addison Wesley, 1986, p. 733; ITT case (adapted).

23. H. Henzler and W. Rall, 'Facing up to the Globalisation Challenge', *The McKinsey Quarterly*, Winter 1986. McKinsey & Co. Inc. N.Y. 10022.

24. O. Gur-Arie and J. R. Taylor, 'Portfolio Analysis of the Brand Level: Methodological Issues and Analytical Tools', *Proceedings of 9th International Research Symposium in Marketing*. Aix-en-Provence, France: IAE, 1982.

3
Modes of international market entry and operations

3.1   Direct and indirect exporting

Introduction

The exporting of finished goods is still commonly carried out through agents overseas, particularly by small- and medium-sized companies. (Over half of world trade,
by value, was still handled by agents in 1987.) Compared with some other (indirect)
modes of exporting, costs are high, but profits are not shared. There are certain fixed
costs of direct exporting which can make a small volume of export sales uneconomic.
These include the costs entailed in meeting government regulations, product adaptation costs, and the direct costs (travel, etc.) involved in controlling agents. On the
other hand, the company retains greater control of operations in direct exporting, and
can develop some 'in-house' expertise in export marketing. There is also an important
distinction to make here between exporting directly to an overseas country by using
agents or distributors based there, and direct selling overseas by the manufacturer's
own sales staff; this will be fully explained shortly.

It cannot be stressed too much that market intelligence and analysis *must* be carried
out in order to keep the company's management up to date on changing market
trends, access and competition (from both local suppliers and other exporters to the
target country). British Overseas Trade Board (particularly UK regional offices of the
Department of Trade and Industry) and Chambers of Commerce are set up to assist
and advise firms and to provide such market intelligence. And any company intending
to develop a substantial export business must understand and make appropriate
changes in products, marketing policies and practices, management skills and attitudes and the utilization of plant, design and financial resources. Product policy,
especially, needs to be kept under constant review. There are situations where (as
when fulfilling a large contract order) the demands of the home market are such that
production for export has to take second place; conversely, a company can find itself
in a position where the demand for a product in a single country (such as West
Germany) requires special production arrangements. Furthermore, details connected
with product packaging and presentation must not be overlooked, particularly the
effect of climatic conditions, language use, transit times and storage problems.

In managing direct export operations, the question of whether a separate export
organization is required will depend on such factors such as the size of firm (in the

case of a small firm, the answer is almost certainly 'No'), the volume of export business contemplated, the range of products to be exported and the experience/expertise of staff. In any medium- or large-sized firm with substantial exports, it is most unlikely that the home and export sales functions would be combined; in some cases there are quite separate companies or divisions for exports. However, such units can cause problems, in that they can become too bureaucratic and too far removed from the mainstream of the firm's operations, eventually finding it difficult, for example, to exert sufficient influence over production planning.

Case example 3.1

A large UK firm, a household name in the consumer goods field, had an entirely separate international company, which in effect bought products from the individual manufacturing companies throughout the UK and then sold these products in export markets. During National Export Year, management decided that a principal theme of the campaign for the group should be to impress on the manufacturing companies, which had their own organization for marketing products in the home market, the vital importance of successful exporting to the future well-being of the group as a whole. The directors of the international company expressed themselves pleased with the results of this campaign and considered that performance had benefited considerably.

In Case example 3.1, this was rectified by a change of emphasis/attitude by management; but in other industries, it has been followed through by major organizational changes, reflecting changes in marketing policies. For example, the international marketing divisions of Baker Perkins in the engineering sector, and Cadbury Schweppes in the drinks and confectionery sector have been dismantled, and the management responsibility for export marketing placed firmly with each trading or manufacturing division/company. In pharmaceuticals, both May & Baker and Roche have recently disbanded their separate companies which were responsible for UK exports, and relocated these responsibilities in head offices in Paris and Berne, respectively.

Nevertheless, for small and most medium-sized companies, the use of agents in overseas markets is the usual mode of operation for export business, offering as it does a high degree of control on a fixed-payment (commission) basis related to the level of sales turnover; such exporting is also the most usual way of initially penetrating a foreign market. Many of the costs of doing business abroad are thereby avoided, although certain fixed costs of exporting (mentioned above) can make export sales in small-volume markets uneconomic.

Exporting can be expensive because it is a management-intensive process. However, it does not involve the capital commitment of direct investment; nor does it put the firm's know-how at risk, as licensing may do. Where the firm has spare capacity, or where the marginal cost of increasing production at home is low, it can be highly profitable. Exporting is also advantageous where the nation of origin has a good reputation for the product in the selected market.

Tariffs and transport costs are major barriers in many product areas, but the exporter must also face up to product adaptation requirements in the target market. Both regulatory differences and differences in consumer tastes must be overcome. In general, the exporter must be sure that his products can be sold profitably in competition with local manufacturers.

Agents

If an agent is to be used, once he has been chosen and has accepted the offer, the agency agreement needs careful consideration, and expert legal advice is essential. One of the most important clauses will be the termination clause, which has to be set out in precise terms without any ambiguity. In some countries it is difficult to terminate agreements without substantial compensation, no matter what is written into the contract. The fact that the agreement is made subject to the laws of the UK does not always help, because sanctions can be applied which could make it difficult for the manufacturer to continue to trade in a country where he has gone against the local law when terminating an agency.

It is usual, but not essential, for the agent to be a national of the country concerned. He will probably operate on a commission basis, within a clearly defined territory. He will no doubt handle other non-competing agencies, but not too many. He may first sell, sending the orders to his principals for handling by them; or he may buy and sell in his own right, carrying stocks; or he could operate with a combination of both methods. He may also handle customer credit. However, although the most usual method of operating is still to use the services of agents, and although that method certainly has distinct advantages over the use of export houses, there can be problems involved. For instance, some agents tend to collect too many agencies, and then neglect those that bring in the least return.

Distributors

Many firms find it best to sell through sole distributors in export markets. This means quite simply that there is one customer only in the country, or group of countries, concerned, which stocks and resells the firm's products to others. In return for exclusivity, the sole distributor undertakes not to handle competitive products and often agrees to a minimum level of annual purchases. A country can be divided into regions, with a sole distributor for each region; or a few 'special' or 'principal' distributors can be appointed, each of whom gets favourable prices in return, for instance, for a minimum purchase commitment. There are a number of variations on the distributorship theme, and it could be wise, where there are several distributors in a territory, to have a local commission agent supervising their activities. In many instances this supervision can be undertaken by visits from head office; or the local agent's supervision can be reinforced by such visits.

Direct selling abroad

The increasing speed of travel has caused many firms to develop direct selling by members of their own staff, particularly in European countries. This has the distinct advantage that the people concerned have much closer contact with the headquarters of the company than is possible in the case of agents based abroad. They can be directly involved in policy-making and planning, and it is often feasible for them to be concerned in the control and guidance of the relevant employees at head office.

The principal problem involved when operating in this way is finding the right people. Attractive as the work may seem, it does involve frequent absences from home, sometimes for long periods, and if done conscientiously it can be arduous. Also, there is an increasing need for those undertaking this sort of activity to be linguists. Buyers, particularly in Europe, are much happier discussing potential business in their own language, and the level of tolerance of the Englishman's traditional linguistic inability has been decreasing remarkably. Many firms have found it advantageous to employ foreigners who are fluent in a number of languages.

For the firm that finds that the cost of employing its own people for direct selling abroad is likely to be uneconomic, it could be worth joining with a few other firms in a group arrangement. The groups concerned comprise up to five or six companies whose products are complementary and, therefore, sold mainly to similar customers. It is necessary for one in each group to act as co-ordinator or secretary, and the manager or representative employed in each case responds to the co-ordinator. The costs—salary and travel—are usually divided in direct relation to the sales in the countries concerned. Those contemplating such arrangements may find it difficult to find other firms with complementary products interested in joining with them; the regional offices of BOTB can help, as can Chambers of Commerce or trade associations. Consortium marketing is of increasing significance and is dealt with in detail in Section 3.2.

Marketing or sales subsidiaries

Establishing a marketing or sales subsidiary is the ideal method of selling overseas if the scale of operations permits. A sound base is set up in the country concerned, where stocks can be maintained if required, and the customers are presented with the easiest way of making contact with the manufacturer. This has advantages where spares and after-sales services are involved. Any such establishment inevitably involves the manufacturer in considerable problems of administration and control, and it is unlikely to be considered unless there is a well established, secure market.

It is sometimes possible to establish a firm which, although not owned by the manufacturer, operates on a basis that gives very much the same result. For instance, some companies have found that the only way to be really successful in the US market is 'sell American'. To this end they appoint agents who are able to appear very much as a branch of the manufacturer. Prices are quoted in dollars for goods delivered to the customer's warehouse, and all invoicing is done through the agents and payments are made to them. Such an arrangement can work very well, and there are US agents who are expert in working for British companies in this way.

In addition, there are courses that lie somewhere between the scheme just described and the establishment of the firm's own office overseas. It is possible, for instance, to invest in an already established business in the country concerned, or to join forces with other manufacturers as already described.

Factors affecting the choice of export mode

It is often difficult in practice to find new distributors or agents overseas who are effective and reliable. Manufacturers who adopt direct exporting will then have two main options:

1. to sell direct in the overseas market;
2. to send their employees to travel throughout the market and obtain orders.

Both options are, of course, costly, particularly if overseas visits are frequent. Certainly, direct exporting has its limitations, particularly if the intent is to build up a strong market position; here the distinction between the company's own sales employees and self-employed agents or distributors overseas is important. A number of points arise for the company's management to consider in determining agency and other agreements.

1. The authority to be given to the foreign agent will have to be considered: shall the agent have authority only to procure and solicit orders that may or may not be accepted by the UK principal, or shall he, beyond that, be entitled to make contracts in a binding manner for the UK company?
2. The specific territory allotted to the agent and the goods he is to represent require careful determination.
3. It may be advisable to appoint the agent in the first place only for a probationary period: he may have other interests, and one can never be certain that he will live up to the principal's expectations.
4. The termination of the agency agreement should be laid down in the written contract, which it is advisable for the principal to insist on, even if it consists of a simple exchange of letters. Many disputes arise when the agency relationship is dissolved, and the contract should be very specific on that contingency.
5. A number of countries, including West Germany, France and Italy, contain protective legal provisions for some types of commercial agents, particularly of the smaller group. These laws provide, in particular, for a goodwill compensation to which the agent may be entitled after termination of the agency relationship; while such a payment is not available in all cases in some legal systems, the principal cannot contract out of it.

In contrast to agency agreements, the main advantage of a distributor agreement is that it gives the exporter certainty to obtain a fixed turnover in the market into which he plans to direct his exports. It is, however, often more difficult to find a very suitable distributor than a self-employed agent. The exporter can conclude two types of contract with the distributor:

1. a basic contract containing clauses about the minimum amount of goods the distributor will undertake to buy annually, territory coverage, probation and termination, obligation of the distributor to sell the goods under the manufacturer's brand name (if that is intended), trademark arrangements, etc.;
2. a specific sales contract by which the above arrangements are actually carried out, providing for, among other details, terms of payment (whether cash or credit), and the agreed margin accruing to the distributor.

The exporter normally refrains from selling directly into the distributor's territory, except if there are 'reserved' customers, with whom the exporter was in contact before he entered into the sole distribution contract, and orders emanating from the distributor's territory are normally credited to him.

So sole agency or distribution agreements invariably provide that the agent or distributor shall have an exclusive territory. That exclusivity may contravene the fundamental concept of the EEC, which is directed against the division of the territory of the Community into separate trading areas. However, the EEC Commission in 1962 granted a 'block exemption' to exclusive agency contracts made with commercial agents. But the Commission's definition of agents is different from that in the ordinary law. An agent is defined as a person who does not take the financial risk of the transaction (except in the case of a *del credere* agency); the text of the EEC Regulation 67/67 goes on:

> The Commission regards as the decisive criterion, which distinguishes the commercial agent from the independent trader, the agreement—express or implied—which deals with responsibility for the financial risks bound up with the sale or with the performance of the contract.

Thus, an agent who keeps a considerable stock of goods or maintains, at his own expense, a service to customers, or has power to determine prices, is not covered by this ruling. What remains prohibited is any agreement preventing 'parallel' imports and exports. This means that an exporter cannot impose an obligation on the foreign exclusive distributor not to buy the goods to which the contract relates in another EEC country, or not to sell them in such a country. He can prevent the distributor from advertising or offering them there, but he cannot prevent the actual buying and selling. In the use of foreign distributors and agents, it is common in some industries, notably pharmaceuticals and automobiles, for the manufacturing company to support the distributor (or agent) with some of its own sales staff in the market.

Of course, there are other indirect methods of exporting which tend to be adopted by 'first-time' exporters or by companies fulfilling overseas orders on a purely reactive basis, with little risk and no investment outlay. Export 'houses' or buying offices in UK or overseas firms are the most commonly used. The former provide a wide range of services for manufacturers, although established exporters use them much less nowadays; as for the latter, manufacturers and foreign extractive industries often have equipment procurement offices in the home countries of supplying firms. Also, some large-scale companies operate multinational buying for foreign operations through domestic purchasing. The situation concerning the British buying offices of foreign firms is somewhat similar; such offices can sometimes prove the only route of entry into a business. (A good example of this is provided by the London buying offices of American department stores.)

An export house is officially defined by the British Export Houses Association (BEHA) as 'any company or firm, not being a manufacturer, whose main activity is the handling or financing of British trade and/or international trade not connected with UK'. There are approximately 700 export houses in the UK, and they handle an estimated 20 per cent of UK export trade. The 'commission', or 'confirming' house, included in this definition is usually 'home-based' and specializes in buying goods on behalf of overseas clients, paying the manufacturer and dealing with transport, payment, documentation and customs for a commission of between $3\frac{1}{2}$ and $8\frac{1}{2}$ per cent. Export merchants who buy and sell on their own account (acting as principals in the export transaction) also fall within BEHA definition.

Finally, two other modes can be considered:

1. foreign buyers employed by foreign state or commercial traders, resident in the exporting country;
2. export company consultants: these provide the manufacturer with the services and expertise of an export department, on a consultancy basis, without the costs and resources needed to provide it internally. Obviously, this is cost-effective, but only in the very short term; for, while the consultant receives a commission on sales, if sales develop well the company may then wish to change to direct exporting; but, while goodwill may have been built up abroad, the company will not have developed any in-house expertise to follow this up.

3.2 Consortium marketing

Introduction

Companies in particular sectors of manufacturing industry have for many years set up consortia to obtain large-scale capital and engineering orders overseas. There are, however, some organizational developments among major industrial competitors of the UK which need, and indeed repay, detailed study, particularly 'federated' marketing, and the role of the international 'trading house' favoured by Japanese industry. It is also a common misconception that export consortia are appropriate only for industrial conglomerates and large-scale engineering companies. In fact, consortia have been used effectively in many parts of the world by small-scale enterprises, as will be explained. And companies that have most often engaged in some form of large-scale joint venture, including manufacturing and/or sales, are to be found in the transport, weapons and weapons systems, chemicals, aerospace and other high-technology sectors and in construction, where finance, management, contracting and equipment supply are combined. Benefits to be derived from a consortium arrangement include:

1. stronger market position to develop long-term sales potential, particularly contracts and tenders;
2. sharing of financial and technical resources and risks, with better financing prospects and terms;
3. increased direct participation in market and more control of the sales operation;
4. strengthening of both technical and market competitiveness world-wide.

Much depends of course on the precise terms of the consortium: there must be technical complementarity, and a joint management task force (usually with a project director) needs to be set up in the early stages. This is particularly so if the project is a large-scale capital or 'turnkey' project, requiring substantial manufacturing investment, export credit insurance, long-term negotiating, etc.; indeed, it is not uncommon at this level for the appropriate section of government foreign trade to participate—in the UK, this was, until recent changes, the Projects and Export Policy Division of BOTB. Recently, a major power plant deal was signed between the Chinese People's Republic government and a UK consortium headed by a senior official of the Department of Trade and Industry.

Many companies in manufacturing industry (particularly in general engineering; paper, board and packaging machinery; food processing equipment; vehicle and vehicle parts; electronic testing and fire control equipment) develop licensing agreements as part of their overseas sales operations. This system works especially well in more distant export markets where the extra costs and logistics of shipping finished machines would make the products uncompetitive (or where the exporting manufacturer may not have the required production capacity). It is a profitable approach to market entry and development, particularly if there are high tariffs on finished imported manufacturers or plant, high costs of setting up wholly owned subsidiaries, and difficulties in the repatriation of profits or dividends. There is still a lot of scope for more profitable licensing agreements for British industry, where technical creativity, innovation and invention have been abundant, but where putting these ideas into production, commercialization and world-wide profitable sales has been somewhat deficient. (Examples of recent new technical ideas in transportation make this point clearly, e.g. linear and electric motors, hovercraft, jet-propelled sea transport, etc.) Licensing and technology are, therefore, developed separately in Section 3.3.

Two further instances of manufactured products illustrate these joint developments. General Motors and Chrysler promote models with standardized subassemblies, castings and components which are manufactured in supply factories in different countries. And Grundig and Philips of Eindhoven have major supply plants in various countries where land and labour are cheaper and more plentiful than in the metropolitan countries. Moreover, economies of scale in research and development as well as in production can be achieved only if there are world-wide sales operations over which to spread such costs, often to the point where the multinational company is heavily dependent on world-wide sales revenues.

On the purchasing side, consortium members are increasingly having to make presentations of tenders, to negotiate with and close the sale of major capital projects to government tender boards or centralized purchasing committees. Not only this, but many overseas governments, in awarding such major contracts, particularly in the Middle and Far East, stipulate some direct government participation, whether technical, managerial or financial. There can also be stipulations about plant capacity and location (for example, in France DATAR directs local and new plants), training of local management, and sometimes a 'buy-back' condition, or one relating to a minimum percentage of the output that must be exported to earn foreign exchange.

One analysis[1] reports the operations and benefits of 'federated' marketing in overseas operations, where a group of three or four companies or divisions of companies, offering complementary, non-competing products or services and selling broadly to the same customers, has set up a joint overseas marketing facility with a co-ordinator company; the costs and risks are shared, and the whole range of products or services receives full-time sales coverage. Sales effectiveness can be improved, the grouping has a synergy, and a sale by one company can open up sales opportunities for others. A grouping of this sort was set up successfully by three manufacturing companies to tackle the USSR food market with the support of a leading commercial bank. A key role is played by the co-ordinator company, which catalyses this joint venture and then provides the administrative and financial services and technical co-ordination that combined operations between independent manufacturing companies require.

Note should be taken at this point of the well documented success overseas of the Japanese trading houses such as Marubeni, which combine operations between manufacturing, banking, contracting and trading. This is in some contrast to the normal structure of the European conglomerate, comprising large numbers of small subsidiary companies, each standing on its own. Indeed, these very diversification policies, which extend product and service ranges, and which spread the product/market risk across many markets, actually tend to weaken the group's ability to concentrate its efforts internationally, rather than reinforce it. Above all, however, such a federated group collectively can deploy resources sufficient to set up a fully manned and effective sales presence overseas at costs which together the companies can afford, and can justify through the total sales revenue achievable.

Choice of markets

This principle of collective effort and sales is growing in importance and applications; but there must be efforts to ensure equal opportunities for the products of all participating firms, particularly if assortments are heterogeneous, so that the same sales organization and the same channels of distribution can be used. The choice of markets is therefore dependent on the types of firms in the consortium—and vice versa.

If potential group members have already been actively engaged in export marketing and have established sales, then the choice of market becomes more complex because these firms might want to

- have those markets included, hoping to strengthen their position with the help of the whole group even if this choice might prove disadvantageous for the rest; or
- have those markets excluded, as the firms are already well established there and are more interested in new market areas, while their prospective partners are especially interested in profiting from the experience gained by these firms.

Again, only a market survey can serve as a basis for the final decision in order to ensure that the best possible market choices for the majority of member firms shall be exploited. Firms that cannot agree to such a decision should be left out. It seems better to limit the number this way than to start off with compromises, which will hamper the commercial success of the consortium.

Some existing groups, like the DELTA Group in Switzerland, have tried to solve this important problem by constituting sub-groups for those member firms who are interested only in certain markets and regions or in certain specified outlets like the department stores or government buying. This certainly is a useful solution, but it seems doubtful whether such a choice is feasible at the beginning of the enterprise when too many complications may jeopardize the efficiency and success of market activities. It should, therefore, be considered as a second stage when the spreading of activities to new markets is planned.

Co-operation with foreign partners

Co-operation between smaller firms of different countries does not seem yet to be very common, but it is likely to grow in importance. If the selection of partners is made carefully enough, not only is such co-operation as good as export marketing with firms of the same country, but it can bring even faster and more profitable results. The foreign partner already has his sales organization established, knows the trade outlets and market conditions well, and has established a reputation of his own which can be of great advantage to the manufacturer who enters into co-operation with the firm. But the risks involved are naturally greater than with manufacturers of the home country who are well known to the firm. A close look has to be taken, therefore, at the following points, which could mean failure or success in co-operating with the foreign partner or partners:

1. position of foreign firm in the market (reputation, strength, channels used, market coverage);
2. production facilities and capacity of the firm;
3. liquidity, financial sources and management ability;
4. marketing policies;
5. assortment range.

The last item is especially important, as lack of harmonization in assortments can easily lead to misunderstanding, unwanted competition with partners, overlapping of efforts and failure of the co-operative venture.

It is easier for manufacturers to co-operate if their products are complementary to each other. If their production programmes overlap, they must endeavour to specialize in such a way that the individual product is manufactured in one factory only, with a resultant lowering of manufacturing costs. An Italian manufacturer of motor scooters, for instance, may enter into co-operation with a Dutch manufacturer of bicycles and bicycle trailers by selling the Dutch products through the same channels of distribution as the motor scooters. In this way the marketing costs are distributed over a large number of products, and the Dutch manufacturer derives advantage from a well established marketing organization in the Italian market. Similarly, the Dutch manufacturer includes the Italian motor scooters in *his* marketing organization and the Italian manufacturer derives a corresponding advantage in Holland.

This type of co-operation can be expanded to other countries in which two manufacturers wish to promote their sales. By employing a joint marketing organization, they will be able to reduce the costs of market research, sales promotion and distribution. Co-operating firms, of course, run the risk that one of the participants may take up the manufacture of the products of one of the others after sales in the product are rising. This risk is particularly serious in the case of international operations, as it may be difficult to take legal proceedings; but the risk may be reduced by arranging for the payment of substantial penalties in case the agreement is broken.

Firms in different countries may also work together in more restricted fields. French, German and British shirt-makers may, for instance, co-operate on advertising their cotton shirts in preference to shirts of synthetic fibres. Firms also frequently combine in arranging specialized international exhibitions. If co-operation is only to comprise a general publicity campaign, then it is of no consequence that the range of products is identical. Collective quotations for large contracts are also frequently submitted. Such contracts often comprise products that are not made by a single manufacturer alone, or are of a volume that exceeds the productive capacity of a single manufacturer. The Belgian GAMMA Group for textile machinery co-operates with manufacturers in other countries as regards both exhibitions and quotations for large contracts.

The fields of co-operation for consortia are therefore considerable, and by no means are confined to manufacturing and selling. An export group may be established for the sole purpose of procuring detailed market information, even though it is nowadays possible to obtain this from public institutions, trade organizations, Chambers of Commerce, etc. It is, however, necessary to adapt such data to the particular interests of the manufacturers in the group. Moreover, such desk research may be the beginning of more extensive co-operation in future. The advantages of co-operation become more apparent when a group undertakes field research on a joint basis. Such research is difficult and calls for larger investments, which are easier to finance if undertaken jointly. Export market analyses are frequently supported financially by public authorities, provided a group of firms will benefit from them and will itself contribute financially.

If co-operation includes sales promotion, the economic advantages become still more obvious. Advertising may well be undertaken collectively even though the participating firms continue individually to canvass their own customers.

If manufacturers do not want to restrict their co-operation to prestige advertising, but wish to extend it to the promotion of individual products, such products should be advertised under a common brand name which should also be used by the individual firms in their own sales promotion, in packaging, etc. Collective advertising can be fully efficient, however, only when group exports are centralized. This may include a central export office and the use of joint channels of distribution in the export markets. In fact, export co-operation will be much more economic and successful if products are sold and distributed through a joint export office. A thorough coordination and centralization of all export functions thus becomes possible and enables firms to get a better return for their marketing costs. It is usually advisable to locate the export office in the home market in order to facilitate the close co-operation between managers of member-firms, but if a group concentrates on a single foreign market with a large turnover, it may be expedient to establish the sales office in that market.

In order to derive full advantage from export co-operation, it is necessary to establish joint marketing channels in export markets as well. An export group is able to procure the best channels of distribution in the individual markets owing to the advantages presented by this type of co-operation to foreign distributors.

Establishing long-term goals

Normally, an export group should begin its life carefully with a selection of possible and, in the long run, desirable operations. Desk research, collective advertising and sales promotion form the basis for marketing groups abroad. Field studies, branded goods policy and product development might follow later when the co-operation has proved successful. A full marketing service should always be the long-term goal, as export groups must offer their members collectively the same competitive weapons that are available to the larger firms individually. In later stages, of course, the group can and should include other fields, such as buying, harmonization of production and basic technical research.

The growing significance of consortium marketing has been highlighted in a recent, authoritative study.[2]

> The most significant change is the increased use of international cooperative ventures or strategic alliances of various kinds to accomplish one or more aspect of the international marketing task ... Because many firms will not be able to enter a sufficient number of markets by themselves, they will form a variety of international cooperative ventures ... to get the international coverage needed. ... [As examples] Siemens joins with Philips [each putting up $400 m and their governments another $400 m] and Honda joins with British Leyland ... These ... international cooperations are not marriages of love but of necessity. The increasing cost of product development is going beyond the resources of even many very large firms.

Case example 3.2 also shows how consortium marketing is being increasingly adopted in major sectors such as pharmaceuticals.[3]

Case example 3.2

Glaxo Holdings and Sankyo, the Japanese pharmaceuticals company, made an agreement in 1987 to co-market two new antibiotics in Japan, including Glaxo's new oral antibiotic. Japan is the world's leading consumer of oral antibiotics. Glaxo's new product, recently introduced as 'Zinnat' in the UK, will be jointly marketed by Glaxo's associate Nippon Glaxo and Sankyo, and will trade in Japan under the name 'Oracef'. At the same time, a new oral antibiotic being developed by Sankyo (code-named CS-807) is to be jointly marketed by Sankyo and Nippon Glaxo. The two companies have also co-operated to date in the successful launch and exploitation of Glaxo's world beating anti-ulcer drug Zantac, marketed in Japan since 1984.

Japan is the world's second largest pharmaceutical market, and Glaxo products, available through a series of co-marketing and licensing agreements with leading Japanese pharmaceutical companies, account for 1.2 per cent of all drugs sold by value worldwide.

3.3 Licensing and technology

Introduction

Licensing, essentially, entails the sale of a patent, technical know-how or processes on a contractual basis, by which a home manufacturer (licensor) grants a licence to a foreign manufacturer (licensee) and receives royalty payments in return. Many companies in UK manufacturing industry (particularly in general engineering, paper, board and packaging machinery, food processing equipment, vehicle and vehicle parts, electronic testing and fire control equipment) operate licensing agreements as part of their plans to develop world-wide sales. The licensing system works especially well in more distant overseas markets, where the extra costs and the logistics of shipping finished machines would make the products uncompetitive, or where the home manufacturer does not have the production capacity to meet overseas orders. Licensing can be a profitable approach to market entry and development, particularly if there are high tariffs on finished, imported manufactures or plant, high costs of setting up wholly owned subsidiaries, and difficulties in the repatriation of profits and dividends (though this can also apply to the remittance of royalties).

The industrial or commercial expertise that is the subject of a licensing agreement can include access to design expertise and industrial designs; commissioning to achieve performance guarantees; product and process specifications; manufacturing know-how that is not the subject of a patent; technical advice or assistance (including the supply of components, materials or plant essential to the manufacturing process); management advice and assistance; and the use of a trademark or trade name. But before any decision to enter into a licensing agreement is made, the manufacturer (who would be the licensor) must check the following in overseas countries:

− market potential and selling conditions;

- the copyright, and patent situations;
- regulations on licensing agreements and royalty payments and on fiscal and exchange control laws (the rate and remittance of royalties may be strictly controlled);
- the level of technical education and expertise available locally to manufacture and market the output (of the licensee), both in his locality and, possibly, to other countries within the region.

Ideally, licensing should combine the skills and expertise of the primary manufacturer (licensor) with the local knowledge, contacts, etc., of the licensee overseas; the licensor there assigns to the licensee, for a royalty payment, one or more of the patent rights, trademark rights, etc., in a particular overseas market or markets. In return, the licensee undertakes:

- to produce the licensor's products to agreed, specified standards;
- to market his output in the territories assigned to him; and
- to pay to the licensor a royalty payment, usually related to sales volume or profits.

There is often also sometimes an initial payment, payable as soon as the licence agreement is signed (often paid to cover the initial transfer of machinery, components or designs, or sometimes simply for know-how).

Clearly, the management of the manufacturing company must, therefore,

1. evaluate the relevance and benefits of operating licensing agreements overseas in particular situations relating to industrial competitiveness, technical developments and expansion of the business;
2. if licensing is adopted, set up a control system as regards both operations and effectiveness, and the continuing technical back-up and support to maintain the necessary standards and quality in the licensee's production.

These two points—evalution and control—are essential to the management of profitable licensing operations, and are now considered in more detail.

Evaluation and control

As for evaluation, much depends on market conditions and available local technical expertise: it may not be possible to identify a suitable licensee in the target country, and obtaining full and prompt payments/remittances may be difficult; costs of knowledge transfer may be high, and the licensor may consider that he is unwittingly creating a competitor. Any evaluation, therefore, should rest on an analysis of the benefits and disadvantages of licensing, leading to a well founded decision in each particular situation. The principal advantage to the licensor is market access: licensing provides entry into markets that are otherwise closed on account of high rates of duty, entrenched competition, import quotas or prohibitions, and high freight costs making any imported products uncompetitive. Furthermore, licensing requires little capital investment and should provide a higher rate of return on capital employed, with (relative to other modes) very low risks; this is especially attractive to firms short of capital or management time. Also, many foreign governments favour licensing arrangements as infusions of new technology; therefore approval and operation are quicker and the licensor is not exposed to the danger of nationalization or expropriation of assets. Local manufacture (under licence) can also be an advantage in securing foreign government contracts, especially defence contracts. And the licensor benefits in two further ways: because of the limited capital requirements, new products can be rapidly exploited, on a world-wide basis, before competition develops, and 'cross-licensing' agreements can provide an additional way of avoiding excessive competition. The advantages to the licensee are access to new technology to strengthen the firm's competitive position; continuing support and advice from the licensor in quality control; promotion and product development; and the financial benefit of increasing profitability of incremental sales revenue (based on the fee or royalty paid).

As for the licensor, there are some negative aspects of licensing arrangements which need analysis. The licensor may be, indirectly, establishing and supporting his future competitor (when the licensing agreement finally expires). Furthermore, the licensee, even if he reaches an agreed minimum turnover, may not fully exploit the market, leaving it open to the entry of competitors, and the licensor then will inevitably lose direct control of the marketing operation. Again, strict product quality control is difficult, and the product will often be sold under the licensor's brand name. Governments often impose conditions on remittances of royalties or on component supply. As for revenue, license fees are normally a small percentage (between 2 and 7 per cent) of the licensee's turnover, and will often compare unfavourably with what might be obtained from a company's own manufacturing operation. Lastly, some arguments can arise, however carefully the licensing agreement is drafted; and a disaffected licensee can be a serious problem.

All these aspects, the last one especially, underline the importance of management control of the licensing agreement by the licensor, particularly as the licensee is operating under the licensor's brand name, using his expertise and developing the market on his behalf. This aspect encompasses a number of steps to be taken in a logical order. Regarding selection of the licensee, the manufacturer needs to have criteria against which he will 'screen' possible licensees; companies should seek out and compare alternative licensees, and not just respond directly to an initiative from one foreign manufacturer. The licensing agreement should be drafted to protect the interests of both parties; the licensor must satisfy himself at first hand not only of the technical competence of the licensee but also that he has genuine up-to-date marketing knowledge and contacts over the whole of the area allotted to him. The licensor should also endeavour, whenever possible, to maintain some degree of control throughout the duration of the agreement. He may, for example, retain the right to supply certain ingredients or key components rather than giving a licence for a complete package; alternatively, he may allow in the agreement for the acquiring of a sufficiently large equity interest to convert the operation into a joint venture (thus also avoiding the possibility of establishing a competitor at the expiry of the agreement). Control, however, must be combined with some motivation of the licensee. Such motivation is best ensured by encouraging a continuing interest on the part of the licensee by a steady flow of technical improvements and sales and marketing support and innovation: in this way, the licensee will always have something of value to gain by continuing with, and adhering to, the agreement.

Case example 3.3

A large manufacturing firm had relied exclusively on the licensing route to enter selected and growing markets in Western Europe and Japan because senior management believed that licensing allowed the firm to enter foreign markets with a minimum commitment of resources, while enjoying a guaranteed level of return. As time went on, however, the management became aware that many licensees overseas had developed extremely profitable business based on the licensed know-how, while the licensor's participation was limited to only a negligible royalty. The management belatedly realized that the direct investment route would have been much more suitable in entering and developing these growth markets. And the firm's position would have substantially improved, even under a licensing agreement, had it insisted on equity participation, rather than a straight royalty arrangement, in return for its technical know-how.

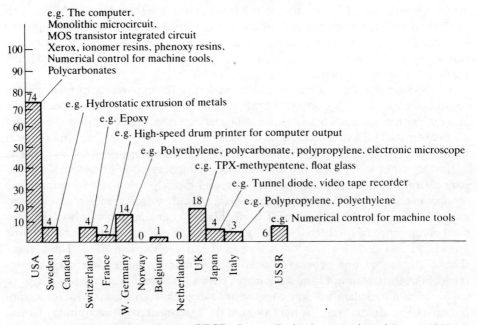

Fig. 3.1 Gaps in technology (*Source*: OECD, *Gaps in Technology: Analytical Report*, 1980)

Marketing technology

The development of new technologies over time and the consequent need to develop appropriate marketing policies is illustrated in Fig. 3.1 as a multi-country comparison in this context, licensing has been increasingly significant: licensors are suppliers of technology, while licensees are the recipients; technology can be defined as any kind of 'know-how' relevant to the solution of engineering and management problems. Two recent studies have explained the role of licensing in both the provision and the control of technology world-wide by manufacturers seeking to develop their international business operations with low risk and capital outlay. The first study[4] illustrates a selection of both industrial licence agreements, and receipts and expenditures on industrial property rights among selected industrialized countries, in Tables 3.1 and 3.2.

This first study explains: 'Table [3.1] shows the dominating position of USA as an exporter of technology; UK marginally in balance; and France, West Germany and Japan as net importers.' The study continues:

[as regards government intervention,] this usually takes the form of political and economic controls deemed to be in the national interest. In Western Europe and North America, licensing thrives mainly on private initiatives within a framework of competition law . . .

Table 3.1 A selection of recent industrial licence agreements (*Source*: A. F. Millman, 'Licensing Technology', *Management Decision*, 21, 3, 1983)

UK licensor	Know-how	Foreign licensee
British Rail (Transmark)	High Speed Train HST 125	Comeng, Sydney, Australia, supplying the New South Wales State Railway
Sinclair Research	Personal computer	Timex Corporation, USA
ARC Concrete	Centrifugal casting process for glass-fibre-reinforced concrete pipes	A number of licensees in Scandinavia, South Africa, Hong Kong and Japan
British Aerospace	BAC III airliner	Banesa Aircraft factory, Bucharest, Romania
Automotive Products	Borg and Beck clutches	ZAZ, VAZ, and AZLK in the USSR
British Nuclear Fuels	Refractory ceramics	Asahi Glass, Japan
Scott Bader	Polyester resins	Licensees world-wide
Lucas Aerospace	Variable feel flying control system	Sumitomo Precision Products, Japan; for the new XT-4 jet trainer aircraft
Conder International	Industrial building systems	Venezuela, Hungary, Brazil, Portugal

Table 3.2   Total receipts from, and expenditure on, industrial property rights for selected countries, 1980 (*Source: Monthly Report of the Deutsche Bundesbank*, 34, 7, July 1982. Converted at £1 = DM4.24)

	Receipts* (£m)	Expenditure* (£m)	Receipts ÷ Expenditure
UK	515	397	1.29
France	212	440	0.48
West Germany	258	619	0.42
Japan	152	569	0.27
USA	2995	324	9.24

* * Receipts and expenditure refer to both related and unrelated companies.

among the technology-importing countries, the most successful example of controlled industrial development is that of modern Japan. Through its Ministry of International Trade & Industry, Japan imposed a tight rein on foreign investment and technology transfer . . .

The study concludes:

While the concept of the patent, and to some extent patent licensing, is relatively well understood, some executives find it exceedingly difficult to extend their thinking to the wider aspects of know-how licensing. . . . Generally, the more international a company is in its outlook and operations, the more likely licensing of technology (in and out) will emerge as a strategic option.

The second study[5] supports this contention and argues that there are indications now that 'more companies seem to have discovered their technological know-how as a marketable commodity and profitable opportunity'. This study cites the trade and financial press as increasingly reporting international technology transactions, often brought about by the mediation of governmental and private agencies, the increasing use of trade fairs and centres where technological know-how is traded, and state-financed facilities in many countries for bringing about industrial technology transfer. This study identifies five types of technology:

1. mainstream technology (also used by licensor);
2. spin-off (by-product) technology (not generally used by licensor);
3. hang-over technology (substituted by mainstream technology; no longer used by licensor);
4. stand-by technology (temporarily unused by licensor);
5. up and coming technology (still in the development stage and/or not yet used by licensor).

In Fig 3.2 this study illustrates the main steps in the licensing process.

It is clear, therefore, in the light of these developments, that companies must understand the process of technology marketing, and must work out new marketing strategies. However, this study explains further that decision criteria by which

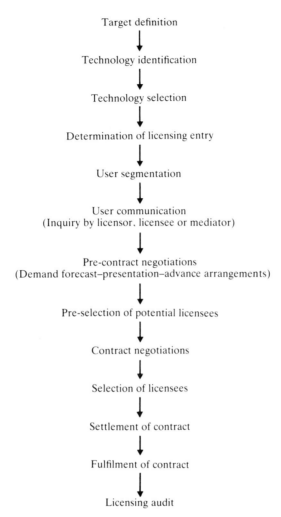

Target definition

Technology identification

Technology selection

Determination of licensing entry

User segmentation

User communication
(Inquiry by licensor, licensee or mediator)

Pre-contract negotiations
(Demand forecast–presentation–advance arrangements)

Pre-selection of potential licensees

Contract negotiations

Selection of licensees

Settlement of contract

Fulfilment of contract

Licensing audit

Fig. 3.2 Stages of the technology licensing process (*Source*: A. Hamman and H. Mittag, 'The Marketing of Industrial Technology through Licensing', *Proceedings of 2nd IMP Research Seminar on International Marketing*, Uppsala University, 1985, p. 6)

management can judge how to identify licensable technology and when to license technology are by no means fully developed yet. While the first aim of effective technology marketing policy is to identify 'technology stock' in a company, definition is by no means straightforward; certainly, some indicators can be used such as (1) physical production facilities (e.g. machines and installations); (2) information reservoirs; and (3) people. But the study also points out that management faces the problem of rating existing, identified technology by its marketability, i.e. its economic prospects as measured by the number and scope of utilizations (e.g. the number of technology users, and the volume of technology utilization). But, it is claimed, the aptitude of a technology for licensing is not stable over time, and it proposes the concept of the technology 'life-cycle' (describing the ageing process of technology). Certain points in this life-cycle can be more effective than others, and the study analyses some highly significant applications of the cycle in the following terms:

> Licensing at the early phases of the technology life-cycle (development and trial phases) is usually difficult because the industrial applicability of technology is either not yet demonstrable or only guided by prototypes or pilot-constructions, and therefore its superiority over conventional technology is not clear. Moreover, the investment necessary to develop viable applications, the time required and the difficulties in estimating future profits may often deter possible users from licensing technology. Licensing in the later stages of the technology life-cycle (maturity and decline) phases may imply the disadvantage that in the meantime other companies have gained know-how from their own R&D so that the number of potential licensees decreases as the number of potential licensors increases. A license can also become unattractive because of its diminished technological and economic prospects.
>
> The conditions to gain market access through licensing and to earn profits seem to be most advantageous at the growth-stage of the technology life-cycle. Interest in a technology increases drastically when it proves to be a viable proposition, and product marketing based on that technology is likely to be very successful. The licensing conditions are not only favourable because potential licensees want to enter the product market as fast as possible, capitalising on the success of the innovator, but also because the technology opens opportunities for further development and for the advancement of their own technology. The proceeds from licensing achieve normally a maximum at this stage in the technology life cycle.

There is, therefore, much scope for senior management, both to identify and develop market opportunities for their companies' technologies, and to identify and develop specific technologies to stages suitable for international licensing arrangements.

3.4   Countertrading

Introduction

'Countertrading' is the term used in international trading to denote transactions by which goods and services are paid for by barter, or by other forms such as part payment in kind and in cash. The various forms of countertrading, such as 'compensatory trading', 'counterpurchasing deals', 'switch trading', 'parallel deals' and 'buyback' arrangements, will be explained in this section. Countertrading has increased in recent years, and it is more complex than is generally realized, even in the business community itself; it is becoming more widely used, and is increasingly specified in many countries, and by many purchasing organizations, as a means of both bilateral and multilateral trade expansion.

There is ample evidence that countertrading is well established in many markets, particularly in trade between OECD countries and other regions. Countries in the COMECON bloc, for example, often demand 100 per cent countertrade on most contracts; and China and many countries in the Third World recognize that establishing a market position in Western countries through countertrading deals is often as important as earning hard currency. Counterpurchase, for example, now accounts for about 65 per cent of all countertrade deals with Eastern Europe: in this kind of arrangement, the Western supplier agrees to buy local products equivalent to a fixed percentage of its own deliveries. The problem here is that the Western supplier is often asked to take technologically outmoded machinery in part payment for its goods and services; in these cases, other modes of countertrading can be used by which the original supplier gets in touch with a third party which can sell the goods in the Third World, where technical sophistication is perhaps not as important as a low price. If the 'bought' product from Eastern Europe is one of the commodities, these are easier to 'offload' in the West. The London Chamber of Commerce and Industry publishes lists of trading houses that will take such things as sugar, edible oils and metals; but the Western supplier still has to pay for the services of a trading house, and if such charges have not been included in the initial costings for the East European contract, it can result in the supplier incurring an overall loss.

Case example 3.4
Cadbury Schweppes has used its international group purchasing resources as a means of entering and establishing a substantial market presence in East European countries. Its Swedish subsidiary manufactured tomato purée, and Schweppes in Britain accepted deliveries of Bulgarian tomatoes as part of a deal to sell its beverages into Bulgaria. And the company set up a HQ team, specializing in this sort of trading, which bought fruit pulp, juices, frozen fruit and aerosols from Bulgaria. These commodities were either used in Britain or sold to other members of the group in other countries. This approach has made it possible to open up a market far beyond anything that could have been achieved in Bulgaria on a direct export basis.

Case example 3.5
Hawker Siddeley (HS) successfully used countertrading to sell military aircraft to Finland. This country is not a centrally planned economy and does not have exclusive strategic material with which to barter; but it used its defence purchasing as a 'lever', knowing that international competition in the sale of military aircraft is fierce. HS set up a 'Finnish Compensation Office', helping the Finns to use HS multinational group facilities to market a wide range of products in Britain and in third countries. Normally a foreign government would insist on a manufacturing involvement in such a deal. It is commonplace for aircraft components to be made locally, in order to reduce the hard currency cost of a defence contract, and to enhance the buying country's maintenance and defence capability. However, in this case Finland had such a small defence production facility that the total value of the aircraft contract was set off against a commitment by HS to arrange for pulp, paper, timber products, handling equipment and medical apparatus and other goods from Finland to be sold internationally.

While countertrading originated as straightforward barter trading (avoiding cash payment on the part of both partners), it has developed into a number of different modes, some of considerable complexity. It is important, therefore, to grasp that countertrading is no longer a 'method of last resort' to encourage trade flows: some countertrade transactions can be used to generate new business in areas where cash payment is not easily effected. Indeed, barter trade (where there is only one contract between buyer and seller, and no third party is involved) was very much a feature of the immediate postwar period and is not at all common nowadays: this is mainly due to the increasing difficulty, in straight bartering, of matching the relative values of different commodities at times of widely fluctuating inflation and currency exchange rates. And the inclusion of barter in an export deal can complicate financing and insurance arrangements: the Export Credits Guarantee Department (ECGD) can hardly cover the quality and resaleability of goods provided in full exchange for export products. Many firms in the UK have come to realize that there are market opportunities overseas which can be opened up by exploiting one or more modes of countertrading. Managers often find, on investigation, that their companies are buyers of materials or components from suppliers who are also potential customers for their products, and who could be influenced to enter bigger deals using the lever of their purchasing power.

Further evidence of the growing importance world-wide of countertrading is provided by a recent US Government report, which surveyed countertrading activities of more than 500 corporations between 1980 and 1984.[6] Its major findings are as follows.

1. The value of US corporations' countertrade with Europe has grown more than fourfold, and such obligations with Asia have more than tripled.
2. Most of US countertrade, about 80 per cent, involves military components; however, non-military countertrade obligations rose from $467 million in 1980 to $580 million in 1984.
3. Half of all US imports resulting from non-military countertrade were shipped from Eastern Europe.
4. The majority of US corporations surveyed claimed that they had derived benefits from countertrade, including larger and more efficient production runs, lower unit costs, increased capital formation and the development of new technology.
5. Almost half of the goods and services imported under non-military countertrade were used internally by US companies that were party to the sales.
6. Nevertheless, some businesses worried about the increasing competition emerging for technology transfer and local procurement conditions enhancing the strength of foreign suppliers.

Types of countertrading

It is now time to consider, in some detail, the various types of countertrading. Straightforward barter trading has already been described, and all the following modes really originated from it.

1. *Compensation deal.* This involves the exporter agreeing to receive full or partial payment (i.e. compensation) in local goods produced in the importer's country. The countertrade 'ratio' in this sort of deal really splits the transaction into a cash portion (usually paid for immediately) and a barter portion (no money involved), and both these are fixed in one contract. Also, the exporter can, by means of a third party clause, transfer his compensation commitment to a trading house or countertrade specialist.

2. *'Switch' trading.* This has developed out of type 1 but is more complicated, and can involve four or even five parties. It is still, basically, a means of offloading a commitment to take goods, instead of money, for part or whole payment of an export delivery. For example, an exporter may have agreed to accept £1 million of payment from Eastern Europe in the form of manufactured goods but can make use of only half of this amount within his own organization. He sells his remaining credit to a switch dealer at a discount. The switch dealer finds someone who is in need of certain ranges of products that can be obtained from the Eastern European country, and the dealer offers the goods at a reduced price. The outcome is that the Eastern European country has obtained its imports in exchange for manufactures; the switch dealer has made a profit on the difference between the two rates of discount, and the buyer of the East European goods has bought them more cheaply than by going direct. The original exporter has completed his contract, but has had to finance the discount involved in doing so.

3. *Counterpurchase or parallel deal.* This is the most frequently used mode of countertrading today. The term indicates that two separate but related contracts are negotiated between two parties, each being a cash transaction. The first contract concerns the sale of Western products, for instance to the Middle Eastern importer (the export contract); in the second, parallel, contract the exporter commits himself to purchase countertrade (CT) goods

   - amounting to a certain percentage of his export delivery (CT ratio), choosing products from within a certain range of CT goods;
   - over a given period.

This latter part of the negotiations is termed 'purchase commitment' or 'contract of obligation'; in case of non-performance of this part, the Western exporter has to pay a penalty to his Middle East partner. The attractions of this mode of countertrading are clear. The original export transaction is fulfilled by both parties to the contract, and the Western exporter receives full payment for the goods delivered. While his commitment to take goods in return may be stretched over a longer period, giving him more time to select and check quality, nevertheless, his purchase commitment results in a future payment to his Middle East partner, based on the separate (second) contract. And a known ability to buy goods from a foreign market can be a valuable lever in securing a big export contract. For example, a British firm with the intention of buying Czech machine tools might well approach a British exporter of cranes and suggest that the exporter includes machine tools in a counterpurchase deal. (The company in need of the tools can then specify in advance what it requires.)

4. *Buy-back contracts.* This mode of CT applies particularly in countries expanding their industrial infrastructure. It involves the seller of technology or equipment, or the supplier of a 'turnkey' plant, agreeing to accept products manufactured in the plant he has supplied as full or partial payment. For instance, a contractor selling chemical equipment is paid by the future output of the investment, i.e. chemicals. There is the commercial benefit to the buyer/owner of the plant in that he is enabled to pay the construction costs of the plant by using future cash flows earned by selling the resulting output. The supplier/seller of the plant, however, has to face waiting, sometimes for several years, between the erection of the plant and the beginning of cash inflows from product sales, which can be used to pay off construction costs. Also, there can be a difficulty in pricing future products when the market may have changed. A buy-back contract is illustrated in Case example 3.6.[7]

Contributory factors and marketing implications

Case example 3.6

Japanese trading companies are able to handle a multifarious range of goods within the same organization. C. Itoh of Japan gets the contract to set up a synthetic fibre plant in Poland and agrees to purchase back from Poland a proportion of the fibre that will eventually be produced. C. Itoh is, of course, one of the world's largest textile merchanting companies and can make such promises without too much difficulty. The attractiveness of such a deal to the buying country is obvious: it gets its new plant with the sure knowledge that it will increase its own exports and that the plant will earn hard currency to replace the cost of building it.

A recent UK government study has investigated the following factors accounting for CT expansion:[8]

1. opportunities both to finance and to expand trade, which would otherwise not take place in the absence of sufficient commercial credit or convertible currency;
2. the chance to exploit a 'buyer's market' position, which enables importers to obtain better terms of trade or similar benefits (assuming competitive bidding);
3. the protection and/or stimulation of the output of domestic industries both to reduce manufactured imports and to earn hard currencies by overseas sales;
4. an instrument for use in fulfilling political and economic policies by governments aiming at planning and balancing overseas trade;
5. maintenance of a country's own resources to protect its levels of domestic production and employment.

Furthermore, it is arguable that floating exchange rates and unpredictable inflation and interest rates (together with hard currency shortages) have created the conditions that have forced government ministries/agencies to stipulate some form of counter-trading; the growing problem of international indebtedness has accentuated this trend. Eastern European countries, for instance, have economic plans that demand supplies of raw materials and manufactured goods from abroad. The same has been true of some of the OPEC countries, which have embarked on huge industrialization and social improvement schemes that rely upon imported components and materials. Iran has had a policy of using its oil as a form of currency with which to purchase capital goods for defence and industrialization. Many such countries have realized, therefore, that the system whereby their purchases from abroad are restricted according to the hard currency they can earn from the West is highly unreliable, and that, to an increasing extent, CT can circumvent this problem.

As for the marketing implications of CT, it is clear from the evidence already cited that the exporter's willingness and ability to meet his customer's CT requirements is now, and probably more so in the future, a prior condition to the development of international markets. At the same time, another marketing aspect is in evidence: by means of one or more of CT modes, the initial exporter undertakes the marketing of CT goods, working as a kind of sales agent for his partner requiring the CT trans-action. Indeed, there is a strong element of economic co-operation implicit in CT,

– in the field of international project financing, where CT commitments constitute essential parts of the different contractual relationships using primarily buy-back arrangements; and
– in joint venture arrangements that involve close co-operation in a common business venture, where both parties participate in the risks and in the success (and profits) of the corresponding transactions.

In view of these complexities in CT, two types of transaction are illustrated in Figs 3.3 and 3.4, drawing on a recent study of CT developments.[9]

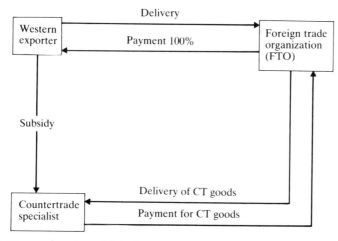

Fig. 3.3 Counter purchase/parallel deal.

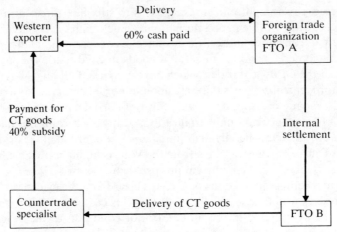

Fig. 3.4 Compensation deal—quadrangular type (*Source*: R. Moser, 'Countertrading: A New Marketing Tool', *Proceedings of the 13th Annual Conference of the International Association of Institutes of Export*, Vienna, September 1986)

3.5 Foreign production operations: contract manufacturing, joint ventures, subsidiaries

Introduction

Many companies recognize that, as their overseas business develops, decisions have to be faced about the extent of investment in and commitment to major markets, in order to secure the company's long-term market position. Such decisions concern investing in and setting up overseas production operations and, sometimes, buying sales and distribution companies locally in order to ensure sales outlets for the required investment in output. Direct investment of this sort is increasingly required to secure a long-term market position, whether or not this has been established by another route, such as exports. In many overseas markets the establishment of such a presence by a manufacturer (production operations, assembly and distribution facilities) can increase local demand. Government incentives in the form of tax concessions and grants will often be available to reduce the costs of capital outlay. World-wide operating costs associated with exporting finished goods can be reduced, and closer links with the market will often enable marketing effectiveness to be improved.

Of course, direct manufacture overseas means financial investment in overseas operations, or perhaps the acquisition of a local manufacturing firm; in either case, there is the element of risk of loss. So the decision to set up local manufacture, in a country previously supplied by imports of finished goods, must be a major step in the international growth of any company. The extent of the commitment will vary according to whether it is full or partial manufacture/assembly or joint venture. Whereas a decade ago the standard advice to the management might have been to set up a foreign plant with 100 per cent ownership (and control), if this was legally permitted, now conditions of both ownership and control are much more complex, and often involve some sort of participation by host government agencies. Also, more use is being made of options such as 'management contracts' (discussed in the next section). In reality, many companies operating overseas increasingly face little option but to consider some form of investment outlay; this is because many host governments, concerned to expand the local manufacturing base and to increase export earnings from output, now operate various forms of tariffs, non-tariff measures and other restrictions and regulations that make direct exporting of finished goods into their countries increasingly costly and difficult. All this requires a positive, rather than a reactive, policy on the part of the international company's management, as Case example 3.7 shows.

Case example 3.7

A manufacturer of industrial equipment had for a long time followed implicitly a policy of undertaking local production only when it was forced into it by competitive pressure or actions of the host government. When management became aware that the company was being squeezed out of some promising markets because of this policy, it reversed its position and began actively to seek opportunities for direct investment overseas. A senior executive of the firm noted that the company was experiencing considerable difficulties in regaining the lost ground, as it was practically locked out of some markets owing to governments' concessions granted to earlier entrants, while in others competition was too entrenched for the firm to develop a viable market position to justify any direct investment.

Assessment criteria

Clearly, a major set of decisions confronts management placed in the sort of situation described in the case example; indeed, such decisions both require and repay research, analysis and planning well before the stage that was reached for that particular company. Research is needed as a basis for planning and decision-making in the following areas:

1. where (which country and which region) to locate/build the plant;
2. demand analysis: is the expected, quantifiable demand likely to make the plant commercially viable when the output can
   - be sold locally?
   - be sold to neighbouring countries/regionally?
3. market access and proximity (as distinct from demand analysis): regional economic communities such as EEC, CARICOM, ECOWAS, LAFTA and ASEAN can provide tariff-free and unrestricted access for output among member countries; type and number bilateral trade treaties;
4. access to sources of supply which can bring economies of manufacture together with improved procurement arrangements for sub-components, materials, etc.;

5. financial aspects: this would include an assessment of the availability and sources of capital (and the terms on which it is available), the expected return on the investment over what period and the position regarding repatriation of profits and dividends;
6. analysis of costs: this of course, covers a spectrum including labour costs, expected operating costs, improvements in raw materials and other supply costs (related to point 4 above);
7. manpower: this refers to the availability, quality and technical levels of local labour and of course, labour costs; all these must be related to estimated levels of productivity;
8. competitor analysis: strengths, weaknesses and assessed marketing policies of both locally based and international competitors, particularly pricing policies and quality/level of service offered;
9. technical and logistical factors: these refer to such items as the availability and costs of distribution channels for the output, quality control standards, energy sources/costs, local availability of chemicals and any other supplies required for manufacturing;
10. fiscal aspects: assessment of the types of customs 'drawbacks', etc., offered by the host government of the proposed country of supply;
11. political factors: many overseas governments favour policies related to import substitution and export development; this means that, once agreement has been reached with the appropriate government agency, continuing support with trade promotion, planning consents, mobilization of labour, direct equity participation and special exemptions from foreign exchange restrictions for the importation of essential supply components, etc., can be forthcoming;
12. Risk assessment: basically, this covers
    - political risks (practically impossible to foresee fully)—change of government, nationalization/expropriation, security measures against terrorism, change of laws, embargoes, strikes, political stability, political relationships with neighbouring countries which are target markets;
    - financial risks—insolvency laws, foreign exchange transfers and delays, level of indebtedness to international banks, currency, inflation and interest rate trends, availability of credit, capital repatriation, etc.;
    - commercial risks—laws regarding contract repudiation of agencies, takeover of partner by competitor, market shrinkage, patent or trademark infringement or revocation, loss of control of technology, product liability risks, performance of technology or equipment, etc.

A more detailed management check-list appears at the end of this section.
   All this research and analysis is needed by management as a basis for

1. the assessment of a country-by-country 'scenario' as to the type of operation most appropriate to achieve the international objectives of the firm;
2. planning and decision-making to make both the manufacturing and the marketing programmes operational, and appropriately resourced.

These scenarios typically encompass a wide range of countries, some at very different stages of industrial development; the key management decision to be made is, quite simply, how best the exporting company can move into some form of overseas investment in order to maintain the competitive position of its manufactured goods. There are a number of scenarios that require decisions about overseas investment. Protective duties and measures to reinforce a weakening exchange rate can steadily increase the landed cost of a finished product to the point where it becomes impossible to compete with local equivalents. There may be technical and other services which go with an exported product so that, beyond a certain volume of business, some form of local assembly becomes necessary. Again, growing restrictions on imports of finished manufactures can lengthen delivery and payment delays to the point where direct sales suffer and some form of direct investment must be considered. In some countries it is possible to take advantage of substantial savings in costs of materials and labour. These, added to savings in freight and duty, can give the company marketing the product more room for manoeuvre in adjusting prices/volumes to improve profits and sales revenues by direct investment; indeed, this latter policy can include supplying the company's home market.

Some of these scenarios are strongly influenced by the policies of governments. Some are negative (i.e., they operate to restrain direct imports), but others operate positively in the sense that they encourage direct investment in manufacturing by foreign companies. An example of the latter is DATAR in France (Case example 3.8).[10]

Case example 3.8
DATAR, the French national government agency for regional planning and development, offers French or foreign firms investing in new plant in certain designated development areas cash grants of between 12 and 25 per cent of the total value of the investment. Extension of existing facilities in those same areas attracts grants of between 12 and 20 per cent; subsidies are also payable for the cost of staff training (50 per cent) and instructor training (100 per cent). Other incentives available through DATAR include tax reductions and tax exemptions, and a proportion of personnel relocation costs. Local government bodies and other authorities offer additional assistance, including the sale of prepared industrial sites at less than cost, and standard factory buildings.

Organizational options

It is now time to consider, in the light of these country scenarios and assessment criteria, the different operational and organizational options/modes facing management. This needs some precision, as the terms 'investment' and 'joint venture', for example, tend to be used loosely. Strictly speaking, an investment requires that capital be sent out of the country, either in money or in kind, and cannot be returned (repatriated) except under strictly defined conditions. A joint venture refers to an agreement by which two organizations (e.g., a manufacturer and a government agency) join forces in a manufacturing/assembling or supply operation, or in a marketing consortium (see Section 3.2 above); in an international joint venture, it is essential to have a detailed mode of operation (control, rewards, conflict resolution, etc.) agreed on between the parties well in advance of manufacturing/assembly operations. A joint venture (manufacturing) is often necessary, and indeed attractive, to companies planning to expand operations where

1. there is insufficient capital fully to exploit market potential;
2. host governments do not permit 100 per cent foreign-owned equity;
3. political and other uncertainties require limiting investment risk;
4. sources of supply must be safeguarded (where a joint venture agreement can be made with suppliers of raw materials);
5. limitations to managerial and technical expertise require additional resources from a partner;
6. positive political factors, such as partnership with the host government, secure the company's long-term market position in that country.

   Closely related to joint ventures is, of course, the management decision about full manufacturing as distinct from assembly operations overseas. There are markets where substantial cost reductions can be obtained by some assembly, thus keeping prices highly competitive; these include lower freight costs, lower import duties on sub-assemblies and other cost advantages brought about by lower wage rates for assembly operations and from local purchase of cheaper components. There is also the point that experience of the market can be built up and assessed prior to any full manufacturing.
   In the case of setting up subsidiaries overseas, even where local partners in a joint venture contribute up to 49 per cent of the equity, this does not make the local company any less of a subsidiary, since the investing company owns more than 50 per cent of the voting shares, and therefore retains ultimate management control. And where such a large amount of new finance is required, it is usually the case that a new manufacturing or assembly is being set up. In some countries, as already explained, host governments do not permit outright foreign ownership/control of new local enterprises. In the case of an associate company, this is where less than a controlling interest is exercised. There is, however, no precise measurement of the level of ownership in an associate company that constitutes effective management control. (One important factor is consolidation of results into the accounts of the investing company.) In practice, there are some ways of exercising control (even though the investor owns less than 50 per cent of the equity) and securing financial benefits, in addition to dividends, for example by royalties related to production or sale, by technical fees and by the supply of equipment and expertise; these can all be regulated by contracts negotiated between the parties. And this is often the case in joint ventures, where (instead of jointly setting up a new plant) the local partner may own existing facilities and machinery, and simply purchase specialized equipment, material or components—

this, plus the use of a brand name or promotional package, licensed to him by the foreign partner who is not then an investor at all.

This last point leads directly to an assessment of a related, but distinct, mode of operations: contract manufacture. This is simply a contract between parties in two different countries for the manufacture or assembly of a product. The company placing the contract usually retains full control of distribution and marketing, and can benefit from limited local investment (avoiding risks such as nationalization), entry into markets protected by tariffs, some possible cost advantages in local supply, the retention of market control and the promotion of a locally made image, which can assist in sales, particularly to government or official bodies. However, the company placing such a contract may have difficulties in controlling manufacturing quality, and/or finding and training sufficient local technical staff; and, if the intention is to develop the market in the long term, the local (contracted) manufacturer can emerge as a strong competitor at the expiry of the contract.

So in evaluating these various modes of market entry and operations, management must have a well researched data base on which to base decision criteria, and these criteria have been discussed in detail. Clearly, the management of a firm expanding international operations must assess the total control of operations conferred by 100 per cent ownership of a foreign subsidiary against the likely rewards and risks. Similarly, in evaluating a joint venture, management must assess the value of the inputs, local market and technical expertise that the partner can bring, together with the lower level of risk and capital outlay involved. As already noted, many governments, particularly those of developing countries (e.g. India), make joint ventures with local capital a condition of market entry. Furthermore, there does seem to be some relationship between full 'parental control' and market success. A study of small- and medium-sized UK companies setting up a foreign production subsidiary for the first time found that firms with 75 per cent or more of voting shares in the foreign subsidiary had a markedly higher record of market success than those whose control was diluted.[11] This study also found that small firms in particular had a low threshold of tolerance for joint decision-making, and that agents (who often initiate moves towards some sort of direct investment) frequently made bad partners. As to be expected, multinational corporations (MNCs) preferred to operate through wholly owned subsidiaries.

The role of marketing management

If the commitment of companies to invest capital, resources, manpower, etc., in overseas operations has correspondingly higher risks than direct and indirect exporting, then this can only highlight the vital role of marketing management. Market research, demand analysis, long-term market prospects and the assessment of sales potential, both in the overseas country and regionally, are all essential prerequisites to overseas operations. Marketing must provide a sound, realistic market data base for planning and decisions. A knowledge level adequate for exporting must be increased and this will cost money; market knowledge of past and present trends and valid market projections must be extended. In addition to research about the company's own products and supply capacity, there must be expert appraisal of the target country's financial and economic prospects. This staff work can be done internally by desk research followed up by some personal, investigative visits, or it can be obtained from outside consultants. (Even abortive studies can sometimes help to improve current marketing methods by the light they throw on market conditions.) And while there is always an element of hazard in market forecasting, the margins of error inherent in this exercise must be clarified at the outset of the research. Indeed, 'sensitivity analysis' should be made of the results in the light of an agreed range of options: should this range be greater than the possible limits of failure and success that the company is prepared to accept; this will serve, on a first or second run of the complete data, either to discard the project before too much time is spent on secondary analysis, or to concentrate the analysis into market sectors (possibly different to those originally set out) that show a greater likelihood of success.

All these tasks are clearly the responsibility of marketing management, together with the actual implementation and evaluation of international marketing programmes, whatever mode of entry and operation is selected; and careful planning has to be balanced against the need for rapid market entry. Timing is often vital to pre-empt a competitor, or to secure a particular contract. Finally, the product range, technical expertise and marketing position of the investing company are themselves likely to be important in determining the viability of a subsidiary, and it is arguable that the foreign entrant should aim for the 'quality' or 'luxury' sectors of the market. Many investors are specialist manufacturers of producers' goods, and 'quality' means producing abroad to at least the same or higher specifications as in the home market, for the following reasons.

1. The higher costs of producing abroad (initially at least) are more easily absorbed at the quality end of the market.
2. Good returns can be earned from a lower volume of production of a quality product (and this would be crucial in the earlier years of the foreign enterprise).

So a dilemma that faces a firm with a foreign subsidiary is the balance of advantage between centralizing decision-making to achieve consistency between headquarters and subsidiary and allowing local management the scope to exercise initiative.

In terms of financial control, headquarters management needs to be well informed of the activities of the subsidiary, otherwise capital, management time and other resources can be wasted. This necessitates the regular submission of budget estimates and accounts from the subsidiary. As multinational corporations have long known, the existence of foreign subsidiaries allows greater flexibility in financial operations. These advantages can be wasted by naive foreign investors. A good example of this is transfer pricing policies. In many firms, internal prices are set on an *ad hoc* basis, rather than being oriented towards clear policy objectives. Often, a similar situation prevails in the choice between the repatriation of dividends and reinvestment in the

subsidiary. Such decisions are strategically important and should be though
at a higher management level.

The issue of control also arises with regard to the optimal number and nai
business functions that the foreign subsidiary should perform, such as markɛ
purchasing, labour training and research. Here it is necessary to distinguish betw
strategy, which must be set by the parent in consultation with the subsidiary management, and contingent decision-making, which, within that policy, is usually best
carried out by local management. It is achieving this division and balance that is difficult.

The successful establishment of a foreign subsidiary is not the end of the process.
The lessons learned must be dispersed throughout the enterprise in order to generate
maximum benefit from the experience.

Each foreign investment is unique, but there are certain regularities in the problems
encountered. Among the most frequently cited are: employment of workers, including
training and supply; problems of control of foreign production, including quality
control; managerial problems, including liaison problems with foreign partners, and
the drain on resources in the parent company; and financial problems including taxation and generating sales in the start-up period.

None of these problems is uniquely an 'international' problem, but all are exacer-
bated by difficulties of operation in an alien environment. However, a learning process is at work, and many firms that successfully establish a foreign unit are often able
to put their experience to good use. Particularly important are lessons of 'managing at
a distance', which often compels firms to formalize and systemize their decision-
making procedures. Second, the importance of having the 'right' man at the top of the
subsidiary is often emphasized by small firms in particular. Third, lessons are learned
on improvements in marketing; and evaluation by foreign investors is often based on
the company's 'sensitivity to local conditions'.

Check-list of major points to take into account when deciding whether, and where, to invest in manufacturing plant abroad[12]

Political
1. Political stability or uncertainty
2. Attitude of host government to private enterprise, and, in particular, to foreign private investment
3. Special inducements for foreign investors, such as tax holidays, grants, loans at favourable rates, tariff protection for newly established industries
4. Membership of a free trade area, or trade agreements with other countries that might offer export opportunities

Legal
1. Legal discrimination against foreign companies or their expatriate employees
2. Percentage of company that may be foreign-owncd
3. Patent protection laws and ease of enforcement

4. Trademark protection
5. Price-control legislation
6. Restrictive trade practice legislation

Cost
1. Cost increases resulting from smaller scale of production, product modification to meet market needs, etc.
2. Wage costs—related to productivity
3. Additional labour costs (e.g. company share of social security payments)
4. Availability and costs of local raw materials and components
5. Availability and cost of transport services
6. Freight, packing and insurance savings (if product previously exported to the country)

Taxation
1. Existence of a double-taxation agreement between host country and parent-company country
2. Withholding of tax payable on remittances to parent company
3. Level of company taxation
4. Method of calculating depreciation allowances, stock valuation, etc.

Exchange control
1. Restrictions on remittances to parent company (e.g. maximum percentage of foreign capital invested)
2. Restrictions on repatriation of capital
3. Convertibility of local currency

Finance
1. Local sources of capital (and interest rates payable)
2. Practicability of supplying capital from the UK
3. External sources of capital
4. Local accounting requirements and conventions
5. Rate of inflation

Personnel
1. Availability of labour (skilled, unskilled, clerical)
2. Availability of local managerial talent
3. Percentage of employees that must be local nationals
4. Availability of work permits for expatriates
5. Living conditions for expatriates (housing, education, medical, etc.)
6. Labour laws and regulations (especially regarding appointment and dismissal of staff)
7. Industrial relations, trade unions, worker participation in management
8. Existence of compulsory profit-sharing schemes for employees

3.6   Management contracts

Introduction

A management contract has been defined as 'an arrangement under which operational control of an enterprise, which would otherwise be exercised by the directors or managers appointed or elected by its owners, is vested by contract in a separate enterprise which performs the necessary managerial functions for a fee'.[13]

Such an agreement, usually valid for five to seven years, can be prolonged, and contract responsibility may be extended to various functions in the local firm, for example to manage production and sale of goods, introduce technical, financial and marketing programmes, and for skills training or management development. The essential point is that it is the foreign firm that is normally responsible for managing and undertaking certain executive and technical functions in another (local) firm without having an equity shareholding. Other related forms of contract can include project management agreements, where the client brings in a contractor to carry out the design and construction phase of the projects, and technical service agreements, where the client draws on special kinds of operational know-how and advice available from the contractor.

Of course, a management contract is only one of the many options open to the firm operating internationally; furthermore, the boundaries between direct investment and other modes of operation discussed in this chapter, such as licensing, are often, in practice, not drawn precisely. Many market opportunities permit combinations, so that management contracts are frequently combined with 'turnkey' projects or licensing agreements; and such a combination helps to ensure the success of the venture. In principle, therefore, the advantages of the management contract to the firm moving into a foreign market are: low-risk market entry, with no capital investment and no expropriation risk; and the fact that the contract capitalizes on management skills and provides a guaranteed minimum income and a quick return. The disadvantages are that the local investor may seek to interfere with the way his investment is being managed; and the managing company may initially lack management resources and marketing expertise to exploit the local market fully.

Management contracts can be associated, therefore, with different modes of entry and operation, involving equity, technical know-how, managerial skills and so on; and the contract provides managerial know-how in a number of different arrangements, or else as the sole agreement, as illustrated in Fig. 3.5. Indeed, direct foreign investment in some countries has in recent years become hazardous, if not impracticable, where governments have legislated directly to regulate the activities of foreign firms, even forcing them to withdraw from certain industrial or economic sectors (for example, Mexico, Nigeria, India and Malaysia); various obstacles such as foreign exchange restrictions have already been discussed (see Section 3.5). The management contract, therefore, has developed as an increasingly attractive mode to companies seeking to strengthen their international market position. It avoids direct confrontation with foreign governments, and provides a useful way of increasing co-operation

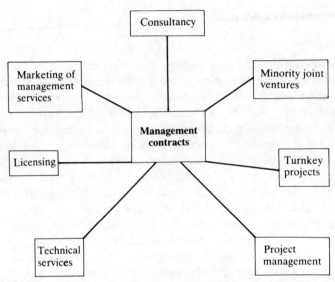

Fig. 3.5 Management contracts (*Source*: J. Holly, 'Management Contracts', *Handbook of International Trade*, Vol. I, Section 3.7(1), Macmillan, London, 1983)

with the local business enterprises to develop the market, whether they are in the private or public sectors. At the same time, any such contractual arrangement must be commercially justifiable compared with the profitability of other modes, such as direct or indirect exporting (discussed in Section 3.1 above). Management contracts can guarantee a satisfactory rate of return to the contractor, even though a rigid comparison of the profit between direct investment and management contract would not be sufficient. In terms of allocating resources and developing appropriate management staff, it is essential for the firm operating internationally to devise some form of acceptable management control, as opposed to control arising from equity ownership; this is also necessary to meet marketing objectives and to minimize risk and uncertainty.

Analysing marketing prospects

In analysing marketing prospects in particular, in having a management contract, the contracting company must take into account opportunities to sell machinery, equipment, technology and know-how in the local (foreign) country. There can also be opportunities to acquire market intelligence and trade contacts, as well as more advantageous local supply arrangements for materials, components, etc. And direct remuneration through fees from a particular contract should not necessarily be viewed as the primary goal; the realization of broader, market-related, goals should be management's aim, and the longer-term value of the contract should be assessed in terms of such factors as

- improved overseas market access, giving better competitiveness;
- realizing a higher share of sales potential;
- local supply and distribution arrangements, bringing higher-quality service and cost benefits to customers;
- longer-term development of a strong overall market position overseas, providing the means to generate/dominate new or key market sectors where demand prospects are high.

As has been pointed out, some management contracts do not separate management and ownership completely. This is an important point. Some companies and countries prefer the contractor to have some small financial involvement (1–10 per cent) or a minority joint venture (10–49 per cent) with a management contract, and the contractor himself may prefer a share in the action. The study cited above argues that pure forms of management contract differ from minority joint ventures in two ways.[14]

1. The foreign contractor makes no significant financial investment in the local firm.
2. In a minority joint venture with a management contract, there is limited ownership-related control of the local firm, and control is vested by the voluntary, temporary delegation of mangerial responsibility by the majority shareholders.

Of course, joint ventures in which a minority partner is contracted to provide management are common throughout both the developed and the developing world. Management contracts, with a fixed term, are therefore used to ensure efficient operation, and to assist in the process of management development and the transfer of technology and marketing techniques. This type of contract is most commonly used either during the initial operation of new joint ventures or during the period after full or part nationalization of a foreign company. Less often, it is used when a local operation overseas has run into difficulty and a foreign firm is invited in to effect a turnround.

There are two further significant aspects of contracting explored and concisely explained in the study already cited.[14]

1. *Countering nationalization.* Many manufacturing companies are forced to sell down their majority holding to a minority position by government policy. In order to protect their remaining equity, these companies endeavour to maintain control through several types of agreements, most particularly management contracts and technical service agreements. The companies not only seek to maintain control through management contracts in order to ensure the good functioning of the former subsidiary and thus receive returns from dividends, but they also seek to maintain the supply of goods from, or the sales of goods to, the former subsidiary. In these cases the function of the management contract is not just to obtain remuneration from the contract but also to secure an overall strategy. The purpose of the management contract is to obtain profits by maintaining or obtaining a market rather than obtaining direct remuneration from the management contract itself. In socialist countries, the contract ensures the maximum foreign control permitted.

2. *Transferring technology.* Usually in a turnkey contract, the contractor has the

obligation to deliver an operating industrial plant to the client without the active participation of the client in the various stages of construction. The contractor may also
have to provide for technical assistance with training and operation of the plant for a
short initial period (that is, the commissioning), and to assist with the marketing of
the product manufactured. If the contract imposes on the contractor an additional
guarantee as to the quantity and the quality of the production over a longer period
(sometimes up to two years), the turnkey contract will become a turnkey-plus-
management contract.

Where expertise is scarce, arrangements must be made to obtain trained and experienced operatives and managers. Technical assistance agreements and management
contracts are, therefore, necessary if the transfer of technology is to be completed.
Contractors can gain from the need for such agreements over and above a fee. The
technology transferred can be tied into a foreign contractor's technology and become
a captive sales market for intermediate goods and sophisticated technical equipment.
Management contracts can arise in connection with the support of licences. The management is provided where the contract enterprise does not have sufficient know-how
to operate a licence. In some circumstances there may be a failure of the licence agreement and the licensor may consider the operation valuable enough to assign management through a contract in order to ensure the continuation of the enterprise. Where
the licensee does not exploit the licence effectively, then the licensor must either
rescind the licence or devote more resources. Devoting more resources may be justified on several grounds, but two seem the most important: the fee that is derivable
from licensing, and the access permitted to a particular market. In the absence of
licensing, a firm may find that another company can exclude market entry at a later
date or can compete in certain markets through exploitation of the asset.

Management contracts may be associated with licensing in other ways. Few technologies can be transferred simply by transferring blueprints, documents and reports.
The negotiation process itself is time-consuming and expensive, and must be followed
by engineering, consultation and adaptation. The early stages of production are
usually characterized by low quality and low productivity. Uncontrolled licensees
may not exploit patents energetically enough, and a licensor's own management can
effect higher sales because of better business know-how. A management contract may
then be used to ensure the efficacious application of a licence and a profitable rate of
return.

To illustrate many of the key aspects of a management contract in operation, Case
examples 3.9 and 3.10 are cited from a recent study of the applications of management contracting in the international marketing of industrial goods.[13]

Case example 3.9
This concerns a Swedish firm, the Scandinavian Dairy Company (SDCo), which
operates in the dairy and farming industry of Sweden. SDCo successfully defeated its
rivals from Europe and the USA for a $40 million turnkey project in 1977 in the

Middle East by entering into a management contract; the company realized that the local firm lacked skilled personnel to establish and operate a modern dairy project. The management contract, moreover, gave SDCo an opportunity to establish a long-term business relationship with the local firm, which in turn helped it to win a much larger contract (worth $100 million) at a later stage for the supply of dairy and farming equipment.

Case example 3.10

Already established internationally through sales offices and subsidiaries, SDCo now acts as a turnkey contractor, assuming responsibility to do feasibility study, technical and market research, etc.; generally, SDCo supply directly only a quarter of the equipment installed in a turnkey project, and purchase the rest externally. SDCo expect four major gains from this particular management contract: (a) increased control over the mode of operation of the local firm and the use of the equipment supplied; (b) use of this management contract as a reference when bidding for turnkey projects in other developing countries; (c) additional business opportunities to sell components and accessories; (d) improved capability to offer, world-wide, a complete dairy and farming system, including managerial services.

The actual project is located in an oil-rich country (though industrially backward with a scarcity of skilled workers); the overall contract incorporates an erection and construction contract, a materials supply contract and a management contract, which is valid for seven years and makes SDCo responsible for the technical operation of the dairy farm and milk plant, and for providing management personnel to the local firm. SDCo receives its remuneration in three forms: (a) it receives a dividend on its financial investment; (b) it is paid a fixed management fee; (c) it receives a tax-free payment (rising from 6 per cent in year 1 to 10 per cent in year 5 and thereafter) contingent on the results realized by the local firm. SDCo has also been receiving non-financial gains in the form of control, export orders, market knowledge and trade contacts.

Developing an international marketing strategy

The most interesting aspect to emerge from these case examples is the importance of the management contract in the context of developing the company's international marketing strategy, specifically in some of the following ways.

1. The development/nurturing of a local enterprise into a flourishing business, coupled with a conflict-free relationship between SDCo and the local firm, is a source of potent and favourable public relations activities for SDCo both in the country and the region.
2. There is a sharper competitiveness of SDCo's product/service offer: the company has developed new solutions and devised software to resolve extremes of climatic situations applicable to other projects in the region.

3. Market access has been opened up in many other countries with a potential for dairy farming and milk production technology.
4. Long-term market development in such target countries is greatly enhanced by the evolution of system sales, and by the ability of SDCo to deliver firm-specific competence by differentiating the company's own solution from solutions offered by competitors in the market. (In practice, this competitive edge is more cost-effective by differentiating software than hardware solutions.)
5. Stronger market presence has been brought about by successful turnkey operations and the establishment of market leadership based on both technology and management expertise.
6. Such a project is valuable in strengthening the firm's base (managerial, technical and financial) to compete for other new turnkey projects.

These marketing aspects underline the wide scope of operations of management contracts in developing a firm's international business operations. For a firm newly entering an overseas market, high start-up costs can make it more expensive to bid for contracts; but the problem-solving and decision-making processes in the local firms (overseas) are likely to be similar to the corresponding processes in the foreign firms with which the local firm has had management contracts. Therefore, the former management contractor, in seeking new contract business, can generally reduce start-up costs at the margin and be more competitive in the market. So firms with previous experience of management contracts tend to have the competitive edge in terms of management expertise, technology transfer and the sale of plant, equipment and components to back up the project; and there is often a clear tactical advantage in securing new or 'follow-on' contracts for the firm that won, and has completed, the initial contract. (Nor should the 'goodwill' generated in the overseas market by the local firm be overlooked.)

3.7   Acquisitions policies

Introduction

There are many different factors that bring about the acquisition of a foreign company; this section is concerned with the marketing implications and outcomes of corporate acquisitions policies. The actual acquisition of a company overseas involves of course, the purchase of all or a majority of the shares of that company (otherwise the operation becomes a joint venture, discussed in Section 3.5).

Any acquisitions policy presupposes that there are, in overseas markets, companies suitable and available for purchase, which is by no means always the case. There may be further complications: for example, local government regulations and attitudes may make acquisition by a foreign company difficult. Some governments are anxious to develop new manufacturing facilities and technology under local ownership, and therefore may discriminate against foreign firms seeking to acquire local ones. The firm considering entry into a foreign market by acquisition is usually in a weaker position to negotiate with the host government than one planning to establish a new operation there. Indeed, foreign government grants of low-interest loans, tax holidays, tariff protection for infant industries, etc., so often offered to incoming investors in new plant, will not normally be available in the case of an acquisition. And the benefit of time-saving sometimes claimed for acquisitions is not universally applicable: location and evaluation of potential candidates for acquisition are often time-consuming processes, and negotiations may extend over lengthy periods.

In particular, the broadening of the company's trading base, the search for 'synergy' by acquisitions in new sectors, the need to find higher-growth sectors of business and the continuing drive to improve overall corporate profitability all have to be appraised on a multi-country basis. Analysis of such acquisitions reveals a situation in which policies are typically pursued by companies for a variety of reasons.[15]

Some companies have a policy of seeking to invest in one or two medium to large strategically strong businesses to act as the core around which a new portfolio will be built. The current businesses are run down or sold off gradually over time, and further acquisitions or new ventures are added to the new strong core. The ultimate goal here is to change the nature of the company through investment acquisitions (that is, acquisitions made primarily on the basis of the financial potential of the 'stand-alone' business). For successful implementation of such a policy, the typical situation would be a 'target' company with fundamental strengths (high market share in certain key market segments, or highly differentiated products) which has shown poor performance often owing to extremely difficult market conditions. So where there is clear scope for improving operating effectiveness, the new parent company will also carry through divestment of marginal parts of the business, thus accelerating improvement in performance. If this is coupled with a recovery in key markets, the results can be dramatic. The problem that often arises is that companies with portfolios like the one described often do not have the resources to acquire a very large, successful business, let alone a series of them.

Case example 3.11 shows how one company invested in developing international business sectors.[16]

Case example 3.11

Electrolux Co. of Sweden, one of the first companies in the world to market vacuum cleaners, pursued its early international expansion largely to gain economies of scale through additional sales. The Swedish market was simply too small to absorb fixed costs as much as the home markets for competitive firms in larger countries. When additional sales were not possible by direct exporting, Electrolux was still able to gain certain scale economies through the establishment of foreign production (spreading R&D and other costs over additional sales and concentrating on standardized production).

And since the late 1960s, Electrolux has substantially expanded international operations by policies of investment and divestment. For example, US subsidiaries were sold off in the 1960s, but Electrolux re-entered US market in 1974 by purchasing National Union Electric (which manufactures Eureka vacuum cleaners). Since then, the company has expanded largely by acquiring firms whose product lines differed from those of Electrolux (to add appliance lines to complement those developed internally). Among fifty acquisitions made in the 1970s are Facit (another Swedish firm, which already had extensive foreign sales and facilities), and (to gain captive sales for vacuum cleaners) cleaning service firms in France and the USA; in addition, Electrolux invested in: Arthur Martin (French kitchen equipment manufacturer), Therma (Swiss home appliance firm) and Tappan (US cooking equipment manufacturer).

These acquisitions mostly involved firms that produced complementary lines (to enable the new parent to gain certain scale economies). However, not all the products of acquired firms were related, and Electrolux accordingly sought to sell off unrelated business. In 1978, for example, a Swedish firm, Husqvarna, was bought because of its kitchen equipment lines. Electrolux was able to divest itself of Husqvarna's motor-cycle line, but could not obtain a satisfactory price for the chain-saw facility; reconciled to being in the chain-saw business, Electrolux management then acquired chain-saw manufacturers in Canada and Norway (thus becoming, by investment, one of the world's largest chain-saw producers).

More recently, Electrolux announced a takeover of $175 million for Granges, Sweden's leading metal producer and fabricator, with 50 per cent of its sales of $1.2 billion outside Sweden; this has opened up the possibility of integrating Granges's aluminium, copper, plastics and other materials into Electrolux's production of appliances.

Contributory factors

The motivations behind international acquisitions can originate not only in the host country, but also in the parent, or 'source', country. These can be positive 'push' factors or negative ones. Among the positive factors can be the desire to diversify risk by having earnings in a variety of foreign currencies, or the need to exploit particular strengths abroad which the firm has built up at home. In certain circumstances, the firm may have under-utilized resources which can be used at very low cost abroad and can earn a reasonable return. Examples of this may arise in internationally skilled managers who can be moved away from routine operations to managing the start, or growth, of foreign ventures recently acquired.

However, the principal strategic advantage of acquisition by total ownership is that it assures greater managerial control over a foreign firm than is possible under a joint venture arrangement. The acquiring firm can implement its own policy and standards in such key areas as financial management, product quality, selection of managerial personnel and the disposition of profit. So with total ownership, the basic conflicts of interest sometimes found in joint ventures are avoided. There are three further substantial operating benefits accruing to the acquiring company: (1) market entry and revenue earning are immediate; (2) the purchase price includes not only the production facilities but also an established marketing and distribution organization, market knowledge and contacts, and some experienced local staff; and (3) the cash requirement for the purchase may be minimal, and it may be possible to issue shares in payment.

So an acquisitions policy can bring about timely entry into a market where sales potential can be exploited quickly through established trade contacts and channels of the acquired company. By contrast, if the firm seeking a presence in the market were to initiate its own venture, a year or two of intensive development effort would generally be necessary before the affiliate/associate company became fully productive. Through acquisition, however, the investing firm can take advantage of managerial talents, technical resources, trade contacts and the labour force of the acquired company, thus avoiding some of the major difficulties of starting a foreign venture. The acquiring firm can also benefit from the sales network and goodwill among distributors and major customers cultivated by the acquired firm during many years of trading. Acquisition can also reduce high risks usually associated with foreign ventures, because the acquired firm possesses a familiarity with the particular industrial environment and competitive conditions in the market.

While there are, therefore, both constraints and benefits in embarking on an acquisitions policy, it is really up to the management of the company to determine what its policy is towards the ownership of foreign ventures/enterprises. Such a policy can be set up only on the basis of

1. a comprehensive market data base on which management can plan priorities in terms of overseas market entry through acquisition and the market potential;
2. the determination of a set of marketing criteria and objectives by which investment decisions, operations and 'pay-back' can be assessed in the light of demand, market access and long-term market development.

Of course, the complexities of international business often frustrate the best laid marketing plans, but it is arguable that if the factors in (1) and (2) above do not measure up to the profit, sales and other criteria of the investing company in particular overseas markets, these should be bypassed in favour of those that do. Sometimes obstacles to trade make access to a promising overseas market practically impossible (e.g., duties making the landed price hopelessly uncompetitive) unless some sort of direct acquisition is undertaken. This sort of operating difficulty is well illustrated in Case example 3.12.

Case example 3.12

A UK firm manufactured a range of very high-precision engineering sub-components for sale to manufacturers of aircraft parts. This product range conformed to the relevant BSI specification, and was sold in large quantities throughout the world on the basis of high quality and minimal reject rates. There was, however, one important country where the range could not be sold because of the existence of a local standard specification which the British products did not meet in one comparatively unimportant detail. There was little doubt that that standard had been arrived at in consultation with the local manufacturers with the sole object of keeping out the world-renowned British products. The British manufacturer was confronted with a choice: to produce a special adaptation of the range for that country, or to opt out of a substantial trade. The problem was solved eventually by the acquisition of a local manufacturer, but not before the expenditure of valuable research and development time.

Other applications

In the situation described in the case example, the company found itself in the position of having to resort to an acquisition in order to gain a market position in a particular country. There are, of course, many other applications of acquisitions policies, and it is important at this point to show how the management of an investing company should adapt these policies to serve distinct and commercially viable marketing objectives. Some of the more generally used applications for management include:

1. to secure the supply and/or improve the cost effectiveness of procurement overseas (this has been a favoured policy in the UK wine trade among brewing, wine and hotel conglomerates seeking to control their supplies to UK and export markets by buying up wine properties and companies in France);
2. to acquire a manufacturing, processing or assembly plant in a potentially lucrative overseas market that would otherwise be dificult to service profitably or competitively owing to tariffs, quotas and other restrictions;
3. to obtain control of trade and distribution networks both within a particular market and among adjacent markets within an economically integrated region;
4. to buy out (i.e. eliminate) a competitor who, as a local supplier, has been taking out substantial business in an overseas market which it would otherwise be impossible for the acquiring company to obtain;
5. to secure 'complementarity' of product range, service offers or technology (acquisition can offer a faster route to extending the product/service offer than investment in new plant or new product development to meet special requirements of some overseas markets);
6. to benefit from the goodwill, trade contacts, local expertise and promotional investment already available in a suitable, acquired firm, rather than incur high initial costs of market development and heavy use of communications/media;
7. to use liquidity to secure the assets of an overseas company with a view to increasing the net international worth of the business, thereby strengthening the financial base and becoming a more attractive company for investors; there are also often tax advantages to be considered;
8. to apply an acquisitions policy on an international scale in order to reshape the business and move into new, high-growth sectors, in countries where it would

otherwise mean massive expenditures and management time to set up new businesses;

9. to achieve a level of expertise and strength in managerial resources, and in technology, so that the group of companies thus formed/acquired can dominate or compete profitably in highly industrialized economies and in high-growth industries. The Hanson Trust Group, for example, scrutinizes and evaluates managerial performance and effectiveness in public companies in basic industries such as food and building materials; where it can identify 'under-performance', under-utilization of assets, deteriorating financial ratios, failure to grow with the market and/or stagnation of business policies, it will acquire these companies, put in more effective management, and sell off those parts in intensely price-competitive markets—all this in the expectation of increasing the net worth of the business.

The internationalization theory

The above-described approaches in using acquisitions as a method of foreign expansion indicate that there are many different company characteristics that influence policies for acquiring foreign firms. Some recent research, however, indicates that three characteristics in particular are significant:[17]

1. the company's degree of internationalization or foreign experience;
2. the intensity of R&D operations;
3. the company's policy towards diversification/integration.

These comprise a well established explanation for acquisitions policies: the 'internationalization' theory.

The internationalization theory is based on certain assumptions. The firm that invests abroad is assumed to have developed a company-specific advantage in its home market, usually cited as superior knowledge/expertise in production or marketing of a product or service. Furthermore, it is assumed that this expertise, as an intangible asset, is developed within the firm, which then tries to exploit it profitably in international markets by acquiring local companies as a base for exploiting market potential overseas. There is also an assumption that the costs of market transactions between independent firms is higher than the administrative costs associated with exploitation within a wholly owned corporate structure. The theory also predicts that this tends to be the case the more knowledge- or technology-intensive the company-specific asset is, and this is reflected in a propensity to invest abroad rather than market through intermediaries. Of course, the greater the uncertainty about the foreign market, the higher will be the co-ordination costs of the investing company, and this in itself tends to reinforce the policy of acquisitions, with lower market uncertainty, more intelligence and contacts and trading expertise provided by the acquired enterprise.

Thus, in the internationalization process, the firm tends to choose acquisitions rather than direct investment in new plant, etc., to get a lower but less uncertain expected rate of return. So the theory predicts a correlation between a firm's degree of internationalization and its propensity to use foreign acquisition as its primary mode of expansion; indeed, the whole theory is based on the view of direct foreign investment as a mode of entry into a foreign market to exploit company-specific assets and expertise.

As far as intensity of R&D operations is concerned, the important point is that, the higher the technology on which the firm bases its asset, the higher is the buyer uncertainty and the more difficult it is to exploit the asset by means of ordinary market transactions; so the theory predicts that foreign direct investment by acquisition will be the usual strategy in technology-intensive firms. As for the degrees of integration/ diversification, the latter is interpreted mostly as entry into new and little known activities; and some research into this aspect clearly indicates that the more remote the new activities are, the greater the uncertainty, and the more likely the firm is to pay for the greater security of market entry by acquisition.[18] A firm that follows a pronounced diversification strategy, therefore, will show a greater propensity to use acquisition as an expanding strategy than will other firms. This tendency will be stronger the more the diversification strategy means going into areas unknown to the firm, whether these areas are in the home market or abroad.

Of course, much depends on the extent of diversification achieved. It is arguable that repeated diversification by going into a new activity or a new country will decline the more diversified the firm already is, because there is an upper limit to the number of business areas that the firm can handle. These findings are set out in a recent research study, which also discusses the 'network theory' approach to acquisitions based on inter-organizational relationships.[19]

Integration and divestment

It is the effective managing of both interfirm relationships, with suppliers, customers, etc., and intrafirm relationships, particularly in the acquired company, that will determine the long-term success of acquisitions policies. And advantages associated with taking over an existing organization and managerial personnel can, in part, be offset by the problems of integrating the acquired firm and its management personnel into the parent organization. This process of integration is complicated by basic differences in managerial philosophy and orientation arising from cultural and environmental variations, and the climate of insecurity often found in acquired firms.

Case example 3.13 shows how a recent foreign investment was made both to strengthen market position in the USA and to achieve 'synergy' in the newly formed organization.[20]

Case example 3.13

The purchase by Unilever in the USA of Chesebrough-Ponds (CP) in 1986 for $3.1 billion came at a time when Unilever's US food business was thriving on its success in margarine, and its household products division was holding up well against rival Procter & Gamble. The significance of this investment is that Unilever's health, beauty and cosmetics interests will benefit substantially from the strong product and market positions which come with CP's renowned brands like Vaseline, Cutex and Q-tips. So there is a synergistic aspect to this investment. Also, the extra profitability of the new group is expected to fund a large new product development programme, and more than treble Unilever's health and beauty sales in the USA. CP will bring a heightened profile in US drugstores and supermarket personal care departments; also, its profitable packaged food division fits neatly into Unilever's branded food-stuffs business. The best 'fit' of all is the skin care market. Unilever's success with skin care products like Fair and Lovely in India and Dawn in South Africa will now be complemented by the relative strength of CP's Vaseline brand (including Vaseline Intensive Care) in the USA and other Western markets. Application of the Vaseline brand to new products will also be considered; but, given the known difficulties of promoting internal growth in Unilever's weakest areas, the best option may be further acquisition.

At the same time, there has been divestment of businesses that do not fit the group's refined 'core operations' policy. Accordingly, much of CP's chemicals division will be sold off, and footwear and sporting goods interests will also be disposed of.

But there are situations in which investment policies can fail to bring about the financial benefits and market dominance that management planned in the first place. Such an outcome is often followed by divestment. Sometimes the new parent company insists on rapid cash pay-back on its investment, thus weakening the long-term competitive position of the acquired business by preventing it from keeping pace with growth in existing market sector(s). Alternatively, the new parent sometimes presses for growth from its newly acquired business, generating high profits: the acquisition can then weaken its own market boundaries, sometimes moving from a dominant position in a sector to a weak position in the total market. An investment policy also depends for its success on a realistic and up-to-date reading of the company being bought, particularly its competitive position *vis à vis* its market sector, and in the total market. For instance, the acquiring company must be alert to what may appear to be a dominant competitor in a market segment in reality being a weak competitor that has produced above-average performance by concentrating on those customers whom the truly dominant competitors have ignored. If that customer group were to continue to grow, or if growth in the overall market were to slow down, the truly dominant competitors would turn their attention to the neglected customer group. Profitability of the investment would fall precipitously, and divestment would almost certainly have to follow.

Finally, Case examples 3.14 and 3.15 show how the acquisitions policies of new businesses produced very different outcomes and why.[21]

Case example 3.14

US General Motors Corporation (GM) recently acquired Electronic Data Systems (EDS), a small competitor in the emerging robotics/production control industry. GM has gone to great lengths to maintain the strategic independence of EDS treating it purely as an investment acquisition, while at the same time providing it with major strategic advantages. GM created a special class of common shares to maintain the entrepreneurial spirit and incentive scheme for EDS management. Thus, it is attempting to shield the flexible management style necessary to 'high-tech' competition from the more entrenched traditions of Detroit. At the same time, GM's management intends to develop a communications standard for all computer-controlled production equipment to be used in GM facilities world-wide. EDS is expected to have a substantial share of that market, and thus will maintain its strategic independence while attaining enormous strategic advantage through market share expansion.

Case example 3.15

The Exxon Co. of the USA invested heavily in establishing itself in the office equipment market. The motivation behind this investment programme arose out of the position of Exxon. The world's largest company found itself in markets that were generally stagnant or declining. Management felt a need to establish a position in high-growth areas, and an area that promised dramatic growth was the 'office of the future'. During the second half of the 1970s, Exxon acquired a number of small- to medium-sized office equipment suppliers, many of which were reasonably profitable. The attempt to 'weld' them into Exxon Office Systems immediately gave them a very high profile, and brought them into out-and-out competition with industry giants like Xerox and IBM. Even the formidable financial strength of Exxon could not offset the strategic disadvantages; late in 1984, Exxon announced a major 'write-down' of its investment, and divestment of its office systems interests followed.

3.8   Factors influencing the development of modes

Introduction

In the last two decades, important changes have occurred in the character of international business. While direct exports still comprise a substantial proportion of, for example, UK total foreign sales, other modes of entry and operation have become increasingly used to establish and maintain strong market positions overseas. These include such operations as local manufacturing, licensing, and direct sales and direct investments (Table 3.3).

These developments have created new opportunities as well as some problems for senior management. International business now accounts for an important share of

Table 3.3 UK foreign sales, (1984) (*Source*: Department of Trade and Industry, 1985)

	%
Direct and indirect exports as % of total foreign sales	43.0
Licensed sales as % of total foreign sales	5.5
Foreign production of UK companies as % of total foreign and interfirm sales	51.5
Total	100

the business of many large corporations, as the development of overseas markets has increasingly required long-term commitments of capital, manpower and technology. Of course, there are major differences of approach among different industries and different markets, reflecting regional requirements and corporate market policies: licensed sales, for example, represent over 38 per cent of UK foreign sales in the chemical industry, but only just over 3 per cent in textiles, leather and clothing; and, while licensing represents over 40 per cent of the UK's total sales to Japan, it is only 1 per cent of sales to Canada.

Whatever method is adopted, the company's management is concerned to ensure that the company's products reach every overseas market by the most profitable means possible. Alternative modes, therefore, are the focus of this section.

Historically, research has shown that in practice the international business built up by companies evolved without any deliberate policy guidance or planning by top management. Much of this began in the form of direct export sales in response to enquiries from distributors overseas. Export sales were traditionally handled by export or shipping managers who did not have senior, and in some companies not even middle, management status. However, as a company's foreign markets grew, it began to encounter difficulties in supplying these markets through export operations because of import quotas and other restrictions imposed by foreign governments on finished goods. And, typically, management, faced with the alternatives of abandoning an overseas market or undertaking local production, usually chose the latter, once the market potential had been assessed as sufficient to justify the commitment. In fact, the initial impetus for such direct investment has often come from the overseas distributor who, understanding trading conditions and prospects at first hand, wished to benefit from a more permanent tie with the foreign firm in the form of a joint venture. Sometimes this can reflect the concern of the distributor at the possibility of losing the market if a competitor succeeds in persuading his foreign supplier to establish local production facilities first. Nevertheless, once a decision is made to enter a foreign market, management must face a number of aspects which require decisions: it must verify economic prospects and industrial or consumer sales potential, must satisfy trade regulations and legal requirements, must undertake complicated financial transactions, and must negotiate with departments or agencies of the host government.

Internationally, some UK companies have been reducing exports and moving production abroad because of government monetary and exchange rate policy. According to a recent report by the Confederation of British Industry,[22] 20 per cent of companies surveyed had withdrawn or reduced their export commitment when sterling was treated as a petro-currency, and 10 per cent had moved output abroad because they were being priced out of export markets owing to the continuing high value of sterling. Clearly, if this trend persisted, future exporting capacity would be reduced, even if, in the short term, companies were to overcome the exchange rate problem by moving output abroad. This survey, therefore, shows the risks of using exchange rates to manage domestic inflation, and highlights the difficulties for government policies in getting the right balance between a competitive exchange rate, interest rates, domestic inflation, export capacity and longer-term investment in overseas markets.

There are many criteria which, in practice, management must use in order to plan as near a rational decision as possible about entry. Not that rationality is everything: judgement, creativity and conceptual aspects all have a legitimate place in the final decision by the company as to which markets to enter and develop. (Certainly, statistics about an overseas market seldom tell the whole story.) But still, criteria are invaluable as a guide to decision-making, and these will be outlined shortly. Meanwhile, the overseas experiences of some companies described in Case examples 3.16, 3.17 and 3.18 illustrate succinctly some of the policy issues involved.[23]

Case example 3.16

The experience of United Biscuits (UB) illustrates how an analysis of competition underlines the need to have a direct stake in an overseas market. While UB was struggling to obtain an acceptable market share in Denmark, rivals Nabisco were taking 40 per cent of the Danish biscuit market through a local subsidiary, Oxford Biscuits. UB had depended on a distribution agreement with Copenhagen Bread Factories (CBF). CBF operated a bread van delivery sales force providing a daily coverage of the smaller shops in Copenhagen, and claimed good access to the co-operatives and multiples through a small national sales force. But these arrangements quickly proved unsatisfactory. The small bakers did not have the volume market for biscuits, and CBF did not have entry to the large high-volume outlets, nor did it demonstrate the determination to gain entry.

Taking account of Nabisco's continuing success, UB took bolder action and set up its own company in Denmark, United Biscuits A/S, which was to be concerned purely with selling (as opposed to selling and manufacturing). Even then, in its first two years' operation, the company failed to meet projected targets. This was due to incomplete utilization of the company's limited resources and ineffective sales management (e.g. haphazard journey planning and excessive efforts expended on selling to small independent retailers). As a result, management changes were made, including appointing as managing director a senior executive from a major competitor in Denmark. Both administration and sales then improved in effectiveness; UB products are now handled by every wholesaler in Denmark, and its share of total UK biscuit exports to Denmark increased from 26 to 53 per cent in six years.

Case example 3.17
Van Heusen (VH), the Taunton-based shirt manufacturers, faced a market situation that practically excluded direct exporting techniques when trying to capture a sector of the lucrative Japanese market. In this case, the management (taking account, of course, of the local trading conditions in their sector of industry) decided against setting up a wholly owned subsidiary, and, after a lengthy period of screening and negotiating, opted instead for a licensing agreement with a Japanese company. The licensee appointed has proved active in utilizing a large network of trade contacts and employs 60 representatives.

VH management recognized, through research and analysis of the market, that the company would make no headway in Japan without a licence agreement, because most retailers there, especially the large department stores, would not accept the product unless it was on a sale-or-return basis, and the company clearly could not cope with that condition on the basis of direct supply from Taunton. In fact, the licensee, Nissho-Iwai, produces about half a million shirts a year, and employs more marketing staff than the UK company. Yet it is this that now provides the back-up and market coverage essential in Japan.

Case example 3.18
A leading European consumer goods manufacturer, impressed with the rapid growth of the Japanese market, and anxious to beat its competitors in establishing operations there, hurriedly negotiated a joint venture with a local firm and, after obtaining government approval, constructed a new plant. The European management's objective, wrong as it turned out, was that, once it had established this foothold in Japan, it could then devote its attention to various operating problems. In fact, when operations got under way, the management found itself confronted by serious operating problems owing to severe local competition, the intricate web of business relationships governed by tradition, and the difficulties of breaking into the well entrenched distribution system. There was little that management could do to correct these problems, and the performance of the subsidiary remained at a level substantially below what the parent company had expected it to be.

Relevant criteria

The case examples illustrate some of the hazards of international market entry and underline the importance both of planning (discussed in Section 2.1 above) and of using researched and realistic criteria in making decisions about entry and mode of operations. First, there are 'company-specific' criteria to be set: these include corporate objectives, size of company, product line and nature of the product, company's market position and the level/intensity of competition. General criteria or factors relatively independent of the company include the following.

1. *Number of markets.* Different methods may have to be used to secure comparable coverage in different markets: a wholly owned foreign subsidiary may not be allowed in some countries, and in others licensing may not be possible because there are no qualified licensees.
2. *Penetration within overseas markets.* Quality of coverage is as important as extent of coverage; the structure of 'sub-markets' within the total overseas market can indicate specific opportunities. The degree of 'access' must be established, both by direct and non-direct methods, and, last but not least, demand analysis and an overall view of sales potential/prospects must be carried out.
3. *Market feedback.* Facilities for market reporting and intelligence, and forms of channel management and market infrastructure, must be established.

Then there is a set of financial and administrative criteria specific to the company which management must apply in appraising operations. Clearly, more direct involvement in market management enhances learning by experience; but there are other factors.

1. *Control.* The range of control depends on the channel: if the company has to exercise strong price control/leadership, then it must choose/use a channel that permits this. Channel use may change over time: the optimal mode today may have to be reviewed in three years.
2. *Incremental costs.* Clearly, marketing outlays and working capital will vary directly with the channel chosen. (With indirect exporting there are practically no additional costs; with own subsidiary, substantial costs.)
3. *Profit possibilities.* Management must estimate long-run sales volume and costs associated with each method as a basis for decision-making. (The highest profit margin may be the best only in the very short term.)
4. *Investment requirements.* This does not refer just to plant investment: there are some capital outlays needed for inventories and extension of credit. Investment is often the most important decision point for companies: criteria for determining 'pay-back' period and risk analysis (political and commercial).
5. *Administration and personnel requirements.* These include coping with international trade regulations and documentation and legal/contractual criteria, plus criteria relating to international management resources and skills needed to develop the business (transferability, acculturation, rewards, taxation, etc.).

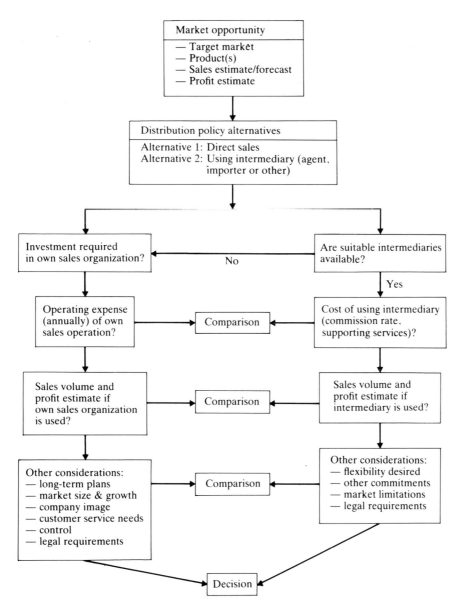

Fig. 3.6 Decision model: direct export sales *v.* sales through intermediary (*Source*: International Trade Centre UNCTAD/GATT, Geneva)

So, in determining which strategies for market entry and operations to adopt, management must take into account:

1. changes in trends, structure and access in overseas markets which may require a corresponding change in modes of entry and operations;
2. developing different modes of operation to penetrate overseas markets which are at very different stages of economic and industrial change;
3. choosing strategies for which the parent company has, or can acquire, the necessary financial, technical and managerial resources, and in particular the marketing expertise and trade networks appropriate to different countries;
4. setting marketing objectives and operating according to realistic financial targets in each of the company's overseas markets.

Finally, in getting involved in direct investments overseas, management faces another important decision: that is, it must determine the firm's policy towards ownership of foreign ventures. The ownership pattern of a foreign venture can range from no equity (i.e. only a contractual relationship, and/or debt financing), minority ownership, 50–50 split majority, to 100 per cent ownership. An investing firm can obtain equity participation in a foreign venture through a variety of ways, such as through contributions in cash, technical assistance, equipment, brand names, managerial know-how and stock of the investing firm. Combinations of any one of these alternatives is entirely possible. In fact, some of the most intricate financial arrangements are known to have been employed in acquiring equity in a new foreign venture.

Although the participation of local interest in foreign ventures is required in some countries such as India, Mexico and Japan, management has considerable flexibility in determining ownership patterns in other important markets, including those in the European Common Market.

There is a wide diversity in managerial attitudes towards ownership of foreign ventures. Some firms insist on, or at least prefer, complete ownership of their ventures, while others actively seek the participation of local interests. Although there are various ramifications to the ownership issue, the basic choice lies between total ownership and joint ventures. The advantages and limitations of each choice of mode require careful assessment, and have been given special attention in this chapter. Figure 3.6 also illustrates some of these factors when making decision about the modes shown.

References

1. C. Claxton, 'Federated Marketing', *Marketing*, December 1979.
2. Vern Terpstra, 'The Development of International Marketing', *International Marketing Review*, Summer 1987.
3. 'Glaxo Marketing Agreement in Japan', *Independent*, Market Report, 20 February 1988.
4. A. F. Millman, 'Licensing Technology', *Management Decision*, **21**, 3, 1984.
5. P. Hamman and H. Mittag, 'The Marketing of Industrial Technology through Licensing', *Proceedings of International IMP Research Seminar on International Marketing*, University of Uppsala, September 1985.

6. *US–Europe Countertrading*. Report of International Trade Commission. US Department of Commerce, Washington, DC, 1985.
7. S. Paulden, 'How Barter Trading Works', *Marketing*, April 1977.
8. *Countertrading*. Report by Department of Trade and Industry, Project and Export Policy Division. London: HMSO, 1985.
9. R. Moser, 'Countertrading: A New Marketing Instrument?' *Proceedings of the 13th Annual Conference of the International Association of Institutes of Export*, Vienna, 1986.
10. L. S. Walsh, *International Marketing* (2nd edn). Macdonald & Evans, 1981.
11. G. D. Newbould, P. J. Buckley and J. Thurwell, *Going International: The Experience of Smaller Companies Overseas*. Associated Business Publications, 1979.
12. Walsh, *International Marketing*. Checklist reproduced by permission of Pitman Publishing Ltd, London.
13. D. D. Sharma, 'Management Contracts and International Marketing in Industrial Goods', in E. Kaynak (ed.), *International Marketing Management*, Chapter 7. New York: Praeger, 1984; also in University of Uppsala, Reprint Series 1985/7 (Department of Business Administration).
14. J. Holly, 'Licensing, Franchising and Other Contractual Arrangements', *Handbook of International Trade*. London and Basingstoke, 1983, Chapter 3.7–02.
15. J. J. Boddewyn, 'Foreign and Domestic Divestment and Investment Decisions', *Journal of International Business Studies*, **14**, 3, Winter 1983.
16. J. D. Daniels and L. H. Radebaugh, *International Business: Environments and Operations* (4th edn). Reading, Mass.: Addison-Wesley, 1986, pp. 217–19.
17. B. D. Wilson, 'The Propensity of International Companies to Expand through Aquisitions', *Journal of International Business Studies*, Spring/Summer 1980.
18. R. Caves, *Multinational Enterprise and Economic Analysis*. Cambridge University Press, 1982.
19. M. Forsgren, 'Foreign Acquisition Strategy—Internationalisation or Coping with Strategic Interdependencies in Networks?' *Proceedings of International IMP Research Seminar on International Marketing*, University of Uppsala, September 1985.
20. C. Parker, 'Putting on a New Face in the USA', *Financial Times*, 3 December 1986.
21. J. V. Guineven, 'Establishing an Acquisition Policy', *European Management Journal*, **3**, 2, 1985.
22. *A Survey of UK Monetary Policy's Impact on Business*, Confederation of British Industry (CBI), London, July 1987.
23. K. Westall, 'Why Overseas Subsidiaries are worth the Headaches', *Business Administrations*, October 1977.

4
Managing international operations

4.1 Organization and systems

Introduction

Many different forms of corporate organization have been developed over the years by companies operating world-wide to enable them to develop, in a planned way, their international operations. The type of organization chosen will, of course, depend on many different factors, both internal and external. Every company will have certain internal organizational strengths and weaknesses; for example, a company can derive strength, organizationally, from

1. well established and productive trade links in some overseas countries;
2. organizational structure which both reflects and reinforces strong expertise in managing particular types of overseas operations such as manufacturing or licensing;
3. strong product positions in certain overseas markets and a strong corporate image, both the result of consistent, planned investment in product development and communications;
4. a strong commitment to and investment in research and development, reflected in the management structure.

Internal factors, therefore, are essentially all about resources: managerial, financial, technical and product. The essential point, of course, is that the external business environment is changing constantly, and what may have been organizational strengths, in terms of international competitiveness, two or three years ago can become redundant as business conditions change; so new organizational strengths must be built up to combat these changes.

Some of the external factors influencing changes in any enterprise seeking to maintain competitiveness include

1. increasing levels of national indebtedness in the world economy, and the corresponding need to develop special financial expertise in the company to cope with the problems of non-payment, late payment for goods and deteriorating foreign currency reserves in many overseas markets;
2. the growth of local supply and manufacturing bases overseas, particularly in the designated 'newly industrializing countries' (NICs), requiring changes in manage-

172

ment structure and skills which reflect the need for joint ventures, the export of improved technology, and productivity drives at home to maintain competitiveness with local suppliers and other foreign suppliers;
3. growing price competitiveness in international trade, and the impact of this on the company's organization in terms of improved productivity, investing in new technologies, currency management, and improvements in product/service quality, particularly the design function;
4. the growing importance of political, cultural and fiscal factors in opening up and maintaining market access in international operations, and the need to have these and related skills reflected in an appropriate management organization.

A first step in organizing effectively for international operations is the compiling of a management audit for international operations, encompassing, in detail, all those internal and external factors mentioned above.

The nature and extent of these key business factors clearly influence the shape of the organization and the management structure of the company operating internationally. Furthermore, management must also be concerned with achieving strategic targets, and many companies operating in distinct sectors of overseas markets adopt the concept of strategic business units (SBUs) to resource and direct task forces to exploit significant market sectors with high sales potential, particularly in the case of companies marketing specialized or industrial products. Another interesting approach is to organize the company's customer sectors under 'market' as distinct from 'product' managers; the rationale here is to make the company's organization more responsive and competitive in that it will reflect directly the structure of the company's major customer sectors. Product management, traditionally concerned with the development and sales of product lines (each controlled by a product manager across the whole spectrum of markets), has been judged by some companies to be increasingly ineffective in penetrating international markets because of its 'fragmented' structure.

Case example 4.1
An indication of the way some larger companies are moving to market management is provided by the Metal Box Co. Formerly this company was organized in three main product groups: open top cans, general line metal containers, and paper and plastic packaging. This meant that, in each of the major markets, customers typically had three independent sales operations servicing their requirements. This was a sales organization which did not encourage market development outside a factory's or division's product interest. However, with the market (and market management) organization that has replaced it, the total market is broken down into: (a) the beverage market; (b) the food market; and (c) general packaging (paint, cosmetics, pharmaceuticals, etc.). A complete product service world-wide can now be offered and developed by the 'market managers' concerned to each of the three key market/customer sectors.

In organizing for international operations, companies must ensure that the management and overall corporate structure are shaped to ensure continuing competitiveness. Clearly, organizational effectiveness alone is not enough: planning and control have an important part to play in sustaining overall competitiveness within planned parameters, timing and targets. Planning provides the system and operating procedures, and control ensures that performance against targets is monitored, and any corrective management action taken in good time. The organization provides the framework, and the nature of the organization will be influenced by such factors as: the level of international expertise, the level of involvement in international markets, the number of markets the company operates in, the overall size of the business, the nature of the products and services sold and the corporate goals set for the company in developing its international business. The essential aim of every organization is to achieve 'synergy'. But this does not come about on its own: managers must make it happen by integrating the various functions and separate national operations into a co-ordinated enterprise. While the principles of effective organization are as valid in multinational as in domestic operations, special problems can arise in the former because of communication gaps.

Approaches to international organization

There are a number of different approaches to international organization reflecting the different aims and conditions described above; clearly, there is no one optimal form. The two basic alternatives are

1. the separate/specialist approach—the international division;
2. integration—the global approach for the world company.

To take the international division first, the advantages of this approach are: centralization of all specialist skills and expertise; centralized focus and viewpoint to develop business; more effective allocation of resources; and more objective and realistic analysis of market potential by major world sectors. The disadvantages are that sub-optimization can result from the dilution of corporate resources; a growth of bureaucracy and inertia in the international division, resulting in too much analysis and rigidity; and management remoteness from 'front-line' trading operations. Also, there can be friction between international and domestic divisions. Regarding the integrated approach by the world company, there is no distinction between domestic and international business, the only discrimination being in terms of market size; also, while there is great potential to optimize performance, potential efficiency and profits, this is rarely fully achieved, owing to managerial inflexibility.

Nevertheless, the drive towards centralization can be hazardous, as Case example 4.2 shows.[1]

Case example 4.2

A few years ago, the Cinzano Company found itself faced with an ageing customer profile, particularly in Europe, North America and Australasia. It decided to apply the 'global' remedy by appealing to the world's youth (emulating the world-wide strategy of Coca Cola Co.). Under Swiss-based management, all important marketing decisions were made centrally. This proved to be both costly and frustrating for the marketing managers in the regions. For example, consolidating research from a common data base to achieve world-wide agreement and support was not easy: every idea or proposal from head office had to be 'bounced off' all the major markets for comment (usually by telephone or telex). The real cost in terms of time, money and management effort was in the planning process and putting together the centralized marketing plan. The company has now dismantled this centralized structure and is considering other approaches under the new ownership of International Distillers & Vintners (IDV).

Within these two main approaches, there are a number of different operating divisions which provide senior management with the following options.

1. *Area structuring*, or dividing the world geographically into regions (see Fig. 4.1): this appeals to marketing-oriented companies with relatively stable product technology, e.g. pharmaceuticals and automobiles. The advantages of area structuring are: easy communications; grouping of expertise; quick identification and rectification of area problems; exploiting political and economic groups, e.g. EEC. The disadvantages are: some inefficiency and duplication in management (i.e., several areas = several organizations); possible friction between areas and headquarters, and the emergence of gaps between countries in one area (increasing friction); and limited communication between areas.

2. *Product structuring*: this entails the division of global responsibility by product line, and it appeals to companies with diverse and unrelated product ranges, as in Fig. 4.2. The chief advantage of product structuring is flexibility: new divisions can be added easily. The disadvantages are: possible conflict between divisions at

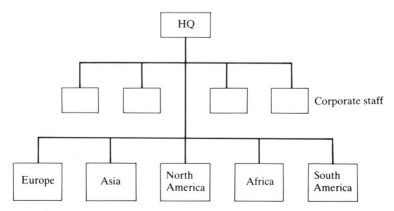

Fig. 4.1 Area organization.

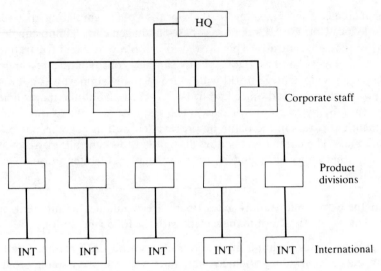

Fig. 4.2 Product organization.

board level; the structure is difficult to manage efficiently at board level; and effect-ive co-ordination is complex.
3. *Functional structure*: this involves the top executives responsible for the major function (finance, marketing, production, etc.) each having global responsibility. It is an approach that appeals to companies with narrow product lines, where prod-uct expertise is not a variable, and where regional variations are not significant; but it is not an approach in common use.

The matrix organization

Global problems with area, product and functional approaches have led to more complex approaches, and in particular to the development of the matrix organization, favoured by some multinational corporations. The matrix approach involves dual rather than single command chains; it gained support in the 1970s, but is not now so widely used as it is difficult to manage in practical terms. A topical example of the matrix approach is provided by Philips NV of Eindhoven. There are five tiers in its global organization:

1. the board;
2. product divisions with global responsibility for R&D, production, marketing;
3. service divisions with global responsibility for staff;
4. regional bureaux with liaising responsibility;
5. country organizations with 'on-the-ground' responsibility.

Clearly, there is no one ideal organizational format for international operations: some compromise is essential. After all, technology, size, mode of marketing operation and management, etc., are all variables. The objective is the format that best meets corporate goals, while minimizing the organizational problems.

Marketing operations: to centralize or not to centralize?

The single most important function discharged by an organization operating globally is marketing: the analysis of demand across national markets, and the resourcing and direction of marketing operations to exploit and meet this demand profitably. Marketing involves managing the product/market strategy and the communications mix (see Sections 2.2 and 2.3). In this respect, the organizational structure must ensure that management expertise and resources are transmitted continuously from headquarters to the region. In particular, marketing should tend to be a decentralized rather than centralized function; this is because it relates specifically to numerous overseas markets, and requires continual adaptation of the organization to the needs of each market. Also, it is increasingly recognized that commercial success depends upon skilful marketing rather than just product attributes.

If, therefore, the organization is essentially about the division of labour in management of a company, then the issue of centralization and decentralization is about the division of labour between headquarters and field operations. In setting up and implementing marketing policies at the corporate level, headquarters has the following responsibilities:

1. setting objectives/policies for world markets;
2. playing a major role in planning;
3. acting as a focal point for the development of new ideas, and back-up resources;
4. co-ordinating and integrating national programmes.

Under a decentralized organization, the local subsidiary

1. implements the plan within broad guidelines;
2. conducts market research;
3. has some initiative in product policy and pricing;
4. selects and administers distribution channels;
5. manages sales operations;
6. directs promotional programmes;
7. ideally, has dual reporting—local and headquarters management.

Depending on the size and complexity of the operations, some international companies prefer to centralize on regional offices rather than on one international headquarters. Regional headquarters have the following outline tasks:

1. to service and co-ordinate individual country programmes;
2. to report to and liaise with international headquarters;
3. to give specific support to business development within the region;
4. to ensure that regional management benefits from decentralization of marketing and control.

But, as noted in Case example 4.2, attempts by management to erase existing lines of communication and responsibility and 'redraw' them so that they converge on the centre are fraught with difficulty. The risk is not simply monetary: the company may also end up jeopardizing the goodwill of key local management in the process. So to overcome this problem, a number of multinational corporations are, in practice, looking at a compromise solution. Unable to choose between strong local organizations with autonomous marketing functions and a central marketing department responsible for several countries at once, management has increasingly settled on an organization with the two systems in tandem. The reasoning behind this approach is that an international marketing department superimposed on the network of local subsidiaries will provide 'the best of both worlds'. In practice, this does not always happen. In any kind of international advertising, there is a need for a central department that can mediate between various local/regional interests: but its ability to do this is entirely dependent on its influence within the organization and the extent of its control of budgetary allocations.

These hybrids of central and local marketing organizations take a multitude of forms, as is illustrated in Case examples 4.3, 4.4 and 4.5.

Case example 4.3

American Express has been running international advertising for many years, mainly in magazines such as *Time* and *Business Week*. This has given its European marketing department considerable power. All marketing strategies are formulated at the centre, since it markets itself to a homogeneous group throughout the world; local variations in markets are not wide. However, since charge/credit cards are at a different stage in their life-cycle in each country, local managers are allowed to adapt the strategy to their own needs. So, for instance, there is a Europe-wide advertising strategy, but local companies can determine the execution of the strategy in their own countries. In Britain, therefore, Amex advertisements have used Roger Daltrey, while in France they feature Michel Legrend.

Case example 4.4

By contrast, in Unilever the central marketing department has no operational budget of its own, and its role is therefore reduced to an advisory one. The company is highly decentralized, with each subsidiary setting its advertising expenditure according to its own local targets. The central marketing department sees its main task as providing an information exchange, by picking up ideas from one country and relaying them to subsidiaries in another. While this system has worked for many years, it could prove a severe hindrance if cross-national campaigns needed to be implemented. With each subsidiary looking after its own interests, the difficulty for management at head office will be to decide who is to look after the pan-European opportunities and, more important, pay for them. Management does not contemplate any major resources/

organizational change for the time being; the argument is that having a central budget can create as many problems as it solves. If there is no central budget, there is the problem of allocating the costs of international campaigns. If there is a central budget, this can create more and more pressure for international campaigns, because, effectively, the local companies benefit from free advertising.

Case example 4.5
A compromise between the positions in the two previous case examples has been adopted by Philips of Eindhoven. Unlike Unilever, with its central marketing function, the Dutch group gives its international marketing subsidiaries more responsibility with the necessary resources. The European marketing head has the authority to call in the heads of all the operating companies in his jurisdiction, and to set out the marketing plan and the benefits for each participating country. An international budget is agreed, and is then deducted on a *pro rata* basis from the marketing budgets of the participating countries. While this allows local managements to negotiate the amount of their contributions, it does guarantee a budget for pan-European marketing.

Planning and control

Whatever world-wide organizational structure is adopted, for the effective management of it, there must be a system of planning and control. If companies (whether subsidiaries or associates) market internationally to achieve corporate goals, control is simply the regulation and direction of operations to accomplish these goals. Control therefore involves

1. establishing standards;
2. measuring performance against standards;
3. correcting deviations from standards.

Control is closely linked to planning and organization, and a lack of control in international operations is usually due to communication or delivery gaps. In order to 'close' these gaps, and to minimize international and intercultural conflicts in business operations, there must be a centralization of strategic decision-making, corporate acculturation, systems transfer and personnel transfer. To ensure that this approach to corporate planning and control is actually made operational, it is necessary to implement

1. a standard planning system;
2. a standard reporting system;
3. international control/review meetings/committees;
4. international business publications;
5. business support systems;
6. a rotation of personnel.

In marketing terms, for example, standards should be applied to all phases of controllable operations, including market research, sales, market share/position, market penetration, distribution, the communications mix and the deployment of agents. In expressing the outcome of operations in financial terms (profit, ROI), special account has to be taken of currency movements, taxation, remittances and equity ownership. Setting standards is, however, a complex task, and requires operating plans, reviews and personal contacts among different subsidiaries to minimize conflict. In other words, communication is the key in setting standards that are internationally understood and that will act as measures of both personal and corporate performance. Again, to take the marketing function as an illustration, two specialized measurement techniques available to management are

1. the marketing audit—by which the total marketing effort is examined;
2. distribution cost analysis—which determines the profitability of different parts of the marketing programme.

In directing the development of the total business internationally, there are three major aspects to setting up management systems of overall strategic control; these are shown in Table 4.1.

The question of management development, to ensure implementation of operating systems, has also to be considered. This applies, of course, as much to local managers as to expatriates: while the expatriate clearly has to be mobile, adaptable and dependable, and must remain motivated (sometimes in a difficult working environment), the position of the local manager is increasingly important in view of many governments' policies of 'localization'. The local manager will require intensive or accelerated training, and management experience perhaps outside his own country. Clearly, in both cases special attention must be paid to remuneration and reward systems, the costs to the company of employing expatriates, acclimitization (linguistics and work ethic), special factors in local working conditions, relationships with host governments, the direction and level of investment put into the major overseas markets, and the operating aspects of corporate and business plans in different national environments.

Table 4.1 Setting up management systems for overall strategic control

Data management	Manager management	Conflict resolution
Information systems	Selection of key managers	Decision and responsibility assignments
Measurement systems	Career paths	Co-ordinating committees
Resource allocation procedure	Reward systems	Task forces
Strategic planning	Management development	Issue resolution process
Budgeting process	Socialization and acculturation	Encouragement of creativity

Case examples 4.6 and 4.7 show how an increasing commitment to the global co-ordination of marketing policies is often accompanied by attempts to tighten co-ordination in particular regions.[2]

Case example 4.6

Kodak recently experimented by consolidating 17 world-wide product line managers at corporate headquarters. In addition, the company made marketing directors in some countries responsible for a line of business in a region as well as for sales of all Kodak products in their own countries. Despite these new appointments, country managers still retain profit-and-loss responsibility for their own markets.

Whether a matrix approach such as this broadens perspective rather than increasing tension and confusion depends heavily on the corporation's cohesiveness. Such an organizational change can clearly communicate top management's strategic direction, but headquarters needs to do a persuasive selling job to the field if it is to succeed.

Case example 4.7

Procter & Gamble has established so-called Euro-brand teams which analyse opportunities for greater product and marketing programme standardization. Chaired by the brand manager from a 'lead country', each team includes brand managers from other European subsidiaries that market the brand, managers from P&G's European technical centre, and one of P&G's three European division managers, each of whom is responsible for a portfolio of brands as well as for a group of countries. Concerns that the larger subsidiaries would dominate the teams and that decision-making either would be paralysed or produce 'lowest common denominator' results have proved groundless.

4.2   Management development and control

Introduction

There is a spectrum of relationships which can be described as running from 'open' to 'closed' in the degree of control exercised by the parent company over its subsidiaries. The most completely closed relationship occurs when the foreign subsidiaries are managed as if they were extensions of the domestic operations. Their autonomy is no greater than that of an operating unit in the home country and may well be less. At the other end of the spectrum, there exists a purely investment relationship whereby the parent company is the sole principal shareholder in the subsidiary, but is interested only in collecting dividends. Control is exercised purely through the annual meeting and representation on the board. The spectrum itself can be seen as a scale along which any given company, or given relationship within a company, can be placed.

There are still difficulties in placing companies on this spectrum, although this research is being pursued. One of the reasons for this is that degrees of influence or authority have to be assessed, not just the position where a decision is taken. This can be discovered only by extensive research within the company, as the actual degree of authority so often differs from the perception of any one individual. The placing of a company is further complicated by the need to look at the informal as well as the formal situation. In spite of the difficulties, however, enough evidence has come to light to permit some general observations.

A company does not usually have a very open relationship between some units and a closed one between others. Some of the evidence for this assertion has already been widely established. A number of factors are expected to influence the relationship, including the size of the subsidiary, its nationality and its age; also, it is frequently suggested that the relationship will differ according to the function. The question of size is one that contains another paradox. Some companies argue that there is a closer relationship with the larger subsidiaries because of the effect that they can have on the well-being of the group as a whole. Other companies suggest just the opposite: that the large subsidiaries could look after themselves and that close control was reserved for the small ones.

There is also a complex relationship between control in the sense of reporting, and control in the sense of exercise of authority. There is the question of how far the amount of reporting is linked to the degree of centralization of authority. The most significant factors would appear to be as follows: (1) that a large amount of reporting from a foreign, though not necessarily from a domestic, unit forces conformity to head office method, and (2) that companies which exercise a close relationship with their foreign subsidiaries are just the ones that also develop elaborate control systems.

Strategies of control

The current variation in measures of control exercised by head office, particularly in Western industrialized countries, derives from four strategies which have evolved over the years.

The first of these is the exploitation of natural resources abroad. In Europe this particular strategy has a long history, going back to colonial times. The next strategy is international manufacturing; this includes companies that go abroad to make a wider use of their technical lead. The third strategy is called commercial; it is essentially defensive in character—the building of one or two plants abroad to counter threats to the market—and starts with an open relationship. The fourth strategy arises where some geographical diversification is a main motive and where the parent company regards itself as the holding company. This is called an investment strategy, and the contact between head office and the subsidiary may be really that of consultant to client.

It is difficult to relate centralization to success or failure, since many other issues are involved. But two points are clear. One is that deviations from the norm are usually caused by companies being pressed by particular problems at particular times. The other point is that performance depends not just on a *variety* of factors, but on a combination—the right combination.

Another major aspect is head office's understanding or lack of understanding, of local market conditions. Lack of knowledge of basic market conditions is one of the major obstacles to the development of an effective control relationship between head office and subsidiary in international marketing. When head office commits itself to measure and evaluate subsidiary performance, the decision commits head office to participate in subsidiary planning. Measurement and evaluation of current performance are intrinsically involved in the planning cycle of operations and programmes in future time periods. In order to become effectively involved in this planning cycle, head office must understand the basic characteristics and conditions of the subsidiary market. If there is inadequate understanding, head office may adversely or inadequately influence the design of the country marketing plan for future periods and may misunderstand the significance of operating results in current periods. The result of such a misunderstanding can involve major failures if head office succeeds in imposing an inappropriate plan on subsidiaries or influencing subsidiaries to accept inappropriate objectives.

Perhaps even more dangerously, head office misunderstanding can result in a failure of subsidiaries to achieve their full potential in a market. If head office does not understand the basic characteristics of a market, it will not be able to pinpoint subsidiary under-performance. The problem in international operations is a counterpart of the problem of managing product divisions in different technologies in a divisionalized company. In order to manage a product division, corporate management must understand the basic technology of the products being managed. If they do not understand the technology, divisional management virtually has free rein to develop its plan and explain its performance.

One often finds, when studying companies that are expanding, that head office's understanding of foreign markets is enhanced in one important way: it is actively involved in the subsidiary planning process. This involvement ensures that head office executives learn about each subsidiary and each region's market conditions. A few sophisticated companies are assigned approximately equal numbers of domestic and foreign executives to their international head offices in an effort to obtain an effective mix of home product and system know-how and international environmental knowledge in the head office group.

The other issue is that of consistency. One of the difficulties of control systems in overseas operations is an attempt by headquarters management to apply a consistent standardized approach to world-wide control. There is a view held by some managers that a well run company should evidence the consistent application of tools and practices. If there is a best way to control international operations, should it not be applied on a universal scale?

There is no single best control system. There is a best way to control international operations only if these operations are homogeneous. Most companies that have extended themselves to more than one continent find their operations to be highly differentiated in terms of the kinds of markets they have, the length of experience of subsidiaries and a host of other factors. The skilled and sophisticated international enterprise recognizes this diversity, and develops control relationships with regions and subsidiaries based on the major variables influencing controls. If a subsidiary is large and has a highly developed headquarters staff of its own, if the management of the subsidiary is highly confident, if the market in which the subsidiary operates is highly differentiated from other markets and requires a differentiated response to achieve company sales and profit objectives, then a differentiated control system is needed. If a company's technology, its size and position in markets, its communication relationships, its markets and the competence of local management are uniform around the world, then a uniform control system is appropriate. Since these conditions are rarely if ever achieved, it follows that all control systems should be differentiated to respond to relevant differences. The secret of success is in developing systems that are responsible for, but not unique to, each market.

As far as the management and development of personnel in overseas operations are concerned, policies still tend to be based upon domestic policies or extensions of these rather than on rational choice. Personnel practices are more *ad hoc* and short-term; in short, there is a lack of a more systematic approach to the personnel management function, and this aspect requires early attention by those companies expanding their overseas operations.

Management development policy

Owing to the diversity of the environments in which firms with overseas subsidiaries operate, staffing is subjected to a variety of influencing factors, both internal and external to the firm. These factors affect the choice of an effective management development policy and the subsequent implementation of the chosen policy. This can be shown clearly in a simple three-stage model as in Fig. 4.3.

Research and analysis of overseas operations over a number of years have identified a number of sets of these 'influencing factors'. Foremost among these are the following company characteristics.

1. *Ownership of foreign subsidiaries.* A different policy, and indeed a different kind of person, will be required according to whether the investment is short- or long-term. The investment that is expected to be short-term can be used either as a training place or as a final posting for those about to retire. The latter policy would overcome the problems of reintegration. Similar considerations may apply where minority holdings are concerned; but in joint ventures considerable powers of diplomacy and knowledge of the company may be required. Longer-term management policies are appropriate where the parent company has majority or total ownership. Many companies use skilled international staff in all of these situations.

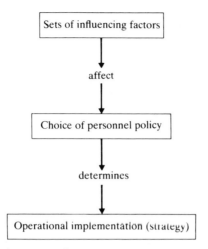

Fig. 4.3   Management development policy.

2. *Industry group.* Policies will vary at least between manufacturing and service industries. The latter may depend more on intangible knowledge from head-quarters, and so are likely to continue to employ expatriates, although this does not necessarily apply to banks, which employ local nationals for their knowledge of local business conditions.

3. *Technology.* The level of the technology in terms of sophistication, together with the amount of the research effort needed to sustain it, will affect the policies of both the technical and the marketing departments. This will apply particularly when the transfer of knowledge virtually requires the transfer of staff. There is some evidence, too, that companies operating in high-level technologies are more likely to transfer other personnel policies.

4. *Market influences.* If the market for the product is purely local and the techniques employed are well within the capacity of local management, expatriates or third-country nationals are much less likely to have a part to play than where global techniques are applicable in world-wide markets.

5. *Age of investment.* The older foreign subsidiaries are likely to have established means of staffing which are hard to change unless problems arise.

6. *Organization structures.* Companies with product group world-wide structure are likely to have more expatriates; those with matrix organizations are almost cer-tain to have some international management development schemes.

7. *Commitment to international business.* A company that does not have a substan-tial part of its business abroad would not consider the more elaborate schemes for international promotion.

8. *Cost factors.* These are debatable, and there is no formula for working out the costs and benefits of the possible programmes. The costs of expatriates of all types, especially third-country nationals, are increasing rapidly; but the benefits

have also been shown to be so great as to make their employment almost certain under some conditions.

9. *The communication and coordination system.* This may affect staffing policies in many ways. One is the use of international transfers, meetings and educational programmes to facilitate communications.

10. *Style of management.* Companies will settle for a distinctive style which suits their business or their personalities. This style is likely to be culture-bound, however, and may cause difficulties.

In addition to company factors, the policies are also influenced by the characteristics of individuals who may be available. These include their life-style, their expectations and their ambitions and can be listed as follows:

– qualifications and experience;
– record of previous performance;
– commitment to international business, including aspirations to international promotion;
– suitability for international business, including ability to adapt to new environments and to show sensitivity to new situations; family commitments.

Finally, there are the host country characteristics.

1. *Level of economic development.* This naturally affects the ability of the company to recruit in a given country either for local or for international posts. On the other hand, there will be pressure on the company to assist the development process by the establishment of educational programmes to facilitate rapid promotion. Applications for permits for residents, wherever they come from, are likely to be scrutinized even more carefully in those countries that have most need of foreign management; the industrialized countries place less obstacles to the movement of managers across frontiers.

2. *Political stability and nationalist sentiments, including the propensity to nationalize or expropriate.* Similar considerations apply, but skilled and experienced management may be required to maintain a presence or get the best possible terms for a withdrawal.

3. *Control of foreign investment and immigration policies.* The control of ownership and the issue of work permits are usually the subject of negotiation, even where there are laws on the subject. If the company has international policies, however flexibly they have to be operated in practice, these will aid negotiations.

4. *Availability of qualified and experienced managers and the need to develop and promote local managers and technical staff.* These considerations apply in the same way as those already listed.

5. *Socio-cultural setting.* There are clearly problems of adjustment across boundaries of culture, race, language and religion. There are equally clearly some boundaries that cannot be crossed; these are mainly political, and they sometimes prove impermanent. In general, these problems are the subject of many myths which are

dispelled in practice. Some of the most difficult cultural boundaries are crossed successfully, and the myths are dispelled after brief examination. On the whole, if other considerations require that a manager move between two incompatible countries, then selection and training can minimize the problem to the point where they become tolerable.

6. *Geographical location.* As with the socio-cultural setting, the location is obviously an important consideration, but it does not make for impossible difficulties for actions that are otherwise desirable.

These influencing factors are by no means exhaustive. They do include some of the more important factors affecting the rational choice of an international management policy. Within each set, variables themselves are interdependent. That is to say, a number of influencing factors within the host country may interact to affect strongly the choice of one particular policy rather than another. Also, each set of influencing variables interacts with the others. In choosing a management development policy, one set may be weighed by itself and, in comparison with the others, especially with a view to reconciling differences between the three parties involved: the company, the individual and the host country.

4.3 Integrating key functions

Introduction

Management practice, as it has traditionally applied to international business, however, still tends to be fragmented. For example, the financial implications of marketing planning are not communicated sufficiently to staff responsible for developing overseas business; nor are the design and technical functions integrated early enough in the planning process. The importance and topicality of a 'task force' or 'integrated approach' to markets by management has been stressed at the highest level of industry:[3]

> Management is itself insufficiently aware of international markets—and more particularly of how the design, engineering, manufacturing and selling disciplines have to be integrated if competitiveness is to be sharpened. A major task lies ahead for management in creating technically literate, professionally skilled and internationally experienced management at all levels in our companies . . . The breadth and experience necessary to develop trade routes has to pervade all levels of a company so that its culture is international.

Management must seek to identify the extent to which European industrial competitiveness can be enhanced by an improved integration of management functions in overseas operations, particularly

- operations management,
- research and technical development,
- design,
- marketing,

– supply,
– finance.

(Effective management of these is illustrated in Fig. 4.4 below.)

Management is faced, therefore, with a number of options in bringing about integration to improve competitiveness:

1. closer integration of key management functions, to bring about better structured decision-making and longer-term planning in international markets;
2. closer liaison between finance and marketing, to produce more competitive offers to international customers and to ensure higher levels of company profitability;
3. 'task force' approach to international markets, to help companies penetrate markets and establish/sustain a long-term position of market strategy, rather than a short-term tactical presence based on individual countries or customers.

There has been some research on management integration, but more is needed. One important analysis[4] found that, in exporting and non-exporting manufacturing firms, a failure to compete internationally was caused mainly by managerial apathy. This analysis provides an important base from which to start, as it focused on the quality of management as a determinant of international competitiveness. Three measurements were used to assess this.

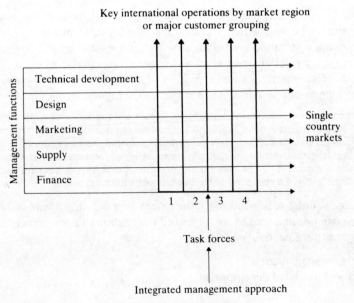

Fig. 4.4   Organizational matrix for international competitiveness.

1. Peer evaluation showed that the firm with superior planning, research and decision-making had procedures to integrate all functions.
2. Self-evaluation by management showed a more aggressive approach to business development internationally.
3. Integrated management practice was found to correlate with firms expanding international trading.

Further empirical research signifying the importance of integration was contained in Barclays Bank International Report, 'Factors for International Success'[5] This found serious undermanning of UK operations adversely affecting the competitiveness of companies; sales staff, for example, were spread too thinly over too many markets (particularly in comparison with France and West Germany, and indeed Japan). This BBI research discovered two other important factors.

1. There were significant differences between the UK and the other two countries as far as the role, status and reward of middle management are concerned. In the UK there was a lower appreciation of middle management's vital role, not only in the development of exports, but also in the attainment of standards of quality of the product, the overall efficiency of operations, and indeed the dynamism of a company depending largely on middle management. In contrast, every encouragement appeared to be given to middle management in France and Germany in terms of status, responsibility and remuneration.
2. British companies appeared to employ fewer people in their international operations than the French and Germans. This is due to the importance given by the latter to the quality of the overseas selling organization. It was not new technology but imaginative and enthusiastic French marketing that brought about that country's impressive expansion of exports during the decade up to 1980.

   Skill in selling was not, however, sufficient by itself. British export sales specialists were compared favourably with their French and German counterparts—but large British companies in the sample employed fewer people in their export departments than in their home sales departments.

The main objective, then, is the identification and quantification of benefits in terms of increased international competitiveness through better integrated management organization for planning and business development. The focus is on effective management organization as a competitive weapon for European industry. Undermanning in one vital sector, for example sales, is a direct consequence of inadequate management organization to cope effectively with increasingly sophisticated demands of overseas customers in a competitive world.

The question remains, How can management bring about better integration? Two practical options arising out of some of the research so far quoted are:

1. setting up task forces, which can be deployed in key overseas markets, and which are made up of sales staff supported by design and technical staff, who can respond

to customers' requirements as a team and present a 'package' to overseas customers which is technically up-to-date, competitive in design and range, etc.;
2. assessing benefits of closer interfaces in all overseas operations, particularly between finance and marketing and technical development and marketing.

Task forces

Planning and organization have been looked at in Section 4.2. The entire concept of building task forces and setting up teamwork in international markets must of course encompass the financial as well as other functions.

The task-force-orientated approach is illustrated in the matrix in Fig. 4.4. There are responsibilities for management to grasp in implementing the concept in it.

1. The financial and marketing implications of export policy need to be set up in a co-ordinated way.
2. The typical management structure leans towards 'separation' rather than 'integration' of functions.
3. Export marketing staff need to have greater financial expertise and support if they are to develop profitable business overseas.

Closer interfaces between functions

Particular attention needs to be paid to the interface between technical development and marketing. New technology such as robotics and microcomputer-based designs and controls now make it possible not only to maintain volume production and quality but also to offer more varieties of products of consistent quality at comparable unit output costs. There is also the extent to which information technology (IT) is being used effectively by management for analysis and world-wide communications (e.g. accessing international product codes and data retrieval). The implications of these for marketing management's planning are significant and show the extent to which company competitiveness can be sharpened by integration. There is also the interface between supply and marketing: surveys reported by British Institute of Management and Cranfield Institute of Technology[6] suggest that poor supply performance by UK firms reduces promotional effectiveness, and that this can be improved by more investment in new technology such as flexible manufacturing systems (FMSs).

Case example 4.8

A British company manufacturing prefabricated building materials and components for sale to the Far East, having previously used only sales staff abroad, decided to send out a senior designer to accompany the sales staff. The result was that customers' special requirements could be redrawn overnight, and new design concepts introduced and discussed on the spot, avoiding lengthy correspondence and consultation with the home base. Technical service and design quality for customers improved substantially, and within three years the company had doubled its export turnover in this region by penetration at the expense of competitors.

Management must assess the performance of these key tasks, with the focus on improving the terms offered to overseas customers so that the company's competitive position is strengthened and profitability is ensured. As the company's involvement overseas grow in the more successful markets, so investment decisions in new plant, direct representation and large-scale financing have to be made.

An earlier research study published by the Royal Society of Arts highlighted the importance of the interface between marketing and supply.[7] This report singled out production problems as being often the biggest limitation to international sales growth. It reported supply shortfalls and an irregular flow of components as responsible for many bottlenecks, and cited instances where 300 per cent higher prices were being paid for imported components—to speed up orders to overseas customers. (The lack of adequate steel supplies, for example, was singled out as frequently responsible for unduly long delivery dates and loss of overseas orders.) Since this research was carried out, there are still indications that supply management requires a thorough overhaul and, above all, much closer integration with marketing planning and operations. And management is having to operate under conditions of increasing uncertainty in international markets, such as political risks, commercial risks and competition from newly industrializing countries (NICs). Added to this are financial uncertainties, particularly in the movements of interest rates and currencies.

These external factors alone demand the closest possible collaboration between the finance and marketing functions: the financial implications of alternative export marketing strategies must be set out in terms of offering not only an attractive product range but also a competitive set of financial offers. Indeed, planning marketing activities for overseas demands the most careful financial interpretation of the objectives set and the means of achieving these objectives. This approach is essential

- to 'out-market' competitors with a superior 'total package', and
- to secure improved financial returns to the exporting company.

Financial considerations

The financial package offered by the company has become a vital part of its offers to customers, and there is clear evidence that the nature of competition has been changing and that the management tasks and organization need to be reappraised. Longer credit terms are essential to sustain a position overseas: this is an investment decision (tying up money) as well as a marketing decision. Furthermore, the financing of additional capacity or the setting up of subsidiaries abroad means investment on a more substantial scale.

The net effect of these considerations is that international trading must increase demands on the company's financial resources under conditions world-wide where the profitable use of these resources is less certain. Of course, the effect can be offset to some extent by government services in making exporting more profitable through the provision of low-cost finance, remission of some internal taxes, financing of exports, credit insurance and the facilitation of international transactions. But it is up to the company to organize its export operations more profitably, using the findings of this research, and it can do this only if analysis and planning draw on the joint expertise in the company. Consider, for example, the assessment of long-term prospects of an international market and the expected return on the company's investment over a given period, the impact of inflation on pricing policy, and market potential. These and other vital questions require both financial and marketing expertise to resolve. Yet in many manufacturing companies (on the basis of some empirical research already cited), management organization is such that there is woefully insufficient dialogue between finance and marketing staff, let alone decision-making to raise competitiveness.

Case example 4.9
A British company could have helped his French buyer as follows. The exporter had sold to France in sterling, and the period from date of order to date of payment was approximately six months. The French buyer, wishing to cover his exchange risk, approached his bank in Paris in order to buy the sterling forward six months. He was told, however, that he was only allowed to buy forward up to two months and he was thus exposed to an exchange risk for the remaining four months. The British exporter, on the other hand, should have invoiced in French francs and sold forward on the London money market up to twelve months, if necessary; had he done so, he would have secured the order in the first place, whereas in fact the French buyer delayed confirmation, with a resultant loss to the exporter.

Case example 4.10
Another case with a more successful outcome occurred in 1980, when a British exporter, although requested to quote in sterling, was encouraged by his advisers to quote for a large contract in Germany in both sterling and D-marks. At the time, the three-year-forward premium on the D-mark was equivalent to no less than 15 per cent on the face value of the contract, and so the exporter was able safely to reduce his D-mark quotation by 5 per cent. Confronted by the two quotations, the Germans converted the sterling price into D-marks at the spot rate and were then surprised to find that the D-mark quotation was cheaper than the one in sterling.

Keeping the sales staff informed
Sales staff take orders, but find that they are unable to match interest rates or credit terms offered by their competitors, as a result of which the order is not confirmed; or they accept orders on unprofitable terms. Such lapses can be avoided by more detailed briefing by financial staff, and by using government financial support for visits and missions overseas.

Take, for example, Schedule 2 of the ECGD, which is sent regularly to policy-holders. This schedule is a confidential document containing vital information on

1. the credit and foreign exchange status of all export markets covered by the policy and their financial prospects;
2. lines of credit available to finance bilateral trade agreements and the markets concerned.

Many sales and marketing staff never see, let alone consult, this document, which is sent to and held by the financial controller; some have never even heard of it. In the light of these and other instances of management 'separation', management should consider setting up 'overseas task forces' which bring together operationally managers in key sectors such as marketing and finance (one might add design and supply), so that a total policy to penetrate markets and maximize profits and cash collection can be set up and implemented.

Developing a policy of integration

Management should take steps to ensure that their companies gain from a policy of integration rather than separation. These steps can include the following (and each involves at least three functions).

1. Set out marketing objectives, methods of penetration, pricing and market follow-up, with the full financial implications.
2. Review full sales potential of each overseas market, and determine investment in technical and design work beforehand, so that financial returns can be maximized and the company's market position or prospects safeguarded.
3. Analyse and remain alert to improvements in the price thresholds perceived and accepted by overseas customers in the light of non-price benefits and of competitors' offers.
4. Study competitive design and supply capabilities, and improve both through integrated management action.
5. Critically review the competitiveness of trade terms (e.g. INCOTERMS) offered as part of total marketing 'package'.
6. Set up and maintain closer working relationships among financial management and export marketing staff and, where appropriate, export supply and design, so that the company has a controlling overseas project group responsible for total implementation, including major contracts.
7. Set up or buy in management expertise so that the company can get and offer the best terms in foreign currency dealings, and know what it is doing.
8. Ensure that all marketing staff working abroad are better equipped—to understand their customer's business and provide advice on business development, and to undertake negotiations successfully with overseas customers, using financial as well as sales expertise.

Management v. the professionals

The need to develop some policy about management integration, particularly for international operations, is given more immediacy by some new trends in management organization. First, there is the challenge of the 'professionals'. Peter Drucker, recently addressing the American Management Association (AMA), has warned of the coming domination of the corporation by two potentially conflicting cultures; that of managers and that of professionals. There is growing unease in many European companies over the rising presence and influence of new professional employees—engineering, computer, finance, design, research and other specialists. Professionals account for more than a fifth of total employees in the EEC and a third of those in USA; and companies are cutting down on traditional managers and skilled, unskilled and semi-skilled workers who no longer fit in with new strategies.

In addition to cultural clashes, the advance of the professionals presents problems of organization. Just where do the new professionals fit in? Who manages whom? What is the professional's pay in relation to the manager's? Pension schemes, performance rewards, management training and promotion policies are all having to be reworked. Those relatively few professionals employed in companies in the past enjoyed a certain autonomy, freedom from business management roles and a status afforded by outside professional affiliations. Even so, managers conflicted with scientists over plans or budgets for new technical ideas; management consultants Arthur D. Little have concluded in a recent analysis that leading break-throughs often succeeded in spite of uncooperative managers. Such managers do not normally fit into 'the sub-culture that generates, without much discrimination, new ideas, and brilliant breakthroughs', the consultants reported. For the most part, however, managers ran the businesses and controlled the workforce. The few professionals were often alienated, sometimes of their own choice. Companies needing to make better use of these—'professionals'—are those moving away from labour to capital—particularly banking, insurance, computer, and TV and media, and other service sectors.

Another recent research study has warned of 'a negative impact on organizational effectiveness' when proper integration between professionals and the rest of the organization is lacking.[8]

This lack of integration clearly bears some of the responsibility for the 'historically poor competitiveness of Britain's manufacturing industry'. Some companies are finding it difficult to adjust, particularly those in once conservative industries that are now dependent on those with new professional skills—in particular, specialists in mergers, acquisitions, property, computers, international finance, food research and others. Head offices in these sectors are becoming staffed more by specialists who are playing their part in greater centralization; and local branch management is losing its decision-making role and is responding to the centre.

Future prospects are likely to be increasingly coloured by this interface between managers and professionals. The companies are going to turn into the 'flexible firm', according to a model developed at the Institute of Manpower Studies at Sussex University. It will employ only a small core of full-time professionals, with specialized managers running everything from the centre; part-timers and contractors will serve its other needs.

Project management

The other significant trend is the emergence in the 1980s of 'project management', from a specialist function largely confined to the engineering and construction industries, to a common discipline used in a variety of sectors. While many organizations identify and develop more autonomous profit centres, a range of factors often makes it necessary to commission projects that affect the organization as a whole. Common examples include: the introduction of new technology, change of corporate design, development of a new product or new market, an office move, a company takeover, or the design of a new building.

In many organizations, important projects are used as a testing ground for junior or middle managers. Their potential is judged on their ability to define objectives and see these through. The key to this is recognizing and reconciling the interests of everyone who has a stake in the project. This is often a highly delicate process. In the introduction of a new computerized information service, for example, the project leader will have to take into account the view of senior management, who probably will not understand the technical complexities but will have strategic objectives. Departments within the organization will all have different requirements. Staff who operate the hardware will need systems they can use easily, together with tailored training and support. Project leaders need to recruit a team drawn from different departments, functions and even countries. They need the skills to establish a common culture and commitment, drawing in members of the organization who are not directly involved in the project but are concerned with its outcome. The task is therefore highly political. To succeed, project leaders have to develop close working relationships with the senior manager or director to whom they are responsible, and will have access to confidential information.

Conclusion

In conclusion, the role of senior management in bringing about close integration of key management functions is crucial in developing the international competitiveness of the company. All the evidence cited in this section points towards this priority. What, then, are some of the specific tasks of management in this context?

1. Setting up an effective planning process on the basis of a clear international strategy.
2. Ensuring that planning is based on full, valid data, and involves all areas of management.
3. Allocating responsibilities to key teams or task forces, on the basis of the plan, to develop identified sectors of international business.
4. Developing the management organization so that it is responsive to changes in key sectors of its market(s), particularly by the planned use of technical and professional inputs such as R&D, design, technical innovation and international sourcing.
5. Integrating in the management structure the growing roles of 'professionals' and project managers.

4.4   Managing European distribution

Structural changes

Patterns and the structure of distribution, particularly in Europe, have been changing significantly during the last two decades. These changes are now having an impact both on management organization and on traditional trading relationships. This section considers these developments, particularly in the consumer goods and food sectors.

National distribution systems in Europe can be subdivided into three broad types of trade:

1. wholesale/retail;
2. catering and produce;
3. industrial and technical.

Each of these categories requires a particular approach, and this, in turn, should influence the company's choice of distribution channel. For this reason it is important that companies research the distribution network for their product in each European country before they commit themselves to one channel or method.

The structural changes that have been taking place since the mid-1950s affect mainly consumer goods. In essence, the trend is that the role of the middleman is declining in the purchase and the distribution of consumer products, particularly food lines, as wholesale/retail operations become more concentrated in terms of purchasing power and supply organizations. Linked with this has been the rise in self-service. These structural changes are partly a consequence of increasing urbanization, which has brought about a change in buying habits, and partly the result of strong competition among the various distributors seeking to lower the cost of distribution.

This process is most advanced in Sweden and West Germany. Between 1968 and 1980, the proportion of German retail food stores with a turnover of below DM250 000 decreased from 98 to 75 per cent and their turnover in total retail sales dropped from 76 to 30 per cent. This trend towards further concentration is continuing rapidly and includes the wholesale trade as well. At the same time, the average sales area and turnover of the various outlets expanded drastically. The share of self-service in total German food retail sales grew from 84 per cent in 1970 to 87 per cent in 1979, which is about the same level as in Sweden. A similar pattern has spread from food to other products in the UK and the Netherlands.

Structural changes have occurred also through the expansion of the multiples, or chain stores, and through the growth of wholesalers and retailers buying co-operatives (Table 4.2 and Fig. 4.5). Both developments have led to the formation of a small number of powerful groups with central buying units. The number of critical buying points has been reduced throughout Europe: food items have led the way, but the buying of clothing, household goods and furnishing articles has been increasingly concentrated as well.

Table 4.2   EEC retail buying patterns, 1979: percentage breakdown of sales of some types of products by type of retail outlet (*Source*: Organization for European Co-operation and Development (OECD), Paris)

	Belgium	France	Germany	Netherlands	UK
Furniture					
Large stores	25.0	13.1	29.4	15.0	40.2
Mail order	2.6	3.1	13.8	1.6	12.8
Co-operatives	0.5	2.2	0.7	0.1	7.8
Independents*	71.9	81.6	56.1	83.3	39.2
Domestic appliances					
Large stores	50.8	23.1	32.4	33.7	23.7
Mail order	3.0	13.7	24.9	1.5	4.5
Co-operatives	1.3	1.5	2.4	0.3	6.0
Independents	44.9	61.7	40.3	64.5	65.8
Books and stationery					
Large stores	34.2	na	22.3	38.7	45.7
Mail order	6.3	na	18.0	3.9	1.3
Co-operatives	0.1	na	0.1	0.3	–
Independents	59.4	na	59.6	57.1	53.0
Textiles					
Large stores	13.4	18.0	19.0	30.0	26.2
Mail order	2.5	7.8	17.7	2.2	12.0
Co-operatives	0.8	3.6	1.3	0.1	3.6
Independents	83.3	70.6	62.0	67.7	58.2
Footwear					
Large stores**	23.1	23.7	39.8	37.3	63.0
Mail order	1.5	1.5	0.7	0.8	14.0
Co-operatives	75.0	74.3	59.3	61.8	19.4
Clothing					
Large stores	21.2	21.5	44.8	34.9	71.3
Mail order	2.1	3.2	3.2	0.9	10.3
Co-operatives	0.9	1.2	0.4	0.1	2.8
Independents	75.0	74.1	51.6	64.1	15.6

* Including street and open market traders.
** Including multiple stores.

French and Italian distribution networks remain less concentrated, and many shops in these countries are independently owned. A sample survey carried out in 1979 by the Italian National Institute for Distribution found that 40 per cent of Italian retail shops had less than 24 square metres of sales area, only 10 per cent of the shops had a cash register, and the average number of employees was only slightly above two.

The concentration of the distribution system into bigger organizations increases the

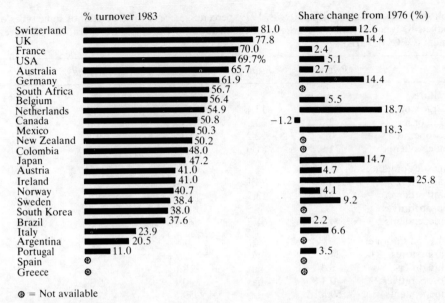

Fig. 4.5 Growth in importance of chains and co-operatives (*Source*: A. C. Nielsen International)

bargaining power of the distributors. The supplier is negotiating less and less with a fragmented trade on which he can impose his conditions. In Sweden, for example, three distribution organizations control approximately 80 per cent of the total retail market for foodstuffs. This concentration has even started spreading on an international scale, with organizations like the Nordisk Handelsforbund, which is a joint buying agent for the co-operative wholesale societies of five Nordic countries. The European voluntary chains such as Spar and Vege, or working combine bodies of associations of the grocery trade like EUROGROUP, will increasingly centralize their future buying efforts on a European scale. This tendency will accelerate with new member countries in the EEC.

Parallel to this concentration of the European distribution trade, a strong movement towards fiercer competition among suppliers has taken place. For a number of commodities, the European market has become a buyer's market, where a variety of similar products within each product category are offered in excess of actual demand and the supplier has fewer possibilities of choosing between a number of different distribution channels. The quasi-oligopolistic position of key buyers enables them to play suppliers off against one another and thus obtain very favourable terms. The success of a supplier's attempt to penetrate a market depends more and more on his success in persuading only a few—perhaps only one—of the small number of dominant distribution organizations to stock the product.

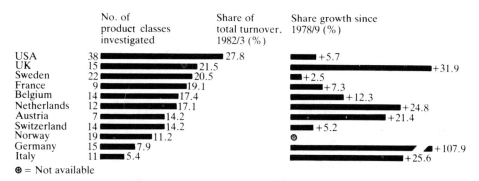

	No. of product classes investigated	Share of total turnover, 1982/3 (%)	Share growth since 1978/9 (%)
USA	38	27.8	+5.7
UK	15	21.5	+31.9
Sweden	22	20.5	+2.5
France	9	19.1	+7.3
Belgium	14	17.4	+12.3
Netherlands	12	17.1	+24.8
Austria	7	14.2	+21.4
Switzerland	14	14.2	+5.2
Norway	19	11.2	⊕
Germany	15	7.9	+107.9
Italy	11	5.4	+25.6

⊕ = Not available

Fig. 4.6 Importance and growth of private label brands (including generics) in selected product classes (*Source*: A. C. Nielsen International)

This factor should be carefully kept in mind when researching the distribution system and appointing a representative. In fact, appointing a representative, such as an agent, may no longer be the right approach. Some big buyers prefer to deal directly with suppliers in order to eliminate one or more layers of profit. They are constantly seeking the lowest possible prices, on a quality-for-quality basis.

Another factor has been the development of their own marketing systems by the various distribution organizations. A salient feature of this trend is the policy pursued by the distributors to market their own branded goods ('private' brand) rather than rely on manufacturers' advertised brands (Fig. 4.6). This trend is growing; large-scale retailers increasingly undertake their own advertising, and make higher margins on their own brands. Nevertheless, in adopting more of the promotional role themselves, the big distributors still expect the suppliers to pay for it, by way of allowances, discounts and similar deals.

A further characteristic that has to be taken into account is the decreasing proportion of specialized shops, as the large supermarkets expand their non-food lines. This development often implies an overlapping of the assortment of products handled by the two basically different distribution circuits; suppliers should investigate carefully which of the two channels it is more feasible to focus on.

Case example 4.11

A large Swiss manufacturer of pharmaceuticals encountered serious opposition when the company decided, in the summer of 1978, to market vitamin C through the supermarkets at a noticeably reduced price. Until this time, vitamin C was sold exclusively through pharmacies. Although a new brand for supermarkets was sold by a differently named subsidiary company, pharmacists threatened to take action against all the other products of the manufacturer.

Assessing correct distribution channels

Special attention should be paid to the degree of self-service facilities in the various countries concerned. Besides foodstuffs, products like textiles, books, cosmetics and 'do-it-yourself' articles are increasingly included in this scheme, and others will consequently follow. As a result, there are fewer salesmen in the shop to influence the customer's buying decision. The supplier's product has to be self-selling and therefore needs good 'shelf appeal'. Product, packaging and display have to be attractive to customers so that they opt in favour of one particular brand from among a number of similar products on the shelf.

Researching the distribution system should therefore be complemented by comprehensive investigations of consumer taste and preferences, competing products on the market, packaging innovations and most appropriate promotional measures, although the thoroughness of such research will depend upon each exporter's budget. If he is dealing with one of the major buying groups or the buying office of a big chain, the buyer can—and will—give him much information on packaging requirements; indeed, the advent of 'visual' shopping requires continuing research by exporters into the visual, in-store impact of their packaging.

The catering trade throughout Europe is relatively disorganized and scattered. It is supplied either directly by European manufacturers or through specialized wholesalers. In the Netherlands alone, 2000 wholesalers specialize in this trade. However, a market trend towards concentration at the wholesale level is under way in most European countries, and the formation of large central buying organizations with cash-and-carry stores is becoming more and more frequent. As a rule, catering wholesalers do not import directly from overseas sources without using the services of an importer, buyer or agent in their own country.

Distribution assessment is a prerequisite in selling profitably to the large sophisticated European market, but it does not in itself guarantee satisfactory sales. The key to successful distribution lies in pricing the product correctly for the end users and the distribution channels chosen, and ensuring that it has quality, design and packing that can compete not only with developing country imports, but with the brands of products produced in Europe. But a product that is correctly priced, designed and packaged will still not sell if the agent or importer is incompetent or if the terms offered to buyers are inappropriate. A clear policy of promotional measures to be performed by an agent or importer must be agreed. Finally, the product must be shipped and delivered on the specified dates. After undertaking market research in Europe, each different country exporter will realize the importance of all the factors listed above and will keep in close touch with his buyer or agent. The exporter will achieve all this more easily and at much less cost if he researches each European market thoroughly before trying to sell.

The importance of understanding how distribution systems work before entering an overseas market is well shown in Case example 4.12.

Case example 4.12

A foreign cosmetics manufacturer encountered difficulties in getting its products distributed in France. These difficulties stemmed from the company's decision to distribute solely through a chain store. By utilizing this method, the company believed that it could achieve maximum market exposure while holding down promotional, distribution and sales costs. While this method may be appropriate in some markets, it did not work in France, because there, 'parfumiers' (small local retailers specializing in cosmetics) are traditionally considered the opinion makers; most manufacturers in France give exclusive franchise to two or three local 'parfumiers'. Word-of-mouth recommendation is vital, and the public relies heavily on the opinion of the 'parfumiers'. When it bypassed them, the foreign manufacturer angered all the 'parfumiers' to the point where they discredited the product and damaged the company's reputation throughout France.

Other factors

But it is probably in the field of distribution of grocery products that the most significant changes in both promotional and purchasing patterns have occurred over the last decade. A recent survey by A. C. Nielsen & Co.[9] shows conclusively that in 25 countries consumers' real purchasing power is increasing steadily, enabling them to spend more; combined with the increasing provision of credit facilities (e.g. retailers' cards), discretionary spending is expected to accelerate into the 1990s. This trend has been reflected by distribution policies throughout Western Europe, in the following ways:

1. increased price competition among the major chain stores and supermarkets;
2. emergence of the discount or bargaining store as the fastest growing sector of grocery distribution;
3. growth of private labels and 'generic products' at the expense of nationally branded products;
4. the continual drive towards increasing productivity in purchasing, warehousing and selling operations through the use of new technology, particularly by hand-held terminals and scanning, e.g. bar-coding.

And while chains/co-operatives have steadily increased their share of food store business, this has strengthened purchasing and bargaining power *vis à vis* brand manufacturers. But here again, there are some differences in distribution throughout Europe. In Switzerland and Sweden, for example, a relatively small number of major chains and/or co-operatives, who do centralized buying, have a very large influence over the success or failure of a given brand. In others, such as Germany, Italy and France, while the small number of chains, buying groups/wholesalers account for some 50–70 per cent of total sales, the product has to be sold to a very large number of individual decision points for it to be in full distribution.

Two other findings cited in the Nielsen survey are of particular interest to management concerned with marketing and distribution policies.

1. Supermarket operators are adding new fields of activity to their stores, e.g. do-it-yourself goods, sporting goods, books, pharmaceuticals, flowers and personal computers, all in order to expand sales volume.
2. Despite the decline in population growth in Western Europe (in some countries

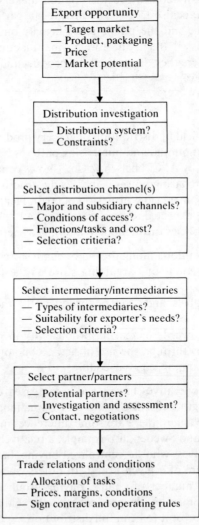

Fig. 4.7   Decision model: Distribution policy formulation (*Source*: International Trade Centre UNCTAD/GATT, Geneva)

population is actually declining), and the decline in the average s
the actual number of households continues to expand. This is due
importance of one- and two-person households, and is leading,
smaller package sizes, with fewer number of servings, in food produ
rapid growth of fast food outlets.

Finally, Fig. 4.7 illustrates, as a flowchart, some of the decision-making ste
in formulating distribution policy.

References

1. A. Jivani, 'Where Global Obstacles Lie', *Marketing*, **4**, July 1985.
2. J. A. Quelch and E. J. Hoff, 'Customising Global Marketing', *Harvard Business Review*, **64**, 3, May/June 1986.
3. Sir Kenneth Corfield, 'World Communications: Tomorrow's Trade Routes'. Conference of British Computer Society and Department of Trade and Industry, London, 1984.
4. W. J. Bilkey, 'An Attempted Integration of the Literature on the Export Behaviour of Firms', *Journal of International Business*, Summer 1978.
5. 'Factors for international success—Industrial and Export performances of France, the UK and Germany', Barclays Bank International, 1979.
6. C. New, 'Managing Manufacturing Operations in the UK, 1975–1985', Survey at Cranfield Institute of Technology, Operations Management Unit.
7. BETRO Trust & Royal Society of Arts, 'Concentration on Key Markets: A Development Plan for Exports', ITI, London, 1973.
8. Proceedings of Research Seminar, Ashridge Management College, 1987.
9. 'Worldwide Trends in Food Retailing', paper presented at 1984 Executive Conference of Grocery Manufacturers of America by Chairman and Chief Executive of A. C. Nielsen & Co. Marketing Trends 1/85 (Nielson Marketing Research Service).

5
Competing internationally

5.1 Innovation

Introduction

The development of new products and new technical processes is clearly critical to the long-term development—indeed, survival—of a company. The process is especially important for firms involved in medium- and high-technology products or services. There are a number of different approaches world-wide to technological innovation, and they will be explored in this section.

Innovation policy is often closely linked to and indicative of the strategic intentions and direction of the company. To allocate resources for innovation strategically, managers need to define the broad long-term actions, within and across operating divisions, that are necessary to achieve policy objectives. To start with basic principles, one leading management thinker defines innovation in the following terms.[1]

1. *Technology-push innovation.* The momentum for the innovation is derived from a technical development (physical, mechanical, etc.) The innovation is developed to its full potential, and then management searches for sales opportunities and all possible alternative commercial uses for it.
2. *Market-pull innovation.* This type of innovation has been developed to fit a specific market need. The innovation is 'pulled' from the company by the needs of the market: the need is first perceived, and the innovation is then designed to fill that need.

The hazard that management must watch under the first of these is that the company may be tempted to develop what is technically interesting rather than what customers require: a technological innovation can appear to have such a lead internationally that the company is forced to pursue its development. Companies run by scientists or engineers are particularly prone to this hazard because 'technical elegance' is more attractive to such professionals than 'market potential'. Faced with a technological breakthrough, such a company tends to develop too narrow a technological base to safeguard the competitiveness of the product range.

And the process of innovation is not simple; numerous studies have been carried out in an attempt to gain a better understanding of this important activity. Innovation has been compared to the blades of a pair of scissors. On the one hand, it involves the recognition of a need, or more precisely, in economic terms, a potential market;

on the other, it involves technical knowledge, which may be generally available, although new scientific and technological information is often required.

As we have seen, in the literature of innovation there are attempts to build a theory predominately on the aspects of technology 'push' or market/demand 'pull'. Some engineers/scientists have stressed the element of original research and invention and have tended to neglect or belittle the market factor. Economists have often stressed the demand side—'necessity is the mother of invention'. Like the analogous theories of inflation, these approaches may be complementary and not mutually exclusive.

It is not difficult to cite cases which appear to support one or the other theory. With regard to the atomic absorption spectrometer, for example, it was a scientist who envisaged the application, without any initial clear-cut demand from the customers. Advocates of demand-pull, on the other hand, tend to cite examples such as synthetic rubber, or the photo-destruction of plastics, where a recognized need supposedly led to the necessary innovations.

And the process of successful innovation has been summarized aptly in an early authoritative study:[2]

> The idea for an innovation consists of the fusion of a recognised demand and a recognised technical feasibility into a design concept . . . if a technical advance alone is considered it may or may not result in a solution for which there will be a demand.

What is clear from the many studies on innovation, some of which are cited in this section, is the importance of innovation as the basis for sustaining competitive strength, and the need to ensure very close liaison by management between the marketing function, and the research and development, innovation and design functions. This management task is by no means an easy one in the face of increasing levels of specialization, larger organizations and rapidly changing international environments. Some steps that can be taken effectively to manage innovation in this context will be explained shortly.

So the main objective of innovation is to ensure that there is a continuous flow of commercially successful new products or services to meet changing or developing market requirements. This innovative task may produce products of essentially a breakthrough type, improvement of an already existing product, or simply a copy of a competitor's product. The most common innovations are of the second and third type, the second type being commonly referred to in research as 'process' innovation.

A very large number of new product ideas never reach the market, and of those that do many are not successful. The criterion for a successful innovation is commercial; that is, it must obtain a worthwhile market share and make a profit. An interesting decay curve of new product ideas is given in Fig. 5.1. The percentage decline from product 'idea' to 'commercialization' is extremely high, and to achieve success a well managed process of sequential steps is necessary, ranging from the generation of ideas to their commercial implementation.

Case example 5.1 illustrates the importance of the interface between innovation and marketing in competitiveness.

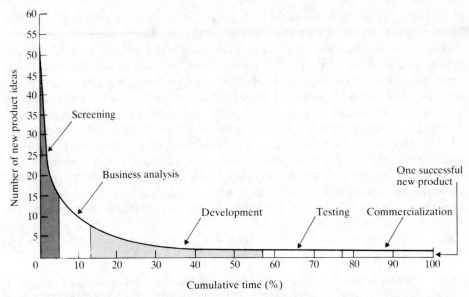

Fig. 5.1 Innovation–decay curve and new-product ideas (*Source: Management of New Products*, Booz, Allen and Hamilton, New York, 1970)

Case example 5.1

Nylon was the first purely synthetic fibre. It was used for making parachutes during World War II. Different applications of nylon—women's stockings, thread, rope, blouses, men's shirts, tyre cord, carpet and furnishing fabrics—were made possible by the ability to process the material in different ways—by circular knit, warp knit, broadweave or textured yarns. However, polyester fibre made substantial inroads in these uses, largely because it was more adaptable in producing different finishes.

ICI have two polyesters: Mitrelle (silk finish) and Terinda (suede finish). Up until a major technical breakthrough by ICI Fibres Division in 1982, a number of markets were effectively closed to nylon because other synthetic fibres were more acceptable, particularly in the markets for lingerie (requiring a 'slinkier' silk-like feel) and sportswear (requiring a more fashionable cotton-like feel). ICI claims that this technical breakthrough has resolved the problem of changing the surface appearance and feel of nylon; this has enabled ICI to compete 'up-market' into more profitable price brackets and to take market share from other synthetic fibres. The new product was first launched in UK before entering European markets. ICI's Mitrelle is at the top end of the silk market and sells in relatively low volume. The new 'silk-nylon' does not compete directly with it, but it enables ICI to move volume in the quality end of the mass lingerie market. The aim with the easier-to-handle 'cotton-like' nylon is to take sales from cotton in sportswear and skiwear. Because of the strong competitive position of continental manufacturers such as Adidas and Fila, the new product was offered to them first. ICI Divisional Marketing Manager is quoted as saying: 'I do not think it is too strong to say that we have rediscovered the importance of marketing in our technical production approach.'

The role of marketing

Every innovation in industry requires a combination of technical feasibility and economic demand; but some research has shown that successful innovation rests on marketing organization and expertise. The Centre for the Study of Industrial Innovation surveyed a total of 53 industrial R&D projects abandoned for non-technical reasons in the electrical, mechanical and chemical industries: the most common cause of failure concerned the nature of the marketing resources of the firm. One of the report's conclusions was that there must be an efficient two-way liaison between R&D department and marketing.

The findings of these reports constitute some evidence of a failure by marketing management to involve itself in the research and development process, and by R&D management in understanding the functions of marketing and the potential contribution that it has to make to successful innovation.

Innovation studies have stressed the importance of identifying a market need and establishing close coupling between functions, particularly marketing and R&D. Remarkably little attention has been paid to the importance and role of top (strategic) management in the innovation process. This would appear to be a major oversight, since one of the primary tasks of top management has to be the structuring of the company/environmental–product/market relationship. This task has to be carried out through the corporate strategic process, which is essentially a two-stage activity consisting of analysis/planning and implementation/control. (See Section 2.1 above for a full analysis of these aspects.)

Research findings

Research on innovation has been undertaken by the Science Policy Research Unit (SPRU) at Sussex University. The Innovation Data Bank at SPRU contains 2100 important innovations introduced by UK firms between 1945 and 1980, analysed by size of company. These data are summarized in Table 5.1. Interestingly, small- and medium-sized firms (500–999 employees) have maintained their share of total innovations made up to 1969, and during 1970–80 small firms actually increased their share by 5 per cent. There are some further points arising out of the data contained in the bottom half of the table. The largest firms (10 000 and over) increased their share of innovations (from 51.8 to 59.6 per cent) between 1960 and 1980; but the next two size categories down (500–999 and 1000–9999) experienced something approaching a halving of their shares (5.1 to 2.9 per cent and 25.0 to 15.1 per cent respectively). While too much emphasis should not be placed on one set of data, this does seem to indicate that the largest companies have succeeded in innovating more than medium-sized companies, with clear implications for the resources—technical, financial and marketing—that are needed to maintain international competitiveness.

Table 5.1 Number of innovations in UK manufacturing industry, by size of innovating unit and by size of firm, for three periods between 1945 and 1980 (*Source*: Townsend, Henwood and Thomas, SPRU Innovation Data Bank, Sussex University, 1981)

	No. of employees										
	1–199		*200–499*		*500–999*		*1000–9999*		*10 000 +*		
	No.	*%*	*No.*	*%*	*No.*	*%*	*No.*	*%*	*No.*	*%*	*Total (no.)*
Innovation by size of innovating unit											
1945–59	103	19.5	76	14.4	56	10.6	213	40.3	81	15.3	529
1960–69	153	18.2	120	14.3	97	11.6	351	41.8	118	14.1	839
1970–80	241	30.7	109	13.9	113	14.4	255	32.9	68	8.7	786
Total	497	23.1	305	14.2	266	12.3	819	38.0	267	12.4	2,154
Innovation by size of firm											
1945–59	63	11.9	37	7.0	27	5.1	162	30.2	240	45.4	529
1960–69	101	12.0	50	6.0	43	5.1	210	25.0	435	51.8	839
1970–80	132	16.8	59	7.5	23	2.9	119	15.1	453	57.6	786
Total	296	13.7	146	6.8	93	4.3	491	22.8	1,128	52.4	2,154

Further research has also been carried out by SPRU into factors accounting for success and failure in managing innovation. The objective of this specific research project was to substantiate or refute generalizations about technical innovations, by the systematic comparison of pairs of successful and unsuccessful innovations. The first stage of the project was a study of 58 attempted innovations in scientific instruments and chemicals. Those in the chemical industry were mainly process innovations, related to intermediates derived from petroleum, while the instrument innovations were mainly in electronics. By 'pairing' attempted innovations, it was possible to discriminate between the respective characteristics of failure and success. Since the project was concerned with technical innovation in industry, the criteria of success was a commercial one.

Two major findings from this project indicate that, on the basis of high levels of innovation,

1. successful firms compete better and understand user/customer needs better;
2. successful firms ensure better linkage/coupling between specialized areas, particularly marketing and R&D.

Further research tends to support these findings, which clearly have significant implications for management in terms of improving the company's competitive position. A government report has recommended that both industry and government (through the Department of Trade and Industry and the National Economic Development Office) should foster conditions that promote, in both the short and the long term, effective technological innovation.[3] The particular objectives that need to be achieved, where this has not already been attempted by management, are summarized in this report as follows:

1. direct linkage of R&D, production and marketing;
2. planned programmes of innovation related to market opportunities;
3. effective technological management to contribute towards sharpening the overall competitiveness of the firm;
4. short, or at least shorter, lead times;
5. balanced use of scientific and technological resources over all stages of the innovative process.

Objective 4 has a particular importance, since the problems of long lead times have proved difficult to resolve. Other research studies have shown that in some industries an average lead time of 19.2 years between invention and commercial production is not untypical.[4] Yet it is the commercialization, the marketing of a new product or process, that provides the international competitive edge: shortening lead times by management can enhance competitiveness only by putting pressure on other suppliers in the market. This, and other managerial implications, are illustrated in Case example 5.2.

Case example 5.2
In 1979 W & T Avery Ltd (in the weighing business for 150 years) concluded that the company was innovating too slowly to meet the market trend towards electronic scales. As a result of a business and product analysis, management launched an aggressive new product development programme, and over 100 new products were launched during the next three years. Two aspects of this policy are noteworthy. First, the latest manufacturing techniques were introduced: this has helped to establish a new high-technology corporate image and ensure growth in the face of fierce competition. Second, the company has substantially improved its international competitiveness, with export sales of its retail scales having more than doubled in the same period. This innovative policy has ensured a strong, technically advanced product range, including platform scales for weighing incoming goods, digital hanging scales for produce, bar code label printers and electronic point of sale (EPOS) systems, all of which can be linked into a total store computer to help the retailer control his business and maximize his profits. For the domestic user, Avery has introduced its innovative health/kitchen scale which calculates the calorie, carbohydrate, fat and fibre contents of over 1000 foods. Industrial scales and systems include analytical laboratory balances, platform scales, printers, indicators and weigh-bridges of 60 000 kg capacity. The company received one of the Engineering Industries Association (EIA) 1985 National Engineering Marketing Awards.

The importance of lead times is borne out by the tendency to 'buy in' feasible innovations. This has been well documented:

[Firms and countries] increasingly seek to overcome long lead times and heavy developmental costs by buying in other people's technological knowledge and by concentrating on the commercial application of important inventions and innovations . . . any firm, or indeed any country, engaged in world trade in advanced industrial products must repeatedly modernise its manufacturing processes and introduce new or updated products if it is not to lose markets and go out of business because of competition from advances elsewhere . . .[4]

After taking into account factors 1–5 in managing innovation, some further research has been undertaken on the diffusion of six new technologies in industry:[5] these included the oxygen process in steel making, continuous casting and the float process of manufacturing flat glass. These innovations have totally changed the manufacturing processes. In some of the other technologies studied, such as the use of tunnel kilns in brick production, research has shown that small-scale trials on a limited basis can be undertaken without heavy investment or fundamental restructuring of the manufacturing processes (as in the case of steel and glass making).

Two further aspects of innovation policy need to be considered: (1) the balance between 'product' and 'process' innovation and (2) the relationship between the rate of technological innovation and the influence of competitive pressure. Both of these aspects have been the subject of research at City University Business School.[6]

1. The development of more efficient manufacturing processes to develop existing markets is characteristic of process innovation, as is the safeguarding of existing products by cutting manufacturing costs. Product innovation tends to characterize firms in a position of market leadership, i.e., firms that typically spend more than their counterparts (the process innovators) on R&D, and are more internationally competitive (export a higher percentage of their sales). The product innovators also (as one would expect) rely more on new products to generate sales revenue, and claim to have a technical lead over their competitors for a higher proportion of their product range.
2. The most frequent form of technological innovation (incremental product innovation) occurs as a result of applying inventions made outside the firm. Where inter-firm competition is not strong and when barriers to entry are high, considerable delays can occur in technological innovation, but when competitive pressures are high it will be necessary for a firm to engage in both product and process innovation.

What makes a firm a successful innovator?

It is widely accepted on the basis of these researches that firms seeking to manufacture and market high-technology products must invest in R&D or accept that their products and processes will be overtaken by competitors from inside the industry or outside it. There remains one fundamental question, however: What management or policy indicators can be adduced to indicate which firms are likely to be more successful in innovating and competing than others? Some analysts claim that the drive or 'will' of management in setting up an innovative strategy is all-important. Certainly, adopting a consistent, planned and positive competitive strategy is likely to be the foundation for success, and competitive strategy is due to its intrinsic importance, dealt with at length later in this chapter (Section 5.4). Certainly, too, generalizations about 'dynamism', 'teamwork' and 'marketing' have only limited value as exhortations to management to become more innovative.

The importance of a recent analytical study of management organization and innovation is especially topical and provides a much needed synthesis based on empirical data (observed results).[7] This study examines those practices/precepts most commonly found in large companies that successfully innovate, as follows.

1. *Atmosphere and vision.* Management understands innovation and develops the company's value system to support it.
2. *Orientation to the market.* There is a strong commitment to competitive marketing at the top of the company, and mechanisms to ensure interactions between technical and marketing people at lower levels.
3. *Opportunity orientation.* Entrepreneurial and innovative companies recognize that the necessary capital can always be found to exploit/develop good new ideas originated by staff.
4. *Organizing for innovation.* Managers need to think carefully about how innovation fits into their strategy, and to structure their technology, skills resources and organizational commitments accordingly.

Case example 5.3, summarized from this analytical study, amply illustrates how these important points can be put into practice.

Case example 5.3

Intel, is a leading US company in semiconductor technology, and it is the declared intention of Intel's management to be the outstandingly successful innovative company in this industry. Intel met the challenge of the last recession with what the management termed its '20 per cent solution': the professional staff agreed to work one extra day a week to help bring innovations to the market-place earlier than planned. Despite the difficult times, Intel came out of the recession with several new products ready to sell (it also avoided lay-offs). In supplying highly technical products to Original Equipment Manufacturers (OEMs), the firm has developed a strong technical sales network to discover and understand customer needs in depth, so as to have technical solutions designed into customers' products. Management has also organized an applied technology group working close to the market-place and a 'cutting edge' technology group that allows rapid selection of available technologies.

5.2 Design

Introduction

In the analysis of international competitiveness, there is increasing awareness of the key contribution to be made by outstanding design. Companies must improve the quality of design in order to compete internationally; indeed, governments are concerned to improve the design of manufactured products by means of techniques known as 'industrial design' so that companies can meet increasingly complex technical and other standards in competitive markets. Some standards are subject to international control, such as CENELEC (electro-technical products) and the Union of Agreement Boards (construction materials); also involved in standards are the Comité Européen de Normalisation (CEN), comprising member-countries of the EEC and EFTA, and the International Standards Organization (ISO), the ultimate international harmonizing body. There is scope, therefore, for companies to develop designs that meet the specifications of such bodies, as this can provide a basis for competitive access to wider markets. This latter consideration can also apply to the design specifications of national industrial bodies such as the West German DIN and Verband Deutsche Elektronik (VBE), where stringent product standards greatly enhance the value of customers' guarantees of performance and design quality.

This introduction to design, however, raises the question of what exactly is meant by the term 'industrial design'. A detailed and authoritative definition has been produced by United Nations Industrial Development Organization (UNIDO):[8]

> Industrial design is tightly interwoven with and dependent on the socio-economic context in which it is exercised. . . . It is concerned with the improvement of usability of industrial products which forms part of the overall quality of a product. From the point of view of industrial design, a product is primarily an object which provides certain services, thus satisfying the needs of the user. . . . It is concerned with 'formal properties' of industrial products. Formal characteristics refer to the overall appearance of a product, including its three-dimensional configuration, its 'physiognomy', its texture and colour . . . It is an innovative activity. It is one special type of technological innovation . . . It is concerned with the marketability of the product in that it relates the product to its market in terms of both raw material supply and product demand.

In brief, industrial design is the design of industrially made products, taking the human factor into account. However, it has even wider implications. It should be noted that a general appreciation of industrial design, as defined above, is generally lacking, even in industrialized countries where the designer enjoys a certain degree of status. To many, industrial design simply means creating industrial products. It is rarely related to manufacturing processes, social patterns, the requirements of the user, the marketing or distribution system through which the product passes, or savings of materials. Yet each of these factors, in addition to many others, is covered by the above definitions and must be taken into account by the industrial designer when he/she creates a new product or redesigns an old one.

A second definition of design concentrates on the role and contribution of the industrial designer:[9]

> An industrial designer is one who is qualified by training, technical knowledge, experience and visual sensibility to determine the materials, construction, mechanism, shape, colour, surface finishes and decoration of objects which are reproduced in quantity by the industrial process. The industrial designer may at different times be concerned with all or only one of these aspects of an industrially produced object.

The industrial designer may also be concerned with the problem of packaging, advertising, exhibiting and marketing when the resolution of such problems requires visual appreciation as well as technical knowledge and experience. The designer of craft-based industries or trades, where hand processes are used for production, is deemed to be an industrial designer when the work produced to his drawings or models is of a commercial nature, is made in batches or otherwise in quantity, and is not the personal work of the artist-craftsman.

Contrast these definitions with the conventional view of the designer as a person whose main concern is with the functioning of a product and its other technical aspects. If the appearance of a product is a key factor in its sale, the 'stylist' is typically called in to create an appropriate 'package' for the 'mechanism' created by the designer, whether it is a typewriter (the housing), a motor car (the body) or a transistor radio (the case). This division of labour is completely misleading, and the concept on which it is based is fallacious. It is the main reason why the industrial designer has often been equated with the 'stylist', to the point of being labelled a 'cosmetician of products'—an even more inaccurate definition. Moreover, the differences between the industrial designer and the engineering designer must be clearly understood by management. The latter has been defined as follows:[10]

> Engineering design is the use of scientific principles, technical information and imagination in the definition of a mechanical structure, machine or system to perform pre-specified functions with the maximum economy and efficiency.

These definitions establish that industrial design is a specialized engineering discipline based on anthropology, ergonomics and visual and tactile relationships. Furthermore, engineering and industrial designers have common goals, and each should make his own technical and social contribution to the competitiveness of the company.

Managing the design function

While research will be cited shortly to show the increasing significance of design in maintaining competitive positions in international trade, further analysis is required at this stage to show how, building on an understanding of the design concepts already explained, the total design function of a company can be effectively managed, and can be used as a competitive weapon. Case example 5.4 shows how West German management achieves this.[11]

Case example 5.4

An exhibition of German design, 'Images of Quality', was held at the Science Museum, London, in 1987. The impact of this exhibition was largely to show that design can be used as an economic tool, and not just a cosmetic exercise. Indeed, the now well-known phrase, 'Vorsprung durch Technik', used to promote Audi cars, indicates much about the role of design in German marketing. (Loosely translated, it means 'Advantage gained through doing things the best way'.) One such exhibit was a Messerschmitt–Bolkow–Blohm (MBB) video communications system (combined into a single office furniture module). This enables conferences to take place on a global scale using audio, video and fax transmission. The design brief was that this installation should not 'over-awe the user'; and as a result, this new package in light blue and white looks like an ordinary desk with two unobtrusive video screens let into it and a large TV screen placed in front. The overhead document copying camera is no more obvious than a desk light. The implications of this piece of equipment are clear to the German designers: direct international communication without the stress and delay of long-distance travel.

Of course, quality has always been paramount in the way Germans manage design: evolution, rather than revolution, protects German manufacturers from over-rapid obsolescence of their products at the hands of cheaper competitors. This is most clearly illustrated in the design of German cars, notably Mercedes-Benz. The cars exhibit not only quality but a 'family' identity of models that goes back over thirty years. The company produces 600 000 units annually and three-quarters are exported. While substantial engineering improvements take place beneath 'the skin', vertical homogeneity is expressed in tiny incremental changes to headlamp and tail-light clusters, and to subtle alterations to the body profile which retain the essential character of the car and prevent any single model from suddenly appearing out-dated.

In managing the design function, then, expertise not available internally can profitably be used; further case examples will shortly illustrate this point. Some aspects of design management in consumer goods sectors must now be considered. There are many such sectors where the quality of a design (especially its aesthetic quality) is the leading factor in a product's attractiveness and competitive market position. These include

1. textiles, clothing and leather goods;
2. ceramics, glassware and cutlery;
3. furniture, household furnishings;
4. housewares, kitchenware and gift trade items;
5. jewellery, silverware, etc.;
6. toys and games;
7. educational products, paintings.

These sectors are highly competitive internationally, and there is a strong brand element in most of them; moreover, in each sector, the innovative element or originality of design plays a key role in the appeal of the product to the buyer. Mass production techniques and unique packaging presentation are of less importance than the design content of the products themselves. In this context, therefore, the management of design involves several discrete, but related, aspects or stages:

1. design for distinctness—the development of innovation design (not necessarily technologically);
2. design for production—to ensure that component parts are made easily and eco-

nomically both in the production process itself; here, the designer must be aware of the production processes, technology, alternative methods and their costs;
3. design for function—value in use implies quality and reliability (the product must satisfy the customer in its prime function over the expected life period);
4. design for aesthetic appeal/appearance—to appeal to the eye and attract customers;
5. design for distribution—to facilitate easy low-cost packaging, and a reduction of handling and storage space.

Liaison with production and marketing

In managing these aspects to gain the best possible competitive advantage, the company must ensure that the designer's ideas are merged with those of the production engineer and the marketing department. So design must liaise with

- production management, to maintain the scheme used for classification and coding; also to review manufacturing methods and investigate component parts proving difficult to manufacture; and
- marketing, to improve standards of finish and design quality; also technical aspects of customer requirements and requests for production improvements.

These linkages in the management of design for redevelopment of a new product are illustrated in Fig. 5.2.

In this particular situation, the process of designing the new product passes through the following stages:

1. preliminary discussion and briefing, which provides the designers with an opportunity to discuss the design and marketing situation;
2. design appraisal, where the designer reviews the feasibility of various design concepts and builds up a conceptual profile for the product while checking market research information. This stage produces a diversity of options, representing different approaches to the same problem;
3. design proposal, which involves a parallel activity between the designer, marketing and production, so that the product profile can be developed into a specific design proposal, detailing the technical features in drawing and model form. The aim is to illustrate as precisely as possible what can be expected from the final product. Consumer research should also be carried out to assess people's attitudinal responses to the product concept. Although this information will be based on existing experiences and preconceptions, it is nevertheless valuable;
4. development, which involves the detailed design of component drawings, prototypes and mechanical and materials testing for production;
5. production, which must, however, be monitored, as it is this final stage that can give rise to several opportunities for compromises which may undermine product quality and lead to product mediocrity.

At the end of the project, where marketing, design and production have all been

Industrial design
— Aesthetic knowledge
— Social and cultural backgrounds
— Environmental relationships
— Ergonomic requirements
— Visual trends
— Insight into aspects of marketing and production

New product

Marketing
— Market research
— Market analysis
— Economics
— Distribution systems
— Promotion

Production
— Technical research
— Technical analysis
— Economic targets
— Production methods
— Ergonomic research

Fig. 5.2 Management of design.

integrated, the company will enjoy the commercial benefits not merely in terms of turnover; if the company is perceived by buyers, retailers and distributors as a manufacturer of attractive, high-quality products, the corporate image and quality will help to strengthen its competitive market position internationally.

Case examples 5.5 and 5.6 show how sound management of design, including the use of some outside expertise, can bring about both improved design and market performance.

Case example 5.5

Some years ago, Allied International Designers (AID) researched a complete redesign for Ever-Ready Co. (now Berec) of a lamp for motorists. The old lamp was a solid square object designed originally to take a square battery. The designers could certainly have restyled that, by changing the colour, altering the handle and so on. The square batteries were not widely available, particularly in overseas markets, and because the lamp itself was bulky, it was difficult to keep and was usually damaged by being knocked about in the car boot; also, new, foreign products, cheaper and more compact, were beginning to take sales from the manufacturer.

What the designers did was first to redesign the lamp to take ordinary batteries, available everywhere. Second, at the expense of the swivelling beam, they made the lamp flat so that now it can be kept in a glove compartment; as an added attraction, the handle was made to move to form variable legs. Third, they simplified the manufacturing process to attack costs. The old lamp had 72 parts and 49 assembly operations: the new lamp has half the number of parts and only 28 assembly operations. It costs 25 per cent less to make, and even with an improved profit margin it meets the price of comparable products. Sales of the new lamp doubled in the first year and export prospects look bright. Interestingly, the company had already analysed the market before this complete redesign was launched; models were used to test the new proposition, and the company even value-engineered the product before tooling. So management knew how the product had to be positioned when the time came for investment. This is unusual in many engineering firms in the UK, where technical staff are expected to develop new products, which production then makes, and only later, at a stage patently too late, are the international marketing staff involved in promoting and selling.

Case example 5.6

As part of UK government's Funded Consultancy Scheme (FCS) through the Design Council, client companies have received design assistance/expertise ranging from a graphic design for tins to an independent verification of the design calculation for an aircraft. All such projects must incorporate some contribution to national competitiveness.

One particular company, Servis, called on the help of Concept Development International (part of AID) to create a new style and range signature for its household laundry appliances. The design brief was to reposition its range to cater to an increasingly fashion-conscious kitchen sector. The group redesigned the facias to tone in with that season's vogue colours, using soft grey with piano key switches and toning blue lettering. In addition, a new control panel was designed which standardized all contact points across the 11 circuit boards and which allowed a single moulding tool to produce all the switch and control combinations. The benefit of the scheme is that it enables UK manufacturers to exploit market opportunities afforded by good design, to sharpen their competitive edge and to create genuine product value/benefits internationally.

Design and competitiveness

So much for the management of design and the design process: as mentioned earlier, there is the strategic question of whether design significantly influences competitive-

Table 5.2   Reasons for trade success

Reasons	%
Lower prices	25
Product superiority	39
After-sales service	12
Product uniqueness and design	24

ness in international trade. Several important studies have been undertaken on this aspect. One, which examined US–West German trade,[12] concludes that only 25 per cent of trade success could be attributed to price factors (see Table 5.2). Another, earlier, study had reported evidence of the importance of quality and design in successful trade.[13] Using US and UK trade data, it showed that over half of UK exports tended to be successful because of non-price or quality components. In a later study it was proposed that, at the design and development stage of product planning, user needs can be itemized and a degree of importance attached to each category. This means that 'Items like price, trade-in allowance, servicing costs, design quality, service user training, delivery date, reliability, flexibility and ease of use and safety can all be given some important ranking.'[14]

The National Economic Development Office (NEDO) has reported that the relatively slow growth in British manufacturing exports can be attributed to the problems of design, quality, delivery and salesmanship, and to some price factors.[15] Import penetration into the UK has also been affected by these non-price factors. In surveying the machine tool industry, for example, NEDO obtained responses from British buyers as to why they chose foreign rather than British machine tools; the responses are shown in Table 5.3.

The main implications of these researches into design and competitiveness require further explanation. In endeavouring to compete in international markets, manufacturers must adapt their products to international design standards and, in so doing, raise their competitive capability (provided that prices, delivery terms and other non-design factors satisfy the requirements of foreign buyers). There is a further aspect: unless a country's manufacturing sector can successfully compete with foreign de-

Table 5.3   Choice of machine tools by UK buyers

Reasons given	%
Superiority of foreign product design	30
Specification unavailable in UK	21
Prospect of reciprocal trade	11
Willingness to meet special needs	8
Better after-sales services	5
Price as the main factor	5

signs, the domestic market will rapidly be dominated by foreign-made products, provided that no obstacles to trade are erected. And if a country's manufacturing industry subsists largely as a result of any such protective measures, its manufacturers are unlikely to develop the design and other expertise needed to penetrate foreign markets.

The case examples already given show how some government-supported agencies can improve manufacturing through industrial design techniques. By way of conclusion, the following considerations largely explain the importance of design in developing competitive strategy.

1. A product that satisfies domestic market requirements may have to be improved or redesigned to compete in international, particularly industrialized, markets.
2. If a newly designed product is to be sold in large volume in many markets in order to recoup development and capital costs, it must embody sufficient originality to ensure that it is not easily copied. Furthermore, a well designed product is more likely to have an extended product life-cycle than a poorly designed product. A long life-cycle means that the product will sell well for several years in many markets before it goes out of fashion, is improved upon by another design, or becomes superfluous. If exported manufactures consistently have long product life-cycles, the economy as a whole stands to earn a better return on invested capital than if its products quickly go out of fashion or otherwise disappear from world markets.
3. Design is a fundamental factor in the entire process of research, development, production and marketing. It also extends to the presentation, packaging and transport of the finished product to the foreign buyer. If a high standard of design is encouraged in the manufacturing sector, all other sectors of the economy dependent upon and supporting manufacturing stand to benefit.
4. Existing productive capacity in some countries is often not fully utilized because of a lack of internal demand. By channelling this unused capacity into production for export, a country improves the efficiency of its industrial investments, provided that the switchover to export-oriented manufacture does not consume more resources than it can pay for with its export earnings.
5. The design of a product is one of the largest, if not *the* largest, value-added component in the product; it consumes less in terms of capital than any other input factor contributing to the creation of the product. Since the design component is synonymous with human creativity, manufactures embodying a high standard of design are mainly dependent upon human resources, hence the importance of effective management of the design process already discussed.

Competing internationally, therefore, requires a strategy on both price and non-price fronts: both aspects need to be competitive. The process of design as a whole must include price as well as quality features, and research cited in this section indicates that product design is, in some industries, just as important as price as a buying factor. Design can also be conceptually considered as a planning process to achieve sales and profits, and this process must begin with a marketing specification; in drawing up this specification, criteria for performance, maintainability, reliability and intended working life, appearance, costs, ergonomic standards and a proposed rate of production must be established. This design specification should seek to integrate market demand with what is technically and financially feasible. So technical excellence and aesthetics, as well as cost considerations and flexibility in operation, are important. And even when development costs are recovered by sales revenue, the design function has a vital and continuing role to play in counteracting product obsolescence and maintaining product competitiveness. (Case example 5.4 has especially proved this point.)

5.3 Manufacturing

Introduction

The management of all manufacturing operations (or 'operations management', as it is otherwise termed) occupies a critical role in maintaining the overall international competitiveness of a company. Many aspects of operations management directly influence this competitiveness, including output prices, labour productivity, cost-effective purchasing and supply, quality assurance, some phases of physical distribution, control of unit costs and efficiency of manufacturing and assembly operations. It is these aspects and their effects on competitiveness that are the subject of this section. Clearly, operations management in all phases has important 'interfaces' with marketing management in servicing international customers cost-effectively and competitively.

These interfaces are sometimes a source of strain in management relationships, and therefore require some brief explanation. If the friction is unresolved, it can lead to a deterioration in the company's competitive position. This is because marketing and manufacturing, in seeking to improve departmental efficiencies, can bring about operational conflicts which reduce the company's service to the customer; this point will be fully explained shortly. Also, the high costs of capital changes in manufacturing processes and the proliferation of automated operations can make it difficult to respond to changing market needs economically and promptly. The quickening obsolescence of many products, combined with the costs of redeploying plant facilities, make manufacturing changes difficult and can lead to declining competitiveness in a company's product/service offer. So managing the 'interface' between marketing and manufacturing becomes all the more important in maintaining competitiveness. An authoritative study of this aspect of management lists the following areas of necessary co-operation, but potential conflict:[16]

1. capacity planning and long-range sales forecasting;
2. production scheduling and short-term sales forecasting;
3. delivery, physical distribution and the level of customer service;

4. quality assurance at a competitive cost;
5. breadth of product line and variety reduction;
6. cost control over operations relating to rapid response and high-quality service to customers;
7. new product introduction and effective design management;
8. adjunct services such as spare parts, inventory support, installation and repair and the associated field service costs.

The study cited proposes that, where such conflicts arise, clear and specific corporate policies can go a long way to resolving if not forestalling them. For example, management can have a policy of full line production, emphasizing only high-volume items, or some other category of products. On the other hand, management can implement a planned programme of 'value analysis' using the expertise of both manufacturing and marketing to improve product quality, add product value and sharpen product performance, while at the same time minimizing/reducing operating costs.

Value analysis

The aim of value analysis is to examine products with the same care and attention that work study has devoted to the activities of people; it is concerned with raw materials, components, work in progress and finished goods, placing the emphasis on the value of the design, and with the objective of reducing costs. The special role of value analysis (VA) in improving the competitiveness of the company's operations is shown in the following aspects.

1. The components of product value: these include

   - The fact that customers with money and unsatisfied wants comprise a market sector;
   - that 'utility' must be provided to such customers, and products must fit the sector;
   - scarcity or exclusivity, reflected in limited range of high quality;
   - total cost to the customer: this is an inverse component of value; given difficulty in attainment, the customer wants to pay the least for overcoming that difficulty;
   - the customer's other options—competitors' offers.

The interaction of these components in value analysis is defined as the value of industrial products determined by the special relationship of utility to cost.
2. Identification of function in VA: function is that property of the product which makes it sell, and the most important step in VA is to identify the function of the product. Rarely does a product in international markets have only one function, although there will be a primary one; however, all its functions need to be identified during a VA exercise.
3. Management can adopt certain tests in assessing value. These include the following.

- Does its use contribute to value (e.g. moulding on a picture frame)?
- Is its cost proportional to its usefulness (e.g. chromium plate on car bumpers)?
- Does it need all its features (e.g. *two* striking sides on a matchbox)?
- Is there anything better for the intended use (e.g. assembling packing cases with nails instead of screws)?
- Can a usable part be made more cheaply (e.g. using offcuts for making tinplate hinges)?
- Can a standard product be found which will be usable in more than one product (e.g. same-size lid for different sizes of small container)?
- Is it made on proper tooling, considering quantities?
- Do materials, labour, overheads and profit total its cost? (Materials cost may be excessive.)
- Will another dependable supplier provide it for less? (Less than a present supplier, or less than the cost of making it?)
- Is anyone buying it for less?

4. Management can also assess the kinds of value that determine the competitiveness of the company's output:

- use value: the price the purchaser will offer in order to ensure that the purpose or function of the product is achieved;
- esteem value: the price that is offered for the product over and above the use value on the basis of competitive advantage (in many cases this goes hand in hand with superior quality);
- exchange value: the conventional purchase price;
- market value: the price the purchaser will offer in the light of the scarcity of the product. Understanding market value helps to avoid reducing cost at the expense of customer acceptance.

Value analysis as a management process is summed up in Fig. 5.3.

Clearly, marketing management should seek to build its programmes round the operational strengths of manufacturing; an analysis of international customer segments must go hand in hand with an analysis of the company's manufacturing capability, so that marketing management understands its competitive strength and constraints. Some recent applications of this concept, cited in the study quoted above, suggest that productive capacity can and must become more flexible in response to changing market conditions.

1. A 'modular' approach, means that the manufacturing function can provide substantial variety to the customer at limited cost by having products designed so that they can be made of interchangeable modules, resulting in greater cost effectiveness.
2. Improved competitiveness can result from managing and refining operations on a more limited scale to precise and quantified sectors of the total market, rather than adapting the volume output of a large plant. One large autoparts manufacturer,

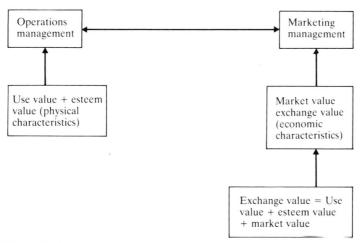

Fig. 5.3 Value analysis.

for example, committed itself to the construction of small (no more than 500 employees) plants designed around specific customer needs and production technologies.

The impact of new technology

The next step is to consider critically aspects of the impact of new technology both on manufacturing and on the operational competitiveness of the company. In this connection, Case example 5.7 is based on recent research at the Industrial Relations Research Unit at Warwick University.

Case example 5.7

Lucas Electrical (LE) drew on 'module production' in order to increase international competitiveness. This is based on the Japanese concept of 'Kanban', and it also involves changing working practices by ending demarcations, and substantial investment in retraining and capital equipment. This research concentrated on one LE plant, BW3, which produces starters and alternators for the automobile industry. The Japanese-based system is a method of 'just in time' production, where stocks and work in progress are closely monitored to fit exactly the production schedule—or a service of 'mini-factories' within the factory based on a self-contained team of workers carrying out a complete stage of the production process. This system is intended to increase production and labour flexibility by reducing set-up costs, by reducing the number of defective parts/components, by continually checking and controlling quality throughout the production cycle, and by transferring (indirect) work to sub-contractors. This methodology, in effect, replaces mass-produced items with little variety with a large variety of high-quality products in small volume, and it has been successfully introduced with major gains in productivity—up to 50 per cent in one case.

The company has set each business unit a 'competitiveness achievement plan', and the introduction of Japanese production methods is an integral part of the drive to beat international competitors, and especially to expand beyond the shrinking UK market into world-wide markets. Moreover, these changes have not been confined to the BW3 plant: the pace of change has been accelerating and has encompassed all the company's divisions.

This case history highlights the contribution of manufacturing management to improving a firm's competitiveness; indeed, superior overall manufacturing capability is widely argued as the main factor underlying the commercial strength of Japanese companies. Furthermore, an industrial company's assets tend to be concentrated in capital plant and technical processes and equipment: changes to improve manufacturing, therefore, require investment decisions, and locating new manufacturing plant to maintain competitiveness is the biggest single investment decision a company is likely to have to face. One recent study, based on extensive research in US manufacturing industry, argues that, in making choices about investments in assets and in planning the manufacturing programme aimed at competitive advantage, management must grasp and act on four principal succeeding stages in manufacturing's strategic role.[17] These stages are shown in Table 5.4.

The paper cited maintains that, while at stage 1 production can offer little contribution to a company's market success, by stage 4 it is providing a major source of competitive advantage. Clearly, the resources referred to earlier need to be utilized in a way that is planned to improve production's contribution to marketing. These include systems and quality control, plant and capacity utilization, labour productivity, procurement and materials handling, physical distribution, process technology (where applicable), human resources (training and motivation), R&D and technical product development. Stage 4 of the table is of particular significance, in that the role of manufacturing is 'externally supportive' in making an important contribution to competitiveness, particularly in 'process-intensive' industries.

The paper contains a typology of companies operating at stage 4, which is quoted now in full:

(a) They anticipate the potential of new manufacturing practices and technologies and seek to acquire expertise in them long before their implications are fully apparent.

(b) They give sufficient credibility and influence to manufacturing for it to extract the full potential from production-based opportunities.

(c) They place emphasis on structural (building and equipment) and infrastructural (management policies) activities as potential sources of continual improvement and competitive advantage.

(d) They develop long-range business plans in which manufacturing capabilities are expected to play a meaningful role in securing the company's strategic objectives. By treating the manufacturing function as a strategic resource, . . . they encourage the interactive development of business, manufacturing and other functional strategies.

Table 5.4 Stages in manufacturing's strategic role (*Source*: S. C. Wheelwright and R. H. Hayes, 'Competing through manufacturing', *Harvard Business Review*, **63**, 1, January/February 1985.

	Objective	*Action*
Stage 1	Minimize manufacturing's negative potential: 'internally neutral'	Outside experts are called in to make decisions about strategic manufacturing issues
		Internal, detailed, management control systems are the primary means for monitoring manufacturing performance
		Manufacturing is kept flexible and reactive
Stage 2	Achieve parity with competitors: 'externally neutral'	'Industry practice' is followed
		The planning horizons for manufacturing investment decisions is extended to incorporate a single-business cycle
		Capital investment is the primary means for catching up with competition or achieving a competitive edge
Stage 3	Provide credible support to the business strategy: 'internally supportive'	Manufacturing investments are screened for consistency with the business strategy
		A manufacturing strategy is formulated and pursued
		Longer-term manufacturing developments and trends are addressed systematically
Stage 4	Pursue a manufacturing-base competitive advantage: 'externally supportive'	Efforts are made to anticipate the potential of new manufacturing practices and technologies
		Manufacturing is involved 'up front' in major marketing and engineering decisions (and vice versa)
		Long-range programmes are pursued in order to acquire capabilities in advance of needs

These stages refer very much to management policy and organization; there is also however, the highly topical question of the new technology available now to manufacturing and its impact on competitiveness. This is termed 'factory automation', but within this general terminology, specific new technologies are growing in importance, including

- computer-integrated manufacturing (CIM) and
- computer-aided design and manufacturing (CAD/CAM).

Most car manufacturers, for example, now use CAD/CAM to shorten the gap between design and manufacture; Peugeot SA claims that, with the 35 CAD/CAM systems in use in its car plants in Britain and France, it now takes one day to complete a new car design, compared with one month previously. And Fiat SpA is usually credited for having the first robotic car plant in Europe, while Volkswagen AG claims to have the world's most advanced assembly plant, 'Halle 54', a CAM facility which produced the Golf model.

Originally, of course, labour savings were seen as the major pay-off of factory automation, but increasingly, companies are coming to utilize it as a competitive weapon. For example, computers can now co-ordinate and monitor the entire production process, from design and specifications through receipt of raw materials or parts and on to final shipment. Managers who effectively exploit this new technology gain unprecedented power, speed and flexibility in such key competitive areas as quality control and inventory management. And by adopting factory automation, while improvements in productivity by a factor of 10 are not uncommon, management has had to become more flexible, and such functions as marketing, design and manufacturing have had to integrate their activities more than ever before.

Much of the pioneering work in CIM-type technology is already under way; indeed, CAD/CAM systems have been widely used since about 1980 to substantially shorten lead times for the development both of new products and of programs to run numerical control (NC) production machines. In the last resort, however, it is really the responsibility of senior management to carry out the development of a manufacturing strategy, using factory automation, which is consistent with the company's product strategy and fits into its overall business strategy.

Case example 5.8 shows how far factory automation can lead to significant improvements in productivity, quality control and operating systems.

Case example 5.8
Three years ago, General Electric (USA) initiated the first phase of a programme to put all ten factories at the steam turbine generator division's New York headquarters on stream with CIM by 1991, beginning with the small parts shop. The aim is to create a 'paperless factory', reducing current manufacturing cycle times by 30 per cent and significantly cutting labour and management costs. GE's system uses a series of computers to process orders from entry through shipment without generating draw-

ings and associated paperwork. The aim is to have, within six years, the entire steam generator complex working from a common computer data base that links all aspects of the business, from quotation and order entry through engineering, process planning, manufacturing, shipment and financial reporting.

GE claims that, with CIM, the small parts shop can now manufacture and ship some emergency parts the day orders are received. Previously, orders of similar high priority took ten days to process and deliver. Management claims that this has led to savings for electric utility customers of hundreds of thousands of dollars a day in replacement power costs during power failures.

5.4 Competitive strategy

Introduction

Two essential points must be made at the outset of this section, and they derive directly from Section 2.1 and Sections 5.1, 5.2 and 5.3 above.

1. The structure of competition is undergoing a profound change. Competitiveness is moving rapidly from national to international—indeed, global—scale; the oil and pharmaceutical industries experienced this years ago. It is clear that, even with government purchasing, fewer segments of industry remain defensible at the national level in consumer electronics, telecommunications, automobiles and industrial machinery; and there is a growing list of sectors where companies are experiencing the benefits of value added from design to sales. In some sectors, it can be in terms of designing products for many markets, thus lowering production costs earlier than is possible for purely national firms. (World-wide designs can cover 80 per cent of customer needs, with 20 per cent for local adaptations.)
2. Competitive advantage, as the basis for strategy, must rest on some clear sustainable product or market factor, controlled by the firm, which is superior to what other companies can offer or deliver. This can relate to one or more of the following: purchasing and supply, research and development, innovation, design, patents, production technology, quality and intensity of promotion, product/ brand performance, pricing, delivery and technical support services, financial terms.

Much of this chapter is concerned with the development of strategy based on point 2. Of course, competitive advantage can also be based on market position: on strength in a particular sector or in some defined area of product/market operations.

There is a further point of general interest, in that a change has come about in the orientation of marketing management thinking in the last decade: there is now more concern with competitors and competitive strategy, compared with, previously, exclusive concern with customers. The building of competitive position and reaction to competitive attack are now accorded a prominent place in planning and plans, where a decade ago they would have been typically eclipsed by the focus on the customer.

The reality behind this change is simple: over-concentration on customers can result in a loss of competitive advantage by which to gain and keep customers. The strategy then is, equally, to gain and to keep competitive advantage, and thereby to secure a sustainable and profitable market position. At the same time, management must be ready to make counter-moves to prevent other firms from eroding this position; indeed, impeding a competitor can still bring greater relative gains, even though the firm's own performance may suffer in the short term. Lowering prices in a market where a competitor would otherwise make high profits can remove his funds from attack on some other front. The importance of some degree of international position is underlined by the danger of allowing a competitor to attack from a secure base. (Contrast, in this context, the failure of the British motorcycle industry and the success of the British ceramics/chinaware industry.)

Competitive analysis by management

Competitive strategy requires, ideally, a process of scanning actual and potential competitors and planning competitive counter-moves to maintain market position. Often the strongest competing company will make the first move (e.g. introduce a new range of discounts), or counter-move (e.g. match, in expenditure and intensity, a promotional campaign). This means that, in initiating competitive moves of its own, the medium-sized company should direct them at firms whose resources and profits are more closely matched to its own. Of course, competitive opportunities or threats can arise from almost any direction, requiring a series of tactics rather than a single move. In general, management should endeavour to allocate resources to maximize the value of its competitive position. This is often easier said than done. Factors to be taken into account include: the closeness of a competitor's position in terms of product and market offering; the financial strength of the competitor and the nature of its market stance (e.g. aggressive, defensive, innovative); the likelihood of direct and speedy retaliation; and the 'distance' of a competitor from the firm's own market position, who appears likely to move closer and reduce the market boundary. Indeed, it is important that management does not draw these market boundaries too closely, but leaves some ground to be occupied by other firms who can then use this factor to counteract what is otherwise a competitive disadvantage.

The scanning and planning process clearly requires rigorous competitive analysis by management as a data base for setting up strategy. This analysis involves several separate, though related, exercises.

1. *Financial analysis.* Reference has been made to the link between competitive advantage and profit, and to the need to reinforce that position. Indeed, the competitive position becomes the company's most valuable asset, and it is this value that determines the worth of the business, not physical assets. A recent authoritative study on financial analysis has shown that volume of sales revenue does not guarantee competitive position, and that, in a declining market, the firm that can trade market share for high profits may well be increasing the value of its present

position.[18] Competitors' relative liquidity and borrowing capacity are also important in determining competitive threats. A high-cost competitor may still be an
aggressive threat if it has the funds and determination to attack and overtake those
who otherwise have the advantage. The paper cited makes this very significant
connection between profitability and competitiveness:

> A business that realise[s] a profit by running down competitive position would in its
> accounts appear no different from a firm that realise[s] the same profit while building its
> competitive position. Yet when competitive position has been improved, it is very likely
> to have meant reducing accounting profit because of the cost of gaining on competition.
> Conversely, increased profit can be a reflection of decay in competitive position as a result
> of higher prices, decreased quality, reducing advertising or any other reduction in spend-
> ing that might have decreased the firm's relative competitive appeal in the market.

2. *Current cost analysis.* Following the points made above, cost analysis too has wide
applications. It can vary from a broad macro type of analysis to highly detailed
micro-cost analyses for each major competitor. In such an analysis, management
should consider: material requirements and estimated costs; manufacturing strategy and cost implications; marketing policy and cost implications; price levels. If
profit data on competitors are available, they provide a useful check on cost and
price data (see Table 5.5).

Table 5.5 Factors influencing average industry profitability

Factor	Influence Will lower profitability	Will raise profitability
Rivalry among competitors		
Structure of competition	Numerous or equal size	One dominant
Growth	Slow	Rapid
Differentiation	Negligible	Significant
Fixed	High	Low
Capacity increments	Large	Small
Exit barriers	High	Low
Diversity of strategy	Significant	Limited
Ease of entry	Easy	Difficult
– scale thresholds		
– access to distribution		
– common technology		
Bargaining power of buyers		
Number of buyers	Few	Many
Purchase volume	Large	Small
Profitability	Low	High
Impact on end-product performance and quality	Unimportant	Important
Potential to back integrate	Significant	Not possible
Ability to switch to substitutes or other suppliers	Easy	Difficult

3. *Business systems analysis.* This is concerned with how a company conducts each key business function: technology, product design, manufacturing, marketing, distribution and service; this approach can be useful at all stages of competitive strategy. (It is more useful in dealing with current and potential competitors than with indirect competitors.)

4. *Analysis of economic value to the customer.* This is done from the perspective of the customer, usually on the basis of discrete, identified market segments. It is useful to a company comparing its products with a competitor's existing or new products, particularly in determining real customer benefits, and how the product should be positioned against competitive products (what benefits should be emphasized in any marketing communication, and how the product should be priced).

5. *Experience curve analysis.* This is useful for helping to identify current cost positions and, more importantly, future cost positions: these, relative to current ones, depend on market growth rates and future market shares. In using the experience curve to predict future costs positions, management should consider:

   - how aggressively each competitor tries to drive costs down the experience curve;
   - whether all competitors have the financial resources to pursue potential experience curve benefits;
   - if competitors have different business systems, the potential experience curve cost reductions may vary across competitors. (The experience curve is referred to again later; see Fig. 5.4.)

6. *Analysis of business/product portfolio.* An examination of a competitor's portfolio of business and product lines can provide some indication of

   - the importance and attractiveness of the business or the product line relative to the competitor's other businesses;
   - the financial and other resources the competitor may be able to draw on to support the business or product line.

   This type of analysis can suggest areas of competitive vulnerability and future competitive actions and reactions.

There are a number of key factors influencing both the competitive position and the strategy of the company. These factors, on the basis of a wide-ranging analysis undertaken at the Harvard Business School,[19] are illustrated in Fig. 5.4. This shows the five competitive forces as a function of industry structure (or as the underlying economic and technical characteristics of an industry). The analysis centres on the effects of competitive forces on the position of the company, and the relationship of these forces to industry profitability. The position of any company striving to improve its competitive position is complicated, therefore, by the strength of the company's suppliers as well as customers, by the threat of possible new entrants, and by competition from substitute products or services. One way in which management can understand

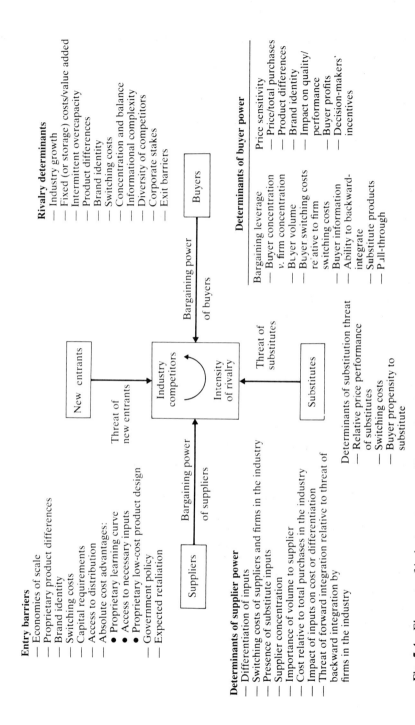

Entry barriers
— Economies of scale
— Proprietary product differences
— Brand identity
— Switching costs
— Capital requirements
— Access to distribution
— Absolute cost advantages:
  ● Proprietary learning curve
  ● Access to necessary inputs
  ● Proprietary low-cost product design
— Government policy
— Expected retaliation

Determinants of supplier power
— Differentiation of inputs
— Switching costs of suppliers and firms in the industry
— Presence of substitute inputs
— Supplier concentration
— Importance of volume to supplier
— Cost relative to total purchases in the industry
— Impact of inputs on cost or differentiation
— Threat of forward integration relative to threat of backward integration by firms in the industry

Bargaining power of suppliers

Threat of new entrants

Bargaining power of buyers

Threat of substitutes

Determinants of substitution threat
— Relative price performance of substitutes
— Switching costs
— Buyer propensity to substitute

Rivalry determinants
— Industry growth
— Fixed (or storage) costs/value added
— Intermittent overcapacity
— Product differences
— Brand identity
— Switching costs
— Concentration and balance
— Informational complexity
— Diversity of competitors
— Corporate stakes
— Exit barriers

Determinants of buyer power

Bargaining leverage
— Buyer concentration v. firm concentration
— Buyer volume
— Buyer switching costs relative to firm switching costs
— Buyer information
— Ability to backward-integrate
— Substitute products
— Pull-through

Price sensitivity
— Price/total purchases
— Product differences
— Brand identity
— Impact on quality/performance
— Buyer profits
— Decision-makers' incentives

Fig. 5.4 Elements of industry structure (*Source:* Reprinted with permission of the Free Press, a division of Macmillan Inc., New York, from Michael E. Porter, *Competitive Advantage: Creating and Sustaining Superior Performance*, 1985. Copyright © 1985 by Michael E. Porter)

w to utilize these factors in setting up competitive strategy, is to itemize the conditions under which the threats are greatest: the opposite conditions will present the most favourable opportunities.

1. Competing products fighting for market share:
    - Market having reached saturation/maturity
    - Slow industry growth
    - Undifferentiated products or services
    - Perishable or short-life products
    - High fixed costs
    - Over-capacity in the industry
    - High 'thresholds' associated with increasing production
    - Large number of relatively equal-sized competitors
    - No competitor with dominant share
    - Competitors having significantly different market strategies
    - Competitors having distinctly different 'brand personalities'
    - No distinct brand personalities established (i.e., all brands seen as similar)
    - Cost of quitting the business high
    - Cost of switching brands by customers low
    - Customer control distribution
    - Buyers' control specification
    - Mergers, or threats of mergers

2. Competition from close or acceptable substitutes:
    - Original product not capable of differentiation
    - Substitutes attractive in price/performance terms
    - Presence of substitutes putting an effective ceiling on prices
    - Substitutes produced by high profit-earners
    - Substitutes produced by companies with excess capacity
    - Substitutes using new techniques to improve performance, reduce price
    - Alternatives made by more efficient producers
    - Competitors' need to keep plant running
    - Competitors operating at a more advantageous scale
    - Dual-sourcing important (and substitutes acceptable)
    - Competitors having better access to distribution
    - No form of protection for original product
    - Producers of substitutes having more market power

3. Threat of possibe new entrants:
    - Capital needs low
    - Products not differentiated
    - No significant economies of scale

- Easy access to sales and distribution channels
- Existing competitors lacking resources or the will to fight back
- No history of violent reaction
- No record or threat of price reaction to restrict entry
- No marked consumer/user franchise
- Lack of excess capacity
- No inherent cost advantages for existing brands
- Government policy which permits or even encourages continued market growth
- Attractive profit prospects
- Market 'explosion' (i.e. rapid, unsatisfied growth in demand)
- Progress possible on technical grounds
- Lack of protection
- Low quality/poor service from existing suppliers
- One-company market
- Brand proliferation (large number of small shares)
- Unbranded markets
- Technology easily copied
- Expiry of patents, protection, licensing arrangements, etc.
- Removal of controls

4. Bargaining power of customers:

- Customers highly concentrated
- Existence of buying groups/associations
- Buyers purchasing in large quantities
- Low-profit products
- Consequences of purchase upon customers' costs low
- Products relatively unimportant to the quality and/or performance of the customer's products or services
- Product accounting for a significant proportion of customer's costs
- Product not saving the buyer money
- Product not a draw line
- Standard or undifferentiated products
- Buyer a middleman (wholesaler/factor, etc.), able to influence the end-user or customer
- Buyer threatening to integrate back into the supplier's business
- Customer accounting for large proportion of your turnover/profits
- Choice from a large number of suppliers
- Some of those suppliers having excess capacity and thus influencing the price at which customers can buy
- Fixed costs requiring plant to be utilized extensively
- Customer controlling technical specification
- Customer controlling distribution channels
- Government supporting customers

- 'Political' buying reasons (e.g. 'Buy British')
- Customers' market intelligence good

5. Bargaining strength of suppliers:

- Suppliers more concentrated than the industry supplied
- Suppliers selling a unique product
- Item required being in short supply
- Suppliers selling a highly differentiated product
- No acceptable substitutes
- Cost of 'switching' high
- Specifications difficult to meet
- Supplier providing an integral part of your expertise
- Expertise which could be sold to your competitors
- Suppliers financially strong
- The terms they offer important to you
- The industry they sell to not important to them
- The possibility that suppliers may integrate forward into their customer's business
- Supplier competing

The full range of possible permutations of these key elements in competitive strategy is not only enormous but also, normally, impracticable. Moreover, the manipulation of too many factors simultaneously can lead to unplanned and possibly unfortunate consequences. In Table 5.6, some competitive options are considered. The simple options involve changing one element while holding the other four con-

Table 5.6 Competitive options

Change	Likely to change (or need change) in association	Hold unchanged
Product	Target segment Communications	Channels of sale Price
Price	Target segment	Communications Channels of sale Product
Target segment	Channels of sale Communications	Product Price
Channels of sale	Target segment Communications	Product Price
Communications		Channels of sale Price Target segment Product

stant; e.g., changing the product but not the target segment, channels of sale, price or what is communicated about the product. However, the *simple* option will normally be unrealistic. Changing the product may well cause it to be of less appeal to the old target market and more appropriate to another. Presumably, the company will want to tell the market about the changes. Obviously, price can change and the changed product may even appeal to different, or additional, sales channels. The three columns thus show a slightly more realistic yet still simplified picture of the changed factor: in the second column, those likely to change in association or most likely to need changes in order to maximize the effect of the lead factor, and in the third, the factors the company can most probably hold unchanged.

The main task confronting management, therefore, is to develop the competitive position of the company and to set up a strategy on the basis of the most profitable options open to it in the light of the five factors illustrated in Fig. 5.4. The significance of these five factors has been summed up succinctly in the analytical study cited:[19]

> [These] five forces determine industry profitability because they influence the prices, costs and required investment of firms in an industry—the elements of return on investment. Buyer power influences the prices that firms can charge, for example, as does the threat of substitution. The power of buyers can also influence cost and investment, because powerful buyers demand costly service. The bargaining power of suppliers determines the costs of raw materials and other inputs. The intensity of rivalry influences prices as well as the costs of competing in such areas as plant, product development, advertising and sales force. The threat of entry places a limit on prices and shapes the investment required to deter entrants.

In identifying and acting on threats and opportunities, then, it follows that the company must formulate a strategy which ensures that profitability is based on a marketing policy that is within the cost resources of the company and that secures some competitive advantage, whether price or non-price. But some companies view competitors as other companies offering the same sort of product or service: such a view is at once too broad and too narrow, as Case examples 5.9 and 5.10 show.

Case example 5.9

A company can be operating in the same business classification and yet not be competing directly; an example of such 'non-competition' is provided by Rolex Co. and Timex Co. Both companies market watches, primarily satisfying a need to tell the time. But their characteristics and competitive positions are very different.

	Rolex	*Timex*
Price range (UK)	£175+	£5–£50
Main mechanism	Mechanical	Electronic
Key sales points	Precision	Value for money
	Reliability	Features
	Durability	Choice
	Associated with success	'Fun'
Main buyers	AB 35+	C2D all ages

Essentially, Rolex sell long-term, quality possessions, valued as much as things to have and display as time-pieces. Timex sell a cheap, functional, ultimately disposable way of telling the time (albeit a Timex quartz watch is probably as accurate as a Rolex Chronometer).

Case example 5.10

A competitor may be in a completely different field and yet represent 'head-on' competition. Grand Metropolitan's brewing division sees as its direct competitor other major brewers such as Courage or Scottish and Newcastle. But Grand Metropolitan's management counts among the company's competitors any other product or service that offers customers an alternative to spending their money on drink. For example the marketing department has been highly concerned at the level of spending on home video players; so part of the company's competitive response is to make pubs more attractive, comfortable places, where the entire family is welcome.

The experience curve

One of the key concepts referred to earlier is the 'experience curve'. It is now time to analyse this in the context of competitive strategy. Indeed, the competitive importance of any company's dominant position in the world market sector(s) should be viewed in terms of cost/volume relationships (experience curves). It is necessary to view this initially in its historical context. A critical aspect of many industries' competitive development recently has been their demonstrated ability to lower a product's supply costs—especially in high-growth economies such as Japan, where firms have usually begun as 'internationally high-cost producers' in most products, but in a few years have become very competitive. This competitive position of Japanese firms is only now being undermined by the rise in value of the Japanese yen and the growth of new low-cost volume manufacturers in other Asian countries such as South Korea and Taiwan.

On the basis of this and other industry studies, the experience curve has become widely accepted as a significant contribution to understanding changes in industry structure and competitive strategy. According to this concept, unit costs in many manufacturing industries, as well as in some service industries, decline 'with experience', or with a company's cumulative volume of production. The causes of this decline are a combination of elements, including economies of scale, capital–labour substitution and other costs reduction investments, and also the learning curve for labour (the efficiency over a period of time by workers through much repetition). The Boston Consulting Group (BCG) and other researchers have demonstrated, for a variety of products, that total costs per unit in constant dollars or other currency will decline by a characteristic amount (usually 20–30 per cent each time accumulated production experience (total amount ever produced) doubles. This analysis of the experience curve is based on an authoritative study carried out by W. V. Rapp.[20] The

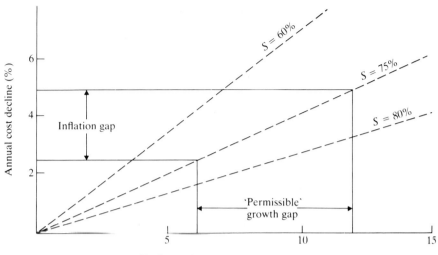

Real growth rate (accumulation rate) (%)

The annual rate of cost decline is equal to the mathematical slope of the experience curve times the accumulation rate. The mathematical slope equals

$$\frac{\log S}{\log 2}$$

where S is the slope of the experience curve. For a 75 per cent curve, $S = 0.75$ and the mathematical slope $= 0.42$.

Fig. 5.5 Real growth and annual cost decline (*Source*: W. V. Rapp, 'Strategy Formulation and International Competition', *Columbia Journal of World Business*, Summer 1973)

analysis also includes a logarithmic relationship between real growth and annual cost decline (Fig. 5.5).

This statistical phenomenon is observed in many regions, including the USA, Europe and Japan; it is an accepted part of cost projection formulations, for example, in the aircraft and semiconductor industries. The cost experience effect over time is more noticeable in new products. Such products have a small experience base and a high demand growth; accumulated production experience can double rapidly, and costs will fall accordingly. In mature industries, the effects of inflation will obscure the decline in real dollar costs. To obtain an accurate picture, one must factor out inflation.

Given the relationship between cost and volume, an individual firm's cost position within an industry depends on its growth relative to the entire industry, i.e. on its market share. Conversely, an industry's ability to lower prices for a given amount of production experiences depends on the market shares of the individual producers, i.e. on the industry's concentration. (With greater concentration, industry experience is spread among fewer producers.)

The implication of the cost experience affect for international competition is that growth directly determines a competitor's ability to accumulate experience and lower costs, and market share determines his ability to lower costs relative to competitors, domestic and foreign. The successful follower is therefore the firm that captures a dominant share of the world demand represented by its home market growth and subsequently by export demand.

Innovators v. followers

The analysis already cited[20] also extends to competitive strategy by 'innovator' and 'follower' companies. For example, if a follower firm accumulates experience at 30 per cent per year, it will double experience in less than three years and will lower real costs 20–30 per cent. If inflation in that firm's country is 5 per cent a year, the firm's current costs will decline between 5 and 15 per cent over the three-year period. If industry demand is growing at 15 per cent per annum, and the industry growth rate has approached industry demand growth, the firm is capturing more than its share of incremental experience: it is gaining market share relative to competitors and is improving cost position. Once it is producing, though, the firm's ability to become internationally competitive is a function of its initial real production costs, the slope of its experience curve, its country's inflation rate, exchange rates, and the firm's accumulation rate.

Conversely, an innovator's ability to maintain price competitiveness and dominance in a product it has introduced depends on an appropriate combination of the following:

1. lower real start-up and initial production costs than the follower;
2. steeper experience curve slope;
3. lower inflation rate;
4. declining value of company's trading currency;
5. faster accumulation rate.

In reality, few of these conditions can be met. The innovator usually has higher initial production and development costs than the follower, given a product's existence and the availability of production equipment and know-how, and the fact that the cost of transferring a given technology decreases over time. The follower need not accumulate equivalent experience to become competitive.

Actual international comparisons by the Boston Consulting Group have yet to show any appreciable slope differentials for the same product between leading industrial countries. Technological factors and industrial organizations at a given stage of development for the same product would seem similar, and cost management by successful firms producing the product are roughly equivalent.

Inflation and exchange rates are macroeconomic variables over which firms have little control. Nevertheless, it must be recognized that rising inflation rates can seriously affect companies' competitiveness.

Despite the above factors, innovators do have some control over follower-firms' ability to capture world market share, to accumulate experience and to become cost-competitive. This is true even if they have not generally done so. Innovators usually have lower current costs when the follower begins production (even though start-up costs in real terms are higher). There is thus a minimum accumulation rate that a follower requires over some time period in order to become cost-competitive. The innovator can remain the dominant and low-cost producer if the follower fails to grow at this rate.

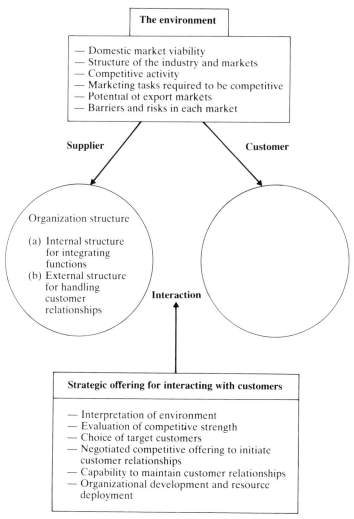

Fig. 5.6 An interactive approach to competitive strategy (*Source*: M. T. Cunningham, 'An Interactive Approach to Competitive Strategy in European Markets', *Proceedings of IMP Research Seminar*, Uppsala University, September 1985)

During the follower's initial production phase, the innovator can rarely accumulate experience as rapidly as the follower. The innovator is the initial producer and has a larger accumulated production base; consequently, he takes longer to double experience. As the follower's smaller market is saturated, however, and as his experience base gets larger, further doublings and cost reductions become more difficult. The innovator must use his initial cost advantage, therefore, to participate in the follower's home market and/or shut off export development. (This strategy may still require moving offshore later, but then production should be concentrated at the new location.) Only in this way can the innovator deny the follower the growth necessary for fully competitive cost reduction. But his time horizon is limited.

An easy way of assessing a follower's competitive requirement is to calculate the 'permissible' growth (accumulation rate) gap allowed by differences in the follower's rate of inflation or by exchange rate movements. (This gap equals the inflation or exchange rate differential divided by the mathematical slope of the experience curve.) Given current costs and prices, if a follower's relative growth exceeds this 'permissible' gap, the innovator's cost position is improving. A smaller inflation differential and/or a steeper product experience curve narrows the 'permissible' growth gap for a particular product; see Fig. 5.5. So one of the objects of a successful international strategy must be to capture enough world market growth so that no foreign (or domestic) competitor can exceed the 'permissible' growth gap long enough to become cost-competitive.

But many US and European innovators have not captured this required market growth. Thus, for many years, follower-firms in Japan and other countries have exceeded the 'permissible' gap in many products. At stable exchange rates, this normally leads to large and persistent foreign exchange surpluses for the high-growth economy, owing to improved relative and absolute cost positions. These surpluses can then be offset by tariff reductions, exchange rate adjustments or other measures. But even though total trade may become balanced, specific products and industries will continue to lose competitive position. Not all products have the same experience curve slopes or are growing at the same rate.

Case example 5.11

Philips NV of Eindoven has responded to the global competitive challenge in electronics, particularly from Japan, in a number of ways. First, it has invested heavily in R&D to maintain expertise of its technology, since it is this that determines the cost and quality of components, and the price of the product. Second, Philips has recently completed a massive programme of restructuring its production facilities (particularly in Europe), from factories producing for national markets to global production centres producing for world markets. And third, Philips has placed top priority on increasing its market position and production resources in the Pacific Basin (notably Japan); the company is about to conclude joint ventures in Japan with a Japanese company for marketing the Philips data network system in Japan, and also for developing and marketing in Japan the company's interactive systems of small home computers.

Table 5.7 Reasons for changing competitive strategy

Demographic	Changes in profile by age, sex, socioeconomic class, geographical location
Psychographic	Changes in the life-styles of buyers and the way these reflect upon purchasing habits
Demand	Fundamental changes in taste, usage patterns, consumption Changes in the relative strengths and profitability of market segments
Technological	New processes on the one hand, obsolescence on the other
Market position	New forms of direct or indirect competition Changes in comparative market positions (strengths and weaknesses in product, service, marketing, etc.)
Distributive	Changes in sales and distribution channels (either as an act of initiative or as a reflection of the way buyers purchase)
Price/profit Relationships	Changes in search of improved results, e.g. low profit/high turnover v. high profit/low turnover
Regulations	Response to laws, codes, standards, regulations, inspectorates

Factors affecting changes in strategy

So far, special emphasis has been placed on: competitive advantage and the effects of the experience curve; the contribution of business analysis, in all phases, to an understanding of competitive position; the financial implications of competitive strategy; and international aspects, notably the different stances of 'innovator' and 'follower'-companies. Having absorbed these policy aspects, management needs to be alert to two particular operating points. The first is the hazard of planning competitive strategy in isolation, that is, without sufficient regard to the company resources and key management functions, such as finance and marketing, that are needed to implement it. In particular, an inadequate data base, especially on markets, can lead to incorrect strategies, and the pressure to innovate can push up the costs with an adverse effect on short-term profits. The second point is that, at the same time, management must remain alert to signals that indicate a possible/desirable change in competitive strategy; these are summarized in Table 5.7.

An interactive approach

Case examples 5.12–5.14[21] serve to illustrate the necessity of having a complete integrated competitive strategy. Research and development alone is not enough; nor is salesmanship. For a competitive strategy to work, R&D, marketing and a sound organizational structure must function together. Both of the firms described in case 5.14 are presently undergoing major reorganizations in an attempt to co-ordinate these activities and make their strategies more effective.

Case example 5.12

By forging a global competitive strategy, Caterpillar Tractor Co. maintained its world leadership in the large-scale equipment business, despite heavy competition. Caterpillar faced increasing pressure from Komatsu, Japan's leading construction equipment producer. Komatsu exported products from centralized facilities with labour and skill cost advantages. Despite this, Caterpillar gained world market share through four defensive moves: a global strategy of its own, a willingness to invest in manufacturing, a willingness to commit finances, and a blocking position in the Japanese market.

How did Caterpillar implement this global strategy? The solution was in erecting two barriers to entry. The first was a global distribution system which served to block off competition; the second consisted of production economies. As a result, no competitor was able to match Caterpillar's production and distribution costs.

Case example 5.13

Chrysler is a US-based multinational, engaged in the manufacture of passenger cars and trucks. Honda Motors is a Japanese multinational which produces motorcycles, automobiles and power products. Both companies are the third largest domestic automaker in their home country. Both spend an almost equal proportion on R&D (Chrysler 2.31 per cent in 1981, Honda 3.13 per cent in 1981). Yet the performance of the two companies is far from similar.

While Honda's world-wide sales are only 45 per cent of Chrysler's, its market share has continued to increase, while Chrysler's has fallen. During 1978–81, Chrysler's market share dropped from 11.3 to 10.2 per cent. Honda's, on the other hand, almost doubled, from 2.4 to 4.6 per cent. During the same period, Chrysler suffered severe losses in its return on equity (ROE), while Honda's ROE averaged 14.7 per cent during this time. These performance measures are typical not only of these two firms, but of the automobile industry as a whole, and they reflect the great contrasts between American and Japanese automakers.

The answer to this disparity lies in the Japanese management style and its global strategy. This emphasizes concepts such as quality control circles and lifetime employment. It is this style that promotes participative management and a human-oriented approach, and it is this style that gets results like those of Honda. Honda developed a comprehensive competitive strategy and an expanded product line to attract new customer segments. Also, Honda erected entry barriers with scale economies by centralizing manufacturing and logistics. The combination of these factors serves as a strong competitive force in Honda's global strategy.

Case example 5.14

Texas Instruments (US) and Matsushita Electric (Japan) are MNCs in the consumer and industrial electronics industry. Both companies experienced phenomenal growth during the 1970s, and much of this success stemmed from their firm-specific advantage in R&D. Matsushita also possesses world-wide marketing skills and a unique (Japanese-style) management philosophy. For years, Texas Instruments was known for its success in adopting a matrix structure along its diverse product lines. Recently, however, both MNCs have experienced difficulties which are evident from their profit figures. For Texas Instruments, net income declined (as a percentage of sales) from 5.8 per cent in 1976 to 2.6 per cent in 1981.

Both Texas Instruments and Matsushita have been 'victims' of their own success. Texas Instruments placed too much emphasis on R&D and ignored other critical factors in an effective global strategy, such as an integrated marketing effort and a sound organizational structure. Instead, its strategy focused only on technological innova tion—'the more the better'. By constantly increasing the amount of R&D, with inadequate regard for the market-place, Texas Instruments had to write off very large investments in products that did not sell. Matsushita made a similar mistake in relying on only one component of a successful global strategy—salesmanship—only to be beaten by competitors.

All of these points underline the need to have a competitive strategy which increasingly takes account of international business.

> When marketing people talk . . . about the potential business opportunities for their companies, they must concern themselves with the fact that the points of competitive challenge are far greater and far more international than even five years ago.[22]

The significance of international aspects has already been underlined by reference to Professor Michael Porter's view of strategy as being the company's interactions with competitive forces arising from new entrants, substitutes, customers' bargaining power and rivalry among existing firms in the industry.

Recent research at University of Manchester Institute of Science and Technology (UMIST) has further developed this concept in an important study which analyses international competitiveness, particularly of UK firms in Europe, in terms of an 'interactive approach'.[23] This is illustrated in Fig. 5.6. The first factor is the environment within which supplier–customer relationships have to be managed. Furthermore, the structure of the different industries in which specific suppliers operate points to the nature of the competition facing suppliers and to the marketing tasks that have to be performed in order to operate successfully. Finally, the size, growth rate and market potential of the different export markets, together with the inter-country trade balances and exchange rate movements, point to the relative opportunities and risks of each market. This comprises the environmental background within which suppliers formulate their sequence of approach to each market (or major foreign customers) and the resources to be committed to each market or relationship.

The second major factor is the strategic offering for interacting with customers. One of the most important considerations for a supplier is the evaluation of the countries to which it will attempt to export and the customers with whom it proposes to enter into relationships. This process is dependent upon how the supplier-company executives perceive the opportunities, competition and barriers to entry into export markets. This derives from their interpretation of the environment. Obviously, for any interaction with customers to take place, the supplier must have a competitive offering. A key feature of industrial marketing is the development of technological expertise and the application of this expertise to solving customers' problems. The competitive offering to accomplish this objective usually involves such elements as

– the innovativeness of the product;
– its price competitiveness;
– the supply capability of the organization as a whole; and
– the technical and commercial services accompanying the product.

It is this offering that will motivate customers to engage in an exchange process with suppliers. Such competitive offerings are often referred to as the 'marketing mix'. In industrial markets, these usually have to be negotiated, rather than being unilaterally imposed by the supplier. Even so, they may account for only short-term exchanges relating to a specific purchase or sale. They do not, of themselves, constitute prolonged interaction, nor are they necessarily the appropriate basis of an abiding relationship between a supplier and a customer. A relationship is really characterized by many more features. One essential feature is the relative importance of the exchange to both parties. Another is the social integration that occurs. A relationship will also consist of the interpersonal communications and adaptations between supplier and customer to achieve mutual benefits. Therefore, the strategic offering for interacting with customers can be considered as involving three interlinked behavioural and economic facets: first, the manager's perception of where market opportunities lie; second, the negotiated competitive offering to initiate relationships; and third, the capability to handle all the characteristics of a satisfactory relationship with customers.

The third factor, which arises from the first two, is the supplier's organization structure. This is the means by which suppliers actually handle their customer relationships. In the first instance, there is the internal organization structure which coordinates and integrates the various types of expertise and functional specializations in the company. This is in order to give effective direction and control over the interaction between these personnel and their counterparts in the decision-making unit of the customer organization. Second, there is the external organization structure, which is the channel of communication, sales activity and distribution between the supplier and the customer.

Relationships with customers, when handled directly through export staff or by agents or subsidiaries, demonstrate differing levels of commitment and resource investments by the supplier. They also permit different degrees of control over the interaction and the relationships.

The research study covered the following industry sectors:

1. raw materials: speciality steels; speciality chemicals;
2. components: industrial components; automotive components;
3. capital goods: pumps, valves and compressors;
4. diesel engines;
5. other capital equipment.

The study grouped the 'ingredients' of the competitive offering as a basis for initiating a relationship with a European industrial customer under the following headings:

1. product design and specification factors;
2. price factors;
3. delivery factors;
4. service factors;
5. quality reliability factors;
6. flexibility and adaptability factors.

And it found that the technical factors of heading 1 predominate both in frequency and 'criticality'. These factors relate to the uniqueness of the product characteristics or its adaptation to meet customers' existing manufacturing processes; thereafter, security of supply, service facilities and price factors are of high importance.

The paper cited also categorized five major competitive strategies typically adopted by UK industrial suppliers.

1. *Technical innovative strategy.* In nine instances, this strategy has been used in obtaining business from particular customers. It occurs where the supplier offers a specially designed product which performs well, meets the customer's specification, but is also supported by high-quality and technical service. Price is of minimal importance.
2. *Product adaptation strategy.* Again, in nine instances this strategy was implemented. It occurs when the supplier's specially designed product interests customers but some design modifications are insisted upon to minimize customer inconvenience and conform to the specification. In order to be a supplier, the offer has to be supported by reliable deliveries, stockholdings and service. Price is of secondary but significant importance.
3. *Availability and security strategies.* This logistic type of strategy was commonly used and occurred in eight instances. The customer is rarely innovative, or the products are well established on the market. The supplier emphasizes risk reduction and reliability in his marketing approach. Quick and reliable delivery is of critical importance, but the product must still conform in all respects to the customer's specification and be at a competitive price. The supplier adapts his supply

system to meet customers' requirements. Of vital importance also is an after-sales service network and ready availability of spares and replacements.

4. *Low-price strategies.* In six instances, this strategy has been used. Here the supplier initially prices his product lower than customers are currently paying in order to attract attention. The intention is to increase price once the business is well established. The offer has to be supported by delivery reliability, adequate quality and acceptable performance of the product on test.

5. *Total adaptation or conformity strategies.* This was somewhat less common and was found in only four instances. The supplier is considered as a second or third supplier only as a result of offering a product to match the performance of competitors and comply with customer specification. Additionally, the supplier has to match competitors in delivery and price. This requires significant technical, commercial and administrative adaptation by the supplier.

Furthermore, research into both marketing and purchasing executives' attitudes to dealing with their customers or suppliers shows that eight factors largely characterize a supplier–customer relationship. Thus, a supplier's strategy should encompass communicating and demonstrating the following eight features:

1. customer orientation;
2. technological expertise (both of marketing staff and of the company);
3. commercial competence;
4. flexibility and adaptability;
5. supply performance capability;
6. price competitiveness;
7. organizational effectiveness;
8. social integration.

The study concludes that strategies 1, 2 and 3 are much more in evidence than the others (but of course, these strategies are not always mutually exclusive).

References

1. E. de Bono, *Opportunities: A Handbook of Business Opportunity Search.* London: Associated Business Programmes/European Services Ltd, 1978.
2. S. Myers and D. G. Marquis, *Successful Industrial Innovations: A Study of Factors Underlying Innovations in Selected Firms.* National Science Foundation, Series 69–17, 1969.
3. *Technical Innovation in Britain,* Report of Central Advisory Council for Science and Technology. London: HMSO, 1980.
4. *Science, Technology and Innovation,* Report to National Science Foundation, 1973; 'The Temporal Mismatch: Innovation's Pace vs. Management's Time Horizon', *Research Management,* May 1974.
5. G. F. Ray, 'The Diffusion of Mature Technologies', *Economic Reviews,* no. 106, November 1983.
6. F. A. Johne, 'Innovation in the Marketing of High Technology Products', *Quarterly Review of Marketing,* Spring 1984.

7. J. B. Quinn, 'Managing Innovation: Controlled Chaos', *Harvard Business Review*, **63**, 3, May/June 1985.
8. G. Bonsiepe, *Development through Design*. Vienna: United Nations Industrial Development Organization (UNIDO), 1973.
9. Report of the Industrial Committee of Societies of Design, Stockholm, 1980.
10. *Engineering and Industrial Design*, Report of Committee of Council for Scientific and Industrial Research. London: HMSO, 1963.
11. M. Pawley, 'Design Makes Class into Classic', Arts *Guardian*, 13 July 1987.
12. I. Kravis and R. W. Lipsey, *Price Competitiveness in World Trade*. New York: Columbia University Press, 1971.
13. D. MacDougall, 'British and American Exports', *Economic Journal*, December 1961.
14. R. Rothwell and P. Gardiner, *The Role of Design in Competitiveness*. London, Society for Long Range Planning, 1982.
15. *Survey of Investment in Machine Tools*. London: NEDO.
16. B. P. Shapiro, 'Can Marketing and Manufacturing Co-exist?' *Harvard Business Review*, **55**, 5, September/October 1977.
17. S. C. Wheelwright and R. H. Hayes, 'Competing through Manufacturing', *Harvard Business Review*, **63**, 1, January/February 1985.
18. K. Simmonds, 'The Accounting Assessment of Competitive Position', *European Journal of Marketing*, **20**, 1, 1986.
19. Michael E. Porter, *Competitive Advantage*, New York: Free Press; London: Collier Macmillan, 1986, Chapter 1.
20. W. V. Rapp, 'Strategy Formulation and International Competition', *Columbia Journal of World Business*, Summer 1973.
21. A. M. Rugman, D. J. Lecraw and L. D. Booth, *International Business: Firm and Environment*, Maidenhead, Berks: McGraw-Hill, pp. 331, 338.
22. Roland Smith, 'International Management', *The Times*, 5 March 1987.
23. M. T. Cunningham, 'An Interaction Approach to Competitive Strategy in European Markets', *Proceedings of International IMP Research Seminar on International Marketing*. University of Uppsala, September 1985.

Index